The Christ Within

Published by BookLocker.com, Inc., Bradenton, Florida.

Printed in the United States of America.

BookLocker.com, Inc.
2014

First Edition

Translation by Maria Baes, Frank Tehan and Pamela Kribbe
Cover design by Janet Witte, www.janetwitte.nl
Cover photo by Gerrit Gielen

A word of thanks

This book is based on channeled messages received in the context of workshops that my husband Gerrit Gielen and I have offered during the past years. I am greatly indebted to Gerrit for his peaceful and clear presence next to me whenever I channel, as well as the countless inspiring conversations we have had about the subjects discussed in this book. In fact, working together with Gerrit in the field of spirituality has always been so natural and so comprehensive, that it is hard for me to distinguish who has contributed what. Although I am the channel, I feel that this book, as well as the others, are a joint creation and the result of our souls' joyful reunion.

The channelings in this book were mostly received in Dutch (apart from a few that I channeled directly in English) and they were translated into English by Maria Baes. I am deeply grateful to Maria for her hard work and her heart-felt connection with the material in this book. Because the channeled messages contained spoken language, they had to be edited in order to make them easy and fluent to read in written language. This was done by Frank Tehan, and I am greatly indebted to him for his skills and dedication. Bringing channeled messages into the world means to bring into material form a high and pure energy that often escapes our human words and concepts. When these messages are written down, the words have to be chosen carefully in order to reflect as best as possible the intent and the radiance of the energy transmitted. I am very grateful to have received the invaluable help of Frank and Maria to achieve this goal to the best of our abilities.

Contents

Introduction

This book contains messages inspired by the Christ energy. The Christ energy was personified on Earth by Jeshua-ben-Joseph 2000 years ago. He planted the seeds for a new awareness, a consciousness based on the heart rather than on the dictates of fear and ego. Jeshua's energy is still alive. The universal energy of love and wisdom that he personified in his life on Earth is also a part of us. In fact, Jeshua's primary goal was to make us aware of this, to *make us aware of the Christ within.*

In 2002, one evening in September, Jeshua started to speak to me. I realize this sounds pretty strange and hard to believe. With my academic background, having finished a thesis in the philosophy of science a few years before, I would heartily agree with that assessment. However, as Jeshua's messages came through, and I slowly opened up to receiving them, my husband and I were struck by the wisdom and healing quality of the information. We decided to write the messages down and after one year, we invited some friends to attend a "channeling session" at our house. I went through a lot of fear, insecurity, and skepticism, but eventually we posted the messages on the Internet, and after some months, people started to send us e-mails in which they told us how touched they were by the Jeshua channelings. They felt as if he spoke to them directly, awakening their hearts, and they felt recognized at a deep level.

Being trained as an academic philosopher, with mainly theoretic interests for many years, I was surprised and sometimes even overwhelmed by these emotional, but heartfelt responses. When I started to channel for small audiences, I was afraid people would attack me by questioning the veracity of my channeling, or the logic of what Jeshua was saying, so I was prepared for skeptical rebuttals. Instead, the energy during the channelings was quiet and serene, and often people were so much touched by Jeshua's words, that they started to cry, both out of joy and out of emotion. The channelings clearly addressed them on another level than the mind.

When Jeshua introduced himself to me, he immediately pointed out that he preferred to be called Jeshua-ben-Joseph, instead of Jesus, and that he was not a kind of deity, but a brother and friend to us. This is how Jeshua introduced himself in one of the first messages I received from him:

*I am the one who has been among you and who you have come to know
as Jesus.*
*I am not the Jesus of your church tradition or the Jesus of your religious
writings.*
*I am Jeshua-ben-Joseph; I have lived as a man of flesh and blood. I did
reach Christ consciousness before you, but I was supported in this by
powers which are beyond your imagination at present. My coming was a
cosmic event - I made myself available for this.*

*It wasn't easy. I did not succeed in my endeavors to pass on to people the
immensity of God's love. There was much misunderstanding. I came too
early, but someone had to come. My coming was like throwing a stone in
a large fishpond. All fish flee and the stone sinks into the deep, though
there are ripples noticeable long afterward. One might say that the kind
of consciousness I wished to convey, did its work underground after that.
At the surface of the pool there were constant ruffles; well-meant, but
misguided interpretations rose to meet and fight each other in my name.
The ones who were touched by my energy, moved by the impulse of Christ
energy, could not really integrate it with their psychological and physical
reality.*

*It has taken a long time before Christ consciousness could set foot on
Earth. But now the time has come. And I have returned and speak
through many, through all, and to everyone who wants to hear me and
who has come to understand me from the quietness of their hearts. I do
not preach and I do not judge. My sincerest hope is to speak to you of the
vast and unfailing presence of love, accessible to you at any time.*

*I am part of a much larger consciousness, a greater entity, but I, Jeshua,
am the incarnated part of that entity (or field of consciousness). I do not
much like the name Jesus, for it has become so caught up with a distorted
version of what I stand for. "Jesus" is owned by the church traditions and
authorities. He has been molded to fit the interests of the church
patriarchs for centuries, so much so that the prevailing image of Jesus is*

*now so far removed from what I represent, that it would truly please me if
you could just let it go and release me from that heritage.*

I am Jeshua, man of flesh and blood.
I am your friend and brother.
I am familiar with being human in every way.
I am teacher and friend.
Do not fear me. Embrace me like you'd embrace one of your kin.
We are family.

(From *The Jeshua Channelings*, p.7/8).

From the start, Jeshua told me his messages were meant for a specific
group of people. He called them "lightworkers" and he said they were at
the forefront of a wave of heart-based consciousness that engulfs the
Earth right now. He said they are pioneers of consciousness and their
soul's mission is to help bring a new awareness to Earth. I did not like
this idea very much. I thought it was kind of elitist to address the
messages to a specific group of people. Isn't the Christ energy alive in
every one of us? Jeshua, however, pointed out that to be a lightworker is
not to have a special status or be superior in any way. Also, every soul
becomes a lightworker at some point, so it is not about a fixed group of
souls. The reason Jeshua insists on addressing this particular group of
pioneers is that he dearly wants to help them remember who they are.
These souls are on the verge of a deep inner awakening, which will make
them become teachers for Earth in the most humble sense of the word.
However, because of the dense energies they encounter in human society,
many of them feel lost, doubting themselves, not fitting in with society,
lonely, and desperate. Jeshua's messages, through me, are meant to make
lightworker souls become aware of who they are, and to give them tools
to heal their inner wounds.

To clarify what Jeshua means by lightworkers, I am going to quote a list
of characteristics that he gave to me in the very beginning of our work
together.

*Lightworkers are souls who carry the strong inner desire to spread light
– knowledge, freedom, and self-love – on Earth. They sense this as their*

mission. They are often attracted to spirituality and to therapeutic work of some kind.

Because of their deeply felt mission, lightworkers often feel different from other people. By experiencing different kinds of obstacles on their way, life provokes them to find their own unique path. Lightworkers are nearly always solitary individuals, not fitting into fixed societal structures.

The word "lightworker" may evoke misunderstanding, since it lifts out a particular group of souls from the rest. It may be taken to suggest that this particular group is somehow superior to the others, i.e. those "not working for the light." This whole line of thought is at odds with the very nature and intent of lightwork. Let us state briefly what is wrong with it.

First, claims of superiority are generally unenlightened. They block your growth toward a free and loving consciousness. Second, lightworkers are not "better" or "higher" than anyone else. They simply have a different history than the ones not belonging to this group. Because of this particular history, which we will discuss below, they have certain psychological characteristics which distinguish them as a group. Third, every soul becomes a lightworker at some stage of its unfolding, so the label "lightworker" is not reserved to a limited number of souls.

The reason we use the word "lightworker" despite possible misunderstandings is because it carries associations and stirs memories within you that help you remember. There is a practical convenience to it as well, since the term is frequently used in your current spiritual literature.

(From: *The Jeshua Channelings*, p.35/36)

Psychological characteristics of lightworkers

From early on in their life, they feel they are different. *More often than not they feel isolated from others, lonely and misunderstood. They will often become* individualists *who will have to find their own unique ways in life.*

x

They have trouble feeling at home within traditional jobs and/or organization structures. Lightworkers are naturally anti-authoritarian, *which means that they naturally resist decisions or values based solely on power or hierarchy. This anti-authoritarian trait is present even if they seem timid and shy. It is connected to the very essence of their mission here on Earth.*

Lightworkers feel drawn to helping people *as a therapist or as a teacher. They may be psychologists, healers, teachers, nurses, etc. Even if their profession is not about helping people in a direct manner, the intent to contribute to the higher good of humanity is clearly present.*

Their vision of life is colored by a spiritual sense *of how all things are related together. They consciously or subconsciously carry memories within them of non-earthly spheres of light. They may occasionally feel homesick for these spheres and feel like a stranger on Earth.*

They deeply honor and respect life, *which often manifests as a fondness for animals and a concern for the environment. The destruction of parts of the animal and vegetable kingdoms on Earth by human doing invokes deep feelings of loss and grief in them.*

They are kind-hearted, sensitive, and empathic. *They may have trouble dealing with aggressive behavior and they generally experience difficulties in standing up for themselves. They can be dreamy, naive or highly idealistic, as well as insufficiently grounded, i.e. down-to-earth. Because they easily pick up negative feelings and moods of people around them, it is important for them to spend time alone on a regular basis. This enables them to distinguish between their own feelings and those of others. They need solitary time to touch base with themselves and with mother Earth.*

They have lived many lives on Earth in which they were deeply involved with spirituality *and/or religion. They were present in overwhelming numbers in the old religious orders of your past as monks, nuns, hermits, psychics, witches, shamans, priests, and priestesses. They were the ones providing a bridge between the visible and the invisible, between the daily context of Earth life and the mysterious realms of the afterlife, realms of God, and the spirits of good and evil. For fulfilling this role, they were often rejected and persecuted. Many of you were sentenced to the stake for the gifts you possessed. The traumas of persecution left deep traces within your soul's memory. This may presently manifest as a fear of being fully grounded, i.e. a fear to be really present, because you remember being brutally attacked for who you were.*

(From: *The Jeshua Channelings*, p.37/38)

These quotes are from The Jeshua Channelings. In that book, Jeshua talks about the history and destiny of lightworkers in depth. The channelings called the Lightworker Series, which make up the first half of that book, are the theoretical background to the messages that followed later, and out of which both the second book - called Heart Centered Living - and the present book were created. The channelings in the second and the present book were all received in the presence of a live audience and much of their contents are related to what people in the audience desired to know. They are a response to the questions and needs of actual lightworkers. The messages therefore often contain practical suggestions for meditations or visualizations which help address inner blockages or hidden emotions.

How does channeling work?

You may wonder how exactly I receive the messages from Jeshua, Mary, Mary Magdalene, and Earth, and what channeling is really about. I wrote an article about this which I published in The Jeshua Channelings and which is also available on www.jeshua.net. In that article, I point out how important it is to look upon channeling as a human endeavor, i.e. as a cooperation between a human being and a non-earthly teacher energy, in which the channeler inevitably influences the information coming through. Channeled information should be assessed in the same way as one assesses other types of information. If the information is clear, inspiring, interesting, and if it feels truthful and uplifting to you, that's a good reason for taking it seriously. What makes channeled material valuable is that it can give us glimpses of another perspective, a very loving, wise, and comforting perspective about our human affairs. In that way, channeled messages can enlighten both our hearts and minds.

However, it is never wise to rely on channeled information, simply because it is channeled and allegedly comes from a higher source. I sometimes feel that in spiritual circles, psychics are put on a pedestal, as if they have privileged access to the truth. But being psychic (clairvoyant, clairsentient) does not make one spiritually evolved, nor does being spiritually evolved make one a psychic, necessarily. One can be psychic and have a very imbalanced ego, or one can be highly evolved, in the sense of being deeply compassionate and wise, without ever seeing an aura or hearing a guide's voice.

I personally feel that channeling has enriched me immensely. It has acquainted me with wider perspectives on life and it has made me aware of the infinite love and joy that is available to us. Whenever I channel, I tap into that huge field of love and lightness and compassion, which is a healing experience and one that always gives me hope and inspiration for the future. My thinking (and worrying) mind goes into the background and I deeply enjoy the clarity and powerful love of the teacher energies running through me. At the same time, I am very human: I have fear, and insecurity, and pride, and anger to deal with in my everyday life. I am growing, but not as fast as I would wish! I experienced a devastating nervous breakdown and depression in 2010, because I could not adequately deal with all the demands and requests for help that I received after the Jeshua channelings came out into the world and I started to work as an energy reader and healer. I was unable to put clear boundaries around me, to say "no", and to basically protect myself against my own perfectionism and fear of rejection. I recovered well from the depression, but I went through a deep and dark night of the soul before I emerged. My connection with Jeshua did help me tremendously, but it was I who had to turn things around, and to allow deep change in myself to occur. The most profound decisions and transformations in our lives are created by ourselves; there is nothing outside us that will do it for us. Teachers, whether alive on Earth or from the spiritual realms, may accompany us, support us, console us, and surround us with love serene and pure, and that is invaluable. However, only we can kindle the light in ourselves, and it sometimes it takes a very deep crisis to get us there.

By all this, I wish to convey that channeling does not offer privileged access to the truth. It may offer glimpses of the truth, like art works, or great novels, or noble people may do. I sincerely hope that the channelings in this book offer those glimpses to you, making you feel safe, loved, and cherished, as you truly are. What we do with those glimpses is up to us. There is no getting around that basic freedom that we all have: to say yes or no, to resist or to surrender, to choose left or right. This freedom is not a burden, but a gift; it makes us into creators instead of victims. True spiritual teachings make you aware of your free nature, of your power to choose. I think that whether channeling is enlightening and valuable should be measured by that standard above all.

The female voices in this book

What is special about this third book of channelings, is that it contains messages from not only Jeshua, but also from two female representatives of the Christ energy, mother Mary and Mary Magdalene. In addition, it contains a fourth series of messages coming from mother Earth, who speaks about spiritual growth and the human journey from her perspective. Thus, the book consists of four parts, corresponding with these four sources of wisdom and inspiration.

In The Jeshua Channelings and on www.jeshua.net, I wrote about how Jeshua came into my life and how I started channeling, with all the ups and downs this process brought along. Five years after I started channeling Jeshua, another energy came to me, at a time when I was feeling rather stressed by the demands my practice put on me. It was a very gentle, fresh, and joyous energy that I felt swirling around me one afternoon as I was sitting in my living room, staring out of the window. It presented itself to me as the energy of mother Mary, the woman who gave birth to Jeshua and who travelled her own path to awakening during her life back then. Her energy felt so sweet and loving that I could not put it aside, even though immediately my mind started to raise objections and the skeptical part of me was guarded and doubtful. I decided I would just see what this energy would bring to me, without doing anything with it in public. Mary's energy proved to be healing and nurturing, helping me to be more gentle and kind to myself, softening up the harsh and critical parts of me. What strikes me most about her energy is the level of detachment in it, which I feel is the key to its joyful vibration. After some time, I felt safe with this energy, and I started to receive channeled messages from Mary, some of which were published in Heart Centered

Living. This current book contains six messages from Mary, which express that particular lightness which I feel is unique to her.

In 2009, I sensed another energy wanting to be heard. This one was different, in that it came not from above, so to speak, but from below. It was the energy of mother Earth. I first connected with her consciously when I was walking in a forest with a friend, and we sat down on the ground quietly, sensing the energy of nature. I felt a warm energy bubbling up into my heart and a very friendly "hello" coming to me from Earth itself. She gave me the image of a road on which groups of people were walking toward the future, and these people were aware of their connection with nature and with each other. The road was leading into a new future, where people would live in harmony with Earth, inspired by the Oneness with everything alive they sensed in their hearts. Mother Earth appeared to me as a young woman with a bright blue aura, expressing the essence of Spring, inviting me to join these people. "Will you come along and help me?" she asked ever so lightly and joyfully. I was deeply touched. Her energy was so positive and uplifting, and her strength so undeniable, that there could be no doubt that this future was going to become real. Her plea for help was real, but it did not come from a place of weakness. I could sense no victimhood, and no reproach or blame in her energy toward humanity. Her confidence and deep sense of joy made me aware that she was a being of great wisdom, looking far beyond what we as humans can see from our limited perspective. Shortly thereafter, I started to receive messages from Earth, and nine of the most powerful ones are part of this book. Mother Earth calls upon us to remember that we are part of Earth, and to honor our human nature, our emotions, our passions. She invites us to let go of the old dualism between heaven and earth, between high and so-called low, and to celebrate who we are in our human form.

In 2011, another energy came to me, and it was the female energy of Mary Magdalene. She was Jeshua's close companion during his life and a very enlightened being herself, although in the bible she is described as being a prostitute and a sinful woman. This misrepresentation of Mary Magdalene seems to be related to the way institutionalized Christianity has treated the female energy in general. While "mother Mary" was made into a saintly, sexless, and rather one-dimensional figure, Mary Magdalene, with her strong and independent spirit, was portrayed as a whore, possessed by demons from whom Jeshua had to liberate her. As I experience the soul energies of Mary and Mary Magdalene, both insist they were real life women, with all the emotions that you and I would have had, were we confronted with the situations they were in. Both present themselves as our sisters and friends. They are not interested in being put on a pedestal. As they speak to me, I can feel a combination of universal wisdom and human warmth. Their souls have evolved beyond the human life they lived two thousand years ago, yet they love to be with us and reach out to us from the heart.

Mary Magdalene's energy presented itself unexpectedly during a workshop we offered in the South of France in 2011. As I was preparing for the workshop, I felt insecure, because I did not sense Jeshua's familiar presence nearby. I felt like I had to surrender to the unknown, and to be sitting in front of an audience with fifty people scared me. As Mary Magdalene started to speak, I could sense a deep power along with a deep sadness overwhelm me. The power came from the original feminine wisdom she embodied, and the sadness came from the repression of that very power throughout many centuries. As she entered and spoke, the room became filled with a sacred energy, an old energy that might move mountains, yet exuded peace and tranquility. Mary Magdalene explained that in her messages to us, she would like to address the female wound, the emotional wound that women bear inside, because of the pain and disrespect they have suffered for centuries. Although Mary Magdalene seeks to empower women, I have been struck by the fact that she does not express any anger toward the male energy. Instead, she often points out that the male energy has become severely wounded as well. Men have for centuries been discouraged from getting in touch with their heart and their feelings and they have become emotionally closed off as a result. This has inflicted a deep wound in them as well. In her teachings in this book, Mary Magdalene pleads for a reconciliation between the male and the female energies, both within ourselves and in our relationships with our partners.

Although each of them has their own unique energy and line of approach, all of the four sources of wisdom - Jeshua, Mary, Mary Magdalene and mother Earth - eventually point to the same universal truth, which is that the key to inner peace, growth, and joy lies within us. The Christ energy is inside of us, waiting to be awakened, nourished, and activated by us.

We are the keepers of Jeshua's heritage. It is now time for us to make the rebirth of the Christ energy a reality, as we give birth to that energy of compassion and wisdom within ourselves. The labor pains may be hard to bear at times, but they are part of a larger current which engulfs humanity right now. This larger current is about the transition from ego-based consciousness to heart-based consciousness on Earth. It is about releasing fear-based ways of living and surrendering to the voice of our soul. All of the messages in this book mean to encourage us to rediscover that voice in our lives and to trust it. The primary aim of this book is to give you the bigger perspective that is so difficult to grasp when you are in the middle of emotional turmoil. It invites you to feel connected again with your soul, the real You, and to live life from its perspective of joy, trust, and surrender.

Teachings from Jeshua

1. Communicating with your soul

Dear friends, I am Jeshua. I am with you. My energy connects itself with yours; feel it around and through you. I am no stranger to you. We are familiar to each other, so feel that familiarity. In your heart there is a flame, an inspiration, a desire, and also a knowing, that this is the life and times in which you want to embody your Christ light here on Earth. You have waited a long time for this opportunity. You have carried this tiny spark within yourself through multiple lifetimes, and you now sense that a new opportunity has come. One of the reasons you wanted to be born on Earth at this time was for the promise of that spark to burst into a flame that is clearly visible to yourself and to others. The desire that brings you here is to form, in one way or another, a channel for the divine soul energy in yourself to be realized in your life on Earth. You want to flow along with the current of your soul, to go within and beyond what has shaped your life on Earth from the outside.

Each of you acquires opinions and beliefs about yourself during your upbringing. You absorb ideas and images from your parents, family, peers, school, etc. You begin to play certain roles without questioning them, and you soon develop something called a "personality": a set of habits, behaviors, and thoughts. But at some time in the course of growing up, something else awakens in you. First, it is no more than a whisper; a memory that you can not place; a knowing that you are more than what is just determined by the world outside yourself. There is something deeper, a layer that can not be contained and understood by the human intellect. Herein lies your core, that which precedes and survives the earthly sphere – your soul.

When your soul incarnates on Earth, it has already acquired a history. The soul carries within itself all kinds of impressions from other lives and experiences in the cosmos. You are not a blank page when you are born; you have already developed wisdom through all your previous experiences. You come into this life with something to give; you are already a unique flower at birth. And life is actually meant to make that flower viable and visible; to bring it into full radiant bloom. However, due to the influences you acquired during your youth, you can be kept back from this unfolding for a long time. You try to conform to what is demanded of you, and that adjustment often brings pain, because you are depriving yourself by doing so. External forces can be very compelling and decisive for you. All who are present here, or who are reading this, want to liberate yourself from these forces. Pressures from your environment try to influence and define you, and keep you in check, but like a butterfly emerging from its cocoon, you seek to liberate yourself from these external forces. And what is it that you are driven by? By a remembrance, a whispering, a knowing that is very slight at first and can not find its fulfillment in the visible world, but only in the depth of your inner being.

There within, you still dare to dream; there within, you sometimes know very clearly who you are. Sometimes you literally travel Home in your dreams during the night to drink from a source so vivid, so familiar, and so pure. When you are there, you can not imagine how you could ever have forgotten – yet it is so. You have lost yourself in Earth life mainly because fear and judgment and negativity are still so prevalent in the world.

Because of their own powerlessness, parents and teachers do not often give their children faith in themselves and in their inner resources – forgive them for that. They, too, have fallen prey to these worldly influences; they have succumbed in part to the illusions prevalent on Earth. But you have come here to shatter those illusions, which makes you a lightworker. Someone who wants to help change consciousness on Earth, so people can begin again to believe in their own unique strength – the soul that transcends their earthly personality – and to bring it into song.

You are courageous. On the one hand, you are wounded through losing your way in this reality, and this painful experience leaves deep inner traces and scars. On the other hand, nudged on by these very wounds, you have opened up to the whispering of your soul. Sometimes it is hard to really trust that voice, because you feel the pull of the old thoughts that keep you small; the feelings of uncertainty and doubt. As a child, you learned that those feelings were correct and true: keep yourself small; do not stand out; do not think beyond the norm; conform; be a good citizen; be a dear partner and a good parent; be responsible.

All those supposedly high values all too often keep you small, and require of you to hide your originality. But once you have started to go inward, you can no longer go back. You can no longer ignore your uniqueness, your strength, and your being different, and this inspires fear in you: "If I follow the voice of my heart, the cry of my soul, will I not become an outsider and be shunned? Who will love me, who will want to accept me then?" I see that doubt in your hearts, and I ask you to first reflect on who you are: that other part that wants to move off the beaten path; that continues to want to go inward; that remembers something: a homesickness, a longing. Feel the energy of that "I", that other part of you. Welcome it on Earth, and feel the power and the wisdom of this part of you. It is your soul that speaks and has tapped you on the shoulder your whole life long and begs for your attention. The soul never speaks with coercion or with judgment, with severity or with threats, such as do the voices of authority. The soul whispers, invites, speaks with joy: "Would this not be nice, would it not be wonderful and inspiring to do this?" Often you are afraid to listen to that voice. "Can this really be? May I then just do and enjoy what I really, really like?" The soul speaks an entirely different language than you are used to hearing.

The soul is no outside power making demands on you; the soul serves you. That might sound strange to your ears, because you are accustomed to thinking: "I must serve my soul, the higher part of me". But the soul equally serves you; it wants to shine through you, lift you up, bring you Home, inspire you to do what you really want and to be happy on Earth as a human being. Invite to yourself the joyous energy of your soul and do it *now*. Let it surround you, feel the gentleness of it – no compulsion, no requirements – just the feeling of being welcomed in a very deep way. Allow yourself to be received by your soul, and feel its presence around your body as a radiant cloak of light. Then ask your soul: "What is important for me to know now? What do I need to know from you at this moment?" And feel its response; you do not even need to hear it in so many words. What kind of feeling, what type of mood does the soul want to convey to you? Let go of all thoughts about how a soul should speak and your ideas about higher and lower. *Your soul is life itself!* It is the living, natural life force and it knows where balance is needed, or the right rhythm, and it wants to give that to you willingly.

When you feel that soul energy flow around and through your body, also observe what may be blocking it in places. Is there a place in your aura, or in your body where the light can not flow through freely and completely? Go to the place that stands out as being most blocked. Have no judgment about it; be like the soul, just observe it, lightly, and with gentleness and openness. See the need in that place in your energy field or in your body, and know that the need does not have to be analyzed or explained in words; simply allow whatever is needed to flow into it.

You all are here today because you want to connect with a teacher "from the other side", for one reason or another. But I say to you, beyond that desire is the greater desire for Home – the heavenly realm you come from – and to bring that Home down on Earth. *That is why you are here!* Feel how good and true that intention is. This desire is the voice of your soul. Your soul wants to manifest more clearly and fully in your life.

Feel how familiar your soul is to you – the lightness and ease of it. That is the voice of love. The "shoulds", the heaviness, the pressure, the duty, are the voices of fear, the voices from outside yourself. The voice of your soul comes from within and often speaks so softly and lightly that you do not hear it. The voice urges you to do what is most natural for you. It whispers gently and quietly: "So simple, is it not?" And it *is* as simple as that! The core of life is uncomplicated and light.

Rejoice now in our common energy; the energy of all lightworkers together. As you read this, and attune yourself to it, you help create a channel for you all. As this channel opens wider, all your soul's energy comes in and it allows you to be yourself completely and without coercion: your beauty, your originality, and the dark or fearful parts as well. The more you communicate with your soul, the more you start to feel Home on Earth.

Have respect for yourself, for your strength, for the courage you have shown thus far. It is not becoming of you to judge yourself, to make yourself small, to criticize yourself, even though you have learned that doing that is "good" or "sensible". Self-worth and self-trust become you; they open your channel to who you really are.

2. The third way

Dear friends, I am Jeshua. I am with you. Through the barriers of space and time, I stand next to you; feel me in your heart. I am so familiar with being human – the heights and the depths. I have explored the whole area of human feelings, and inside that world of extremes, I eventually found a way out; a passage to a different way of looking at things, through which the whole experience of being human presents itself in a different light – a way that creates tranquility and peace in your heart.

It is about this way out, this passage, that I would like to speak to you today. Many of you find yourselves in a dilemma; a struggle you have with yourself. There is an idea alive in your mind that you should be better, and other than what you are now. That you should be more highly developed, holier, and better able to follow certain rules; a higher ideal that you have for yourself – but this is a false ideal. All this working on yourself is based on the idea that you are not good as you are; that you should be different; and that you have the power to change yourself; that you have control over the fact that you are human.

This idea of power and control over your own human nature is one that has influenced many of your philosophical and religious traditions. In trying to mold your human nature according to a pre-set worldview, you tell yourself that you act on the basis of higher principles: moral or even God-given principles. However, behind that pretense of morality resides a deep fear of being human in the first place. Whole ideologies are then built around this fear of life, making it into a worldview that appears as striving for what is good, while in essence, you are trying to control life – both in yourself and in others.

Power corrupts – it alienates you from the natural flow of life that is present in every human being. Power gives you the idea that you can shape life to suit your purposes, but that concept is based on illusion. Life, as you know it, is *not* malleable in that way, and can not be tamed and subdued or restrained by the mind, or by the will. Life does not fit into a worldview or a system, and it can not be organized on the basis of mental processes.

For a long time, you entered into a battle with your humanity – the human condition. Lots of spiritual paths are based on the idea that you must work on yourself, that you have to elevate yourself, and that you have to impose on yourself a planned path of action that will lead you into an ideal situation. But this idea creates much inner struggle. If you start with the idea of a required ideal, you impose standards upon yourself you very well know inside you do not or can not meet – so you fail from the outset.

Feel, now, the energy of this way of thinking: what you are doing to yourself; what energy comes from the need to impose, from the quest to improve yourself, and from the desire to organize life, your emotions, and your thoughts. Feel the energy of wanting to control things. Is that a loving energy? Often, that energy poses as love, as the good and the true, but power always conceals itself in this way so it is easier for people to accept. Power does not show its face openly; power seduces through thought. That is why it is better to not *think* about, but to *feel* what the desire to control life does to you. Look at yourself in your daily life, in the present, in your life now. How often do you still do battle with yourself; do you condemn what arises in you, what happens in you, and what naturally springs up in you and wants to flow? In this state of judgment sits a criticizing energy, a coldness: "this should not be, this is wrong, this needs to go away". Feel this energy – does it help you?

I want to now take you to a different way of looking at yourself; to a place where change *can* occur, but without fighting, without a heavy-handed dealing with yourself. To make this clear, let me give you an example. Imagine something happens in your life that calls up a feeling of anger or irritation in you – whatever you want to label it. Now, you can react to that anger in different ways. If you are not used to reflecting on your emotions, and your reactions are very primary, then there is nothing there *but* anger – you are angry, period. You are engulfed in it, and you identify with the anger. It then often happens that you put the cause of your anger outside yourself – you project the blame onto someone else. Someone else did something wrong and it is his or her fault that you feel angry. This is the most primary reaction – you are identified with your anger; *you* are angry.

Another possibility is what I call the second way to react. You are angry and there is immediately a voice in your head that says, "this should not happen; this is wrong; it is not good that I become angry; I must suppress this." It might be that suppressing your anger has been taught to you through your religious upbringing or from a societal perspective. For example: it is better, nicer, more morally upright not to show your anger to others. It certainly applies to women that it is not fitting to express anger openly – that it is not feminine.

There are all sorts of ideas you have been talked into, causing you to tend to judge anger in yourself. Then what happens? There is anger in you, and immediately there wells up a judgment about it: "this is not to be allowed, this is wrong." Your anger then becomes your shadow side because, literally, it may not come into the light – it should not be seen. What happens to the anger if it is suppressed in this way? It does not disappear; it goes behind your back to affect you in other ways and might, for example, cause you to feel edgy and anxious for no reason. You can not utilize the power that resides in the anger, because you do not allow yourself to use it. You may show your sweet, nice, helpful side, but not that passionate, angry side – the rebellious side of yourself. So the anger becomes locked in, and you think you are different from other people because you have these feelings, so you might even start to distance yourself from others. In any case, the suppression of the emotion creates a bitter conflict inside yourself, and seemingly between two selves, a light self and a dark self. You are caught in a painful game, and it hurts inside, because you can not express yourself. But it is your own judgment that limits you.

Do you really become a better person because of this reaction? Is suppressing your own emotions going to lead you to the ideal of a peaceful, loving human being? When I describe all this to you, you can see very clearly that this type of reaction does not work – it does not lead to real peace, to real inner balance. Yet you all do this to yourself. Very often, you silence your emotions, because they are not good according to the morals you hold, and you do not reflect on these morals – where they come from, and by whom or by what have they been fed to you. So this is what I recommend you do: *to not think about it, but to feel it*. Feel that energy which resides in the judgments you fire at yourself, with your images of what is ideal and what you "should do", which sometimes comes out of seemingly very high motives – *but let that be*. You do not become enlightened by reining in your emotions and by systematically suppressing them.

There is a third way – a third way to experience your own human emotions. The first way was to totally identify with your anger, as in the previous example. The second way was to force out the anger, to suppress and condemn it. The third way is to allow the anger to be *and* to transform it. That is what loving awareness does. The awareness of which I speak does not judge – it is a way of neutrally observing yourself that is at the same time loving and very alive. Now, many spiritual traditions have told you that the way to inner peace is by "knowing thyself", being aware of oneself. I see how you struggle with this notion, because you wonder: how can that be? How can the mere awareness of myself bring about change in the flow of my emotions? You have to realize that the kind of awareness I speak of is something very powerful. It is much more than a passive registering of an emotion – *loving awareness is an intensely creative force.*

Now imagine again that something in the outside world evokes a powerful emotion in you – for example, anger. When you approach it with *loving awareness*, you observe it fully in yourself. You do nothing about it; you do not act upon it, but you do not suppress it, either. You keep watching it with compassion. You no longer identify with the anger; you do not lose yourself in it; you just allow the anger to be what it is. This is a state of detachment, but a detachment that takes great strength, because everything you have learned seduces you into being drawn into your moods, *inside* the emotion of anger or fear. And to make it more complicated, you even get drawn into *judgment* about that anger or fear! So you are being drawn in two ways and pulled away from *loving awareness*, the exit I talked about in the beginning: the exit that is the gateway to inner peace.

Many influences from the world draw you away from that center point, away from that loving awareness, and yet it is the only way out. It is the only way you do not become divided against yourself. By being lovingly aware of what transpires within you – your fears, doubts, negative thoughts – you do not become unconscious, you remain entirely present.

You do not let yourself be drawn in – neither by the emotion, nor by the judgment about the emotion. You look at it in full consciousness and with gentleness: "This is how it is in me. I see anger arise; I feel it course through my body. My stomach reacts, my muscles contract; my thoughts are racing to come up with reasons to justify my emotion. My thoughts tell me I am right and not the other person."

As long as you remain lovingly aware of what happens inside you, you do not go along with it. You do not drown in it; you do not go under. *This is loving awareness – this is clarity of mind.* And in this way you bring to rest the demons in your life: the fear, the anger, the mistrust. You give them strength when you identify with them, or when you fight against them with judgment – either way, you nurture them. The only way to have peace in the midst of heavy or intense emotions is to embrace them with loving awareness – not to fight against them, but to let them be with a sense of compassion and understanding.

What then happens to you? Loving awareness of yourself has a deep impact on your emotional life. You will notice that if you do not nourish your emotional energy, it will gradually dissipate. Your center point, your equilibrium becomes stronger; and your basic feeling becomes more one of peace and joy. Because if there is no longer a battle in your heart and in your soul, the joy comes bubbling upward. You see life with a milder eye. You understand other people more easily and will approach them with more compassion, because what you give to yourself you also give to others. You are not eager to judge any more, and while your emotions calm down, your ability to appreciate life and live it with deep inspiration increases. Know that the ability to be present with loving awareness is something very powerful and strong. This is what it is all about: *this is the exit!*

I invite you now, in this moment, to experience the power of your own awareness – your compassionate self – and the liberation by way of it that allows you to feel *there is nothing you need to change in yourself.* Feel the tranquility and the clarity of this awareness: *this is who you really are.* Put away the false judgments. Let the emotions flow and do not suppress them – they are part of you and some of them have a valuable message. Ask yourself if you have an emotion that you fear, one that is bothering you, one you fight against? Maybe one that has become taboo for you? Allow it to now come forward in your imagination in the form of a child or an animal – to present itself; to show itself. The child might be very expressive, crying or screaming or showing that it is deeply upset. Whatever happens, it *must* be allowed to do everything it wants to do, and to tell you what it feels. You are the loving parent who looks and says, "yes, let me see you; I want to hear your story, do express yourself fully". The story is important, as it tells you what the child or animal needs from you to feel whole and happy again. If the child tells you it is extremely sad, you can offer it comfort and guidance. If the child is emotionally shut down you can ask it what it needs to come alive again. You can talk to your inner child and acquire deeply valuable information from it. The reason you need to honor and lovingly embrace your emotions is that it enables you to restore balance inside yourself. Your emotions are not so much The Truth about a situation, but they are your inner child's truth and to honor that truth enables you to heal the most wounded parts of yourself. Within repressed emotions a lot of life energy is stored, a pure life force that wants to emerge, one that has been choked to death by all the prejudices of judgment. Let the imprisoned child, or animal, come scampering toward you. Receive it with loving openness and the life force will be unlocked and returned to you in a positive and healing way.

Loving awareness transforms – it is the major instrument for change, and yet at the same time, it wants to change nothing. Loving awareness says "Yes – yes to what is!" It is receptive and accepting of all that is there, and this changes everything, because it sets you free. You are now free – no longer at the mercy of your emotions or your judgment of them. Of course, it may still happen occasionally that you are overcome by your emotions and your prejudice – this is to be human. Try not to get stuck there by rebuking yourself: "Gosh, I have not yet attained 'Loving Awareness' – I failed again." If you do this, you start the ball of judgment rolling again. You can always return to the exit, back to the peace, by not fighting with yourself. Observe what is going on inside yourself, have compassion, and make no mistake: not to be drawn in is a great strength. That is the power of true spirituality. True spirituality is not about morality – making yourself behave – it is about letting yourself be in a most active and involved way: the way of love.

3. The center of the Sun

Dear friends, I am Jeshua. I represent the Christ energy, which is now born on Earth in and through you. I ask you to imagine my energy as a sun. Just think of the actual Sun, that radiant image of life and strength. You can also see the Sun as a metaphor, as an image of yourself, of your own being and soul. Focus your awareness for a few moments on the center of the Sun, and enter into it with your imagination – do it very calmly and quietly. Feel the immeasurable power of the energy field that is the Sun and feel yourself in the center of that huge volcano of energy. Feel the silence and tranquility there, and the spontaneous nature of this radiance: the Sun effortlessly radiates its light outward.

Rest, surrounded by light, in the center of the Sun, and feel how right and natural it is that you are supported by this source of power. This light is there for *you*, because you are, in your essence, yourself a sun. Allow yourself to relax and sink into this light. Let this light envelop you in a gentle and loving way that is flowing and warming, but never burning. Allow this light to flow through you completely and to remind you of who you are: a soul, a sun, a star in all the cells of your body. Allow every cell in your body to be imbued with this healing light of your soul-sun.

You can find the center of this sun, your central core, whenever in your daily life you return to the *now* by completely bringing your attention into the present. If you are busy with the past or the future, you go out of your center and you lose connection with your light source – that which carries you. But what is the *now* really? You are asked to be in the *now*, in the moment, in the present, but what is that *now* in reality? Once you talk about it, it is already over. The *now* is not a minute, not a second; it can not be actually named as a unit of time. The *now* evades you when you want to determine what it is. There are no limiting boundaries to the time that is the *now*. The *now* defies ordinary ways of thinking.

In the earthly sense, you can calculate time and count it – there are 24 hours in a day, 60 minutes in an hour, 7 days in a week, etc. That way of viewing time is not natural to the human spirit. The *now* is free from time – what unit of time can describe it? The human mind can not contain or understand the *now*, because it is not subject to the logic of thought, although it is quite understandable to your feelings. You know what it is like to completely lose yourself in the moment; for example, in an instant of enjoyment. There may have been times when you experienced something beautiful and at the same time you realized how special that moment was. You were aware and completely open to the experience that resonated and flowed through your body, soul, and feelings. When that happens, you are one with the experience and one with the *now* – you *are* the *now*!

When you are in the *now*, you are also then in the center of your sun, your soul, and all change takes place from that central core within you. We talked today about fear and how you feel anxious when you are outside your core and away from your center. Fear is linked to thinking in calculable time, the past and the future: "What will happen? What will go wrong?" Anticipating the future from fear is very human, but it can happen only if you have moved from your center, moved from the *now*. Being in the *now* means that all your inner strengths come together and become integrated, and you do this by being completely present in your body, soul, and feelings.

I would like to say a little more about the concept of time, and how it can intimidate and frighten you. During the last few decades, many predictions have been made about dates in the future that are alleged to be spiritually meaningful, for instance about the year 2012. Time is then seen as a sort of line that runs from the present toward the future and on which certain events are fixed or predestined. By accepting that vision of time, you could then be able to prepare for the coming events, and you can do that from either fear or trust. But is this a true image? Is the future really a straight line on which things are fixed in place? Is the future the sum total of all those hours, days, and months that lie ahead of you? Or is this a wholly restrictive way of looking at time and the future?

You who are here and who read this, know that there is more to life than what is just visible in the world. You see the form of things – someone's body, the trees or animals, or even the plants and stones – but you intuit that there is something within all those things that is not visible to the eyes and to the physical senses. You feel something mysterious is there,

an inner life, which creates a unique individual being. You ı
need to look more deeply than just at the surface of things, and ₎uu also
know what it is to experience joy when you penetrate into their inner
world, which is also within you. That is *real* life; that is the reality of all
things. The exterior is only a manifestation of that inner world.

What about time then? If you look at time as a line of quantifiable units
or spaces – days, weeks, months, years – than you look at time only from
the outside, from the perspective of that which you can measure with a
clock or a calendar. But time as seen from the inside, as an *experience*, is
something quite different. That inner perspective becomes evident when
you consider the concept of the *now*. The concept of the *now* can not be
based on the clock or on the calendar; it is based on your conscious
presence, on your awareness. According to your inner sense of time, time
can go very fast or very slow, independently of how the clock ticks.
"Inner time" can stand still when you experience bliss and stretch out
endlessly when you are bored; inner time flows according to the way you
experience things

What about the future and the past? What is their reality when seen from
the inside and not from the outside? Imagine again, for a moment, that
you are in the core of the sun of your soul, where in its motionless center
there is no time – there is only eternity. Although there is movement in
the form of rays radiating out, there is a primordial essence that is always
just there. You can call it God consciousness, if you wish, but it is Eternal
Life, and it is there inside you, deep within your center.

A sun emits rays, and imagine that you are present in those rays that
effortlessly radiate from your sun. By way of those rays, you can manifest
yourself in many lives and be anywhere in the universe. Every ray is a
life in time and space, you might say, in which you have taken on a
specific form: a body. You have experiences in that body; it has a
beginning and an end; it is born and it dies; it is mortal. To live in such a
body, focused in time, you become biologically aware and under the
influence of the concept of time. You begin to see things in terms of the
finite, but *your true center* is in the center of your sun and you, as this
sun, emit countless rays that are possible manifestations of you in the
future – potential lives and expressions of yourself. The future is not

fixed, and although every timeline is a very real possibility in the *now*, you choose to activate one and make it real in your world.

See the past also in this way for a moment. You think there is only one timeline that runs from the past to the now, but seen from the center point of your sun, that is not so. Behind you lies a whole range of timelines, some of which have become activated by you and your choices, and many others which lie dormant, so to speak, but which might still be activated at some time in your future. The past is not fixed and "over"; you can recreate the past by reinterpreting the experiences you had, by interacting with them from the present. This is possible because the past is not something outside you; it is not a dot on a line.

I will give an example to clarify this matter. Let us assume you felt afflicted by your past relationship with your mother or your father; that you felt you were not recognized for who you were and experienced fear and a lack of security in that relationship. You believe your life has been determined by that past and you feel a sense of victimhood because of it. You feel you were made into who you are due to your parents, as a product of your upbringing. But suppose that you, in the course of your life, are going to delve into your consciousness through the process of inner development. You make the connection with your soul and you go into who you are at your core, the sun within you. Through this process you now form a much broader perspective of your life. You now see your parents in the context of *their* past, for example, and you now see *their* powerlessness and *their* images of fear and negative convictions. You have forgiveness in your heart.

This broader perspective helps you to gradually feel less the victim of your parents. Moreover, you start to see that there is a part of you that has never been really touched by what happened to you, a part that has remained whole and unscathed. You increasingly feel your own autonomy and independence. And the more you connect during your life with the center point of the sun within you, the easier will it be for you to let go of the past, such as your relationship with your parents. The way you experienced that relationship was only one ray, one possible timeline, and by changing your awareness of who you really are, you can shift to another experience of the past, and to another timeline.

You are now able to look at the relationship with your mother and father from the perspective of the soul, of which as a child you were not aware. Since you are now more in your center core, you are able to perceive your parents in a different light, in a more understanding and forgiving way. You can explain to the child within you how certain painful experiences helped you grow and how your parents were unaware of the pain they inflicted. Your present consciousness *recreates the past by liberating the energy within you that became imprisoned by it.* You are literally creating a new timeline to the past, which will effect your current relationship with your parents. They will sense a difference in you and if they are open to it, your relationship will change for the better. You have opened up the past through your new perception, and thus created a new timeline in which more understanding and love exist. *This is a real possibility.*

With your consciousness, you can break open time. Time is not fixed and closed behind you; the past is not really over. Whatever you have experienced, even when there were traumatizing events in your past which profoundly influenced you, there are openings available from the present to bring comfort, love, and encouragement to yourself *in that past.* The past is like so many solar rays that come from your core, to which you can still make a connection if you go to the center of your sun.

You can recreate your own past – enlighten *and* lighten it – by looking with more understanding at who you were and at the people who were around you. If you do this, you simultaneously recreate the past as well as create a new future, because shedding light on the past and altering the energy you carry from the past will activate a new and brighter future for you. Neither past nor future are fixed; you can influence both of them from the *now* moment and you can do so most powerfully when you are in your center, which means you are connected to your soul.

Where you stand in the *now* is an *experience* – a living, creative moment – and not a dash on a ruler, nor a dot on a timeline. From the well of the *now*, all timelines spring. The *now* is where you are in the present moment – *where you are with your full attention is the now.* As soon as you are attentive to this most enlightened and present part of you – your center, your soul, your consciousness – then you radiate from this sun-center toward both your past *and* your future, and it all comes together.

Time is *not* a straight line; you can imagine it better as an intricate three dimensional spider web, fanning out in all directions both past and future.

What can you do with this knowledge in the present, in your everyday life? You can become aware of your own strength and potential. Everything is within the range of your power, both the past *and* the future. There is no power outside you; no power that determines your future or says what your past must be – nothing is determined. *You are the creator, always, and in every moment.* In that sense, you are master over your own past *and* your own future. If you remain in your core, you can hold on to this consciousness, this source of light.

In the continual realization of this source of light lies your confidence, safety, and surrender. If you are in the center of this sun, you know you can surrender to it – it is apparent and natural for you to do so. However, once you leave the center and start thinking: "How do I escape my terrible past? How do I create a future in this world that is so full of fear and threat?", you are already out of your center. The art of this transformative process is to go back into your *center and to not want to solve problems through thinking*, but to seek solutions from within the center of your sun, the *now – where there is no time!* This is the Home where *you are who you are*, and where there is nothing outside you that can determine or keep you from your destiny.

I ask you to imagine again that you are in the center of this radiant sun that you are. You feel one with the light and strength that is there, and it is effortless for you to do so, *because this sun exists within you already.* And now imagine that somewhere in that web of rays emitting from your inner sun is a timeline from the past that needs to come more into the light. You do not have to feel or see something concrete, simply imagine that the light from your sun easily fills that dark passageway from the past. And it may be that you do not quite manage to fully rekindle the light there, but the light has made an initial connection with that timeline from the past, so you can come to it again whenever you want to do so.

Say to these past events now surrounded by your sun-light:

> "All that needs light, receive that light from me.
> Old pain and old trauma that want to be resolved and released,
> now come forth into my light."

Let go of all clinging to these past occurrences. They do not define who you are; you are not the darkness you perceive there - *you are the light!* You – operating from the center of your sun – are the redeemer of the past and, thereby, the creator of the future.

Now go to the future. The future lies around you as an immense three dimensional spider web with many threads, and you are at its center. The future is not something that comes to you from the outside. The threads of the web spring from your heart; they are spun effortlessly by the continual thoughts and feelings you have. The inner states create countless possible timelines. You do not have to do anything special to make that happen – *it simply happens because you are a sun that can not help but radiate outwardly*. It is in your nature to be a Creator.

Now, ask the future, ask that web of timelines to show you the brightest thread for you *at this moment*. Ask:

> "What do I need to focus my attention on *now*?
> What do I need to become aware of *now*, in this moment?
> What direction should I follow *now*, so I can walk into a beautiful, light-filled future?"

There will come an urging from the center of this sun that you are, so let yourself be open to it.

Your soul *wants* to reassure you and to encourage you to connect with a powerful, beautiful future that is already lying dormant within you. Be aware of how effortlessly that future will come to you; you do not have to anxiously strive or work for it. *Just stay in the now*. Feel in your heart how the energy of this beautiful, bright future is already a part of you. In this way, you will draw it to yourself with more ease. Feel that beautiful future in your heart and awaken it by simply rejoicing in it. Be open to its lovely vibration. Invite it into your heart and into your hands, and through your open hands, let it flow out into the Earth to be planted there. Let it happen – it will take root naturally. Have confidence in your future and feel your sun power deep within yourself. Feel it in your heart, feel it in your abdomen, feel it in your legs and feet. Allow that sun power to be grounded through your feet and rooted firmly into the Earth.

4. You are society's teacher

Dear friends, I am here with such joy – feel my joy. I love to see you all here united as brothers and sisters. This is what the New Earth is about. When people meet each other with an open heart, when they join together in a circle like this, something new arises, something much more than the sum total of the individuals. So *feel* the energy that you have created together in these past few days. It is *your* energy.

Take pride in yourselves, you are the carriers of the Christ energy today, and I want to pass on the torch to you. Imagine that you are holding a torch in your right hand and hold it out in front of you – do not be intimidated. Now look around yourselves; what is the first thing you see? Do you see other people around you? There are people around you who want to enjoy and receive your light, because your torch burns like no other, you are unique.

Sometimes it makes me sad to see how you hide your own torch, your own light, which is so much needed now on Earth. I appeal to you today to stand up and show your light to the world. It will deeply fulfill you to do so; it is your mission, your true path.

Now, when I say to put your light forth into the world, I know it scares some of you, because your dealings with the world have not been smooth; they have been difficult and painful at times. Some of you would rather withdraw from the world. You feel you do not belong there; you do not feel at home. You feel that you can be yourself only by leaving society behind, but society is waiting for you. You have to travel into the dark to change it from within, and you do this within yourself. I have asked you before to look behind negativity, behind destructive behavior, and see the fearful child within yourself. I ask you to now do the same with society. Do not enter into a struggle with the energies there. Enter into it with a sense of peace. When you struggle with society, you are still in the realm of duality.

You feel there are aggressive powers in society and that you are either its slave or its opponent, but both these roles are within duality. You do not want to be a slave of society and for some lifetimes you have become somewhat attached to the role of warrior, of the rebel fighting against the norms of society. But your true role today is neither of those roles. You are not society's slave; you are not its enemy. *You are society's teacher*, and you teach from the heart. This means that you look beyond outer appearances and go straight to the heart of things, of situations, of people. As a teacher, you know and understand that your energy will not always be received or appreciated, and you accept that, and so you do not feel rejected by society. You are very self-aware and act from love and compassion and, most importantly, you know when to act and when not to act. You do not have to change the world. The need to change things comes from a place of dissatisfaction or even judgment. You are truly here to be teachers of love. I am passing this torch on to you and ask you to be *in* the world and not *of* the world, to always find your truth within, but also to be available and ready to share it with others.

I now ask you to see the energy of society as a child and to give it the face of a child. There is such a lot going on at the moment; the collective energy of humanity is in a state of confusion. Now give it the face of a child. Think of the old structure that is still active: the hierarchies, the misplaced authority. And even if you think it is all very ugly, see if you can find there the face of a child. If you look deeply, you can see a lost child imprisoned within the aggressive male structures of traditional society. It is, in fact, a male child who has become alienated and separated from its own heart. Feel the sadness of this child for a moment. He lost his way a long time ago. He longs for his mother, the mother energy, and at the same time he resists it. He wants to be in control, wants to rule the world with his mind, with his ego. But it is a terrible state to be in and he is not at all happy.

So what would you do with this child? Right now, he is desperate and ready to change. Reach out to see what this child most needs, which is, in fact, *you*. The energy you carry within will heal him. So, talk to this child and connect with him. He is a part of you and a part of humanity, and you, too, are a part of humanity.

You all have played different roles throughout your many lifetimes on Earth. You have had lifetimes in which you were a victim of aggressive male energy on Earth. But there have also been lifetimes in which you were on the other side, in which you yourself expressed this form of male energy. It is part of your journey on Earth to have been both victim and offender. And today you are a teacher and leave both these old roles behind.

We are now here to redefine male energy, and that is what is needed for both humanity and for yourselves. You need your male energy to express yourself in the world, although both the men and women among you have reservations regarding male energy. The male energy has, because of the past, become associated with ego and aggression. But that is not its true nature and we need a new definition, a new feeling about male energy, because it is a necessary part of creation. Male and female are complementary energies.

So I ask you to now look at the male energy within yourselves. See if you can observe the figure of a male inside you. Allow the male energy to express itself in your body, whether you are male or female. Feel the natural strength of the male energy, its clarity, its perseverance, its power to express and manifest. You need this energy to bring your light into the world, so make peace with it.

I just told you that in the distant past you have had lifetimes in which you yourself misused the male energy, lifetimes in which you experimented with the energies of domination and power. On your journey as a soul, you came to deeply regret these lifetimes. You no longer wanted to have anything more to do with that energy, so you entered into a cycle of lifetimes being a victim of aggression and domination, because there was resistance within your heart against defending yourself. But you need both energies in order to have a full human life.

So today, I am asking you to no longer be afraid to use your male energy. Be clear, be visible to others. Dare to speak up, dare to distinguish yourself from others. Your spiritual feminine energy is about connecting with others, and your male energy is there to protect you when needed and to disconnect when it is necessary. Use both!

I would now like to end this talk by simply sharing our energies. Feel the gentleness in your heart and also your strength, your ability to *be* a teacher and to *become* the teacher you are. It is important to meet with others who are on the same path, like the people gathered here today. I want to encourage you to create circles of your own, to be together just enjoying each other's company, sharing your gifts, and telling your stories. Being with soul family helps you build faith and trust in yourselves. That is why I am here. I am here to love and support you as a brother.

5. Love relationships

Dear friends, I am Jeshua. I greet you all sincerely. I feel a deep kinship with you. I am neither more nor higher than you, we are one. We embarked together to plant the seed of the Christ energy on Earth, a seed that over time would slowly grow and blossom into a fully mature flower. This time on Earth is one of completion of that journey. It is a time in which many seedlings begin to develop, and in many ways you *are* the budding flowers. Together we form a unit, a collective of souls who dedicate themselves to the birth of a new awareness. So see me no longer as a master who stands above you, but as a friend who holds you by the hand and wants to share his love with you, because I do deeply love you all.

You have an intense desire for love. You seek it in relationships with others, and also through a connection with the divine. But truly, what you are craving for lies within yourself; it is your own divine nature, the part of you that is one with unconditional love and joy. When you experience this part of you, it feels like coming Home. Everything else in your life becomes easy, light, and joyful. You are at one within yourself and you do not need anything outside yourself to make you feel good. You are a unity unto yourself – and yet you feel connected with everything else in a deep and intimate way.

What is paradoxical about relationships is that you can only be intimately connected with another person if you are able to embrace the oneness within yourself. If you are ready to accept yourself, with the burdens from the past, with your highs and lows, there is then space for another person with his or her unique individuality. You are then no longer using another person in order to come Home. Instead, you share the Home you carry within your heart with that other person. This type of relationship becomes a celebrating together, a sharing, and that is a healing relationship, whether it be with a partner, a friend, or a child; it makes no essential difference. However, love relationships – partner relationships – are the relationships that call up the most in you. They touch you profoundly and stir up deep emotions, because they seem to hold the promise of coming Home as no other relationship does.

Before I talk about love relationships, I would like to remind you that the Home you long for, that original unity from which you were born as a soul, is not far away. It is true that from the perspective of linear time, it was extremely long ago that you took your leave, symbolically speaking, of paradise. That you went on your own path as an embodied soul who chose certain bodily forms in which to manifest yourself and undergo experiences and visit different places in the universe.

When you were born as an individual soul and undertook your journey, you relinquished that primal unity, which you can imagine as a warm blanket of love and light that was so familiar to you. A unity where you always felt the secure presence of a Father-Mother-God, and so you were never afraid of being alone or rejected. These "negative" concepts were not even in your understanding, and yet an archetypal power was at work in God that birthed you out of the womb of this Father-Mother-God oneness.

What was the purpose of that birthing? *So you all could become independent gods!* So you yourselves could become the starting point of a Father-Mother-God source of warmth and love from which an infinity of beings are created and emerge. But the farewell you bid in the beginning came to you as a shock. With this separation from oneness came the realization that in order to truly experience the process of evolvement, you could not know anything in advance. You realized you could only separate from that primal unity by going entirely your own way as an individual soul, who for the first time becomes acquainted with the fear and desolation and darkness of not-knowing and not-understanding.

You still remember that original experience of desolation and solitude, and this memory may be triggered very strongly in the arena of love relationships. But before I address those relationships, I would like to remind you that even though the separation from Oneness happened eons ago from the perspective of linear time, you have the possibility to experience that Oneness *at any time.* When you go into dreamless sleep, you leave your body and connect with the deepest source from which you came, with God, if you want to call it that, and with the deepest core in yourself: that part of you that never left paradise and is still there. Although you left there billions of years ago, the oneness is still within you; it is an inalienable part of your being. At night, if your mind is not too active and you surrender to sleep and to the non-physical realms that you enter, then, as you leave your body, you drink from that Source and so refresh yourself. In your daily life as well, you can make a direct connection with the reality of divine Oneness, of which you are an intimate part. By becoming very still, letting go of worries and fears, you can feel its presence here and now. I invite you to feel how together, as one, we all constitute part of that original face of God.

Imagine that in the middle of your chest, in your heart chakra, is a bright, beautiful crystal. Imagine it there and feel its power: a pure, clear crystal of which all facets simultaneously reflect your many experiences. This heart-crystal is connected with everything around you. The feelings and experiences of other living beings can be perceived by this crystal, and so by receiving their moods and emotions through this crystal, you come to understand them. From this heart-crystal, you share in the experiences of others: their pain and joy, their triumphs and disappointments. Your heart-crystal is connected to the hearts of all other living beings, because we all are one. And yet it is important to be aware that this heart, which you carry in your chest, belongs to *you:* it is *your* soul-heart. Feel how both aspects go together. You are connected on the level of the heart – a horizontal field that connects you with everything alive – so there is no separation as we all are one. Yet you are also "one", meaning that you are *you*, and no one else is exactly like you. You are an individual being and there is a vertical line which connects you directly to your Source, to God. You are in this physical body, which is the bearer of your heart, your own piece of God consciousness.

Feel the vastness of this crystal: the infinite consciousness that belongs to you and yet can go wherever it wants. It is not tied to this body, although it is in this body now, temporarily, but it is such a vast energy that ultimately it is not bound to any form. You *are* this consciousness; you have brought a piece of the divine fabric of the Father-Mother-God along with you here to Earth. You are whole and complete within yourself, and you are the guardian of this heart-crystal. Remember that, while we now look at the theme of love relationships.

all in love with another person, there is often an intense ⸱f delight at the beginning of the relationship. It seems as if someuₙₙ₉ gets torn wide open within you, something that was long hidden and can be only unlocked by the look of that other. Other people do not seem to see that "something" within you, but your lover awakens the real depth of who you are. Your passion and your enthusiasm for life increase, you feel seen and loved, and your eyes are opened to your unique beauty– the wonder of you. This what the experience of "falling in love" brings to you. And although it seems to be about the other, it is really about you, what the other evokes within you, how they make you feel about yourself! It seems that the other's presence magically awakens you to how much you have to give and how much you can be loved.

Although the experience of falling in love can offer you genuine insight into your own potential, it also holds the danger of becoming intoxicated with the awe and wonder of the infatuation. When that happens, you tend to blindly attach yourself to the one who awakened the feeling of bliss within you. She or he has the "magic wand" in their hands, and what first led to a revelation, and a loving feeling toward yourself as well as the other, leads gradually to a flight from yourself, as you become totally focused on the other.

Then begins a struggle with the other. You will want to possess the part of them that makes you feel so good. And the other often does the same with you, and you both become deeply confused by this tug-of-war. In this way, the highest that you can give each other eventually calls up the lowest, namely jealousy, dependency, and power struggles. This is an extremely painful fall that almost everyone has experienced in their life.

How does this fall happen? There are two parts within you. From that heart-crystal I described, there is a love in you that can see the other exactly as he or she is, and can experience the beauty that is there. From this space in your heart, you can enter into an equal and balanced connection with each other, in which you acknowledge the divine in each other and in which you also accept the human in each other. You grant the other their pain, limiting beliefs, disappointments, and resistance.

But from the level of your abdomen there is another energy at work, something that can be a very strong, disruptive force in a love relationship. I call this energy the neglected inner child, who carries a deep and ancient pain within that goes back to the original cosmic birthing pain of leaving the Father-Mother-God oneness. This wounded child awakens as you fall in love, with renewed hope for redemption, and it has many emotions that can obscure your heart. These emotions can envelop the heart-crystal and cloud the fact that *you* are the source of the delight and bliss you experience in the beginning stages of romantic love. Those feelings had to do with *you* and hold the promise of healing and self-love. They were ignited by the other's presence, but the real promise of love between two people is that it can help both of you to love yourself more.

However, the child in you, who is in pain and crying out for the attention, love, and recognition it has missed for so long, may be tempted to take a kind of stranglehold on the partner; it wants to hold on at all costs in order to get for itself what it lacks. In this way, the child and the heart-crystal can end up on two opposing sides. What at first seemed to be pure, unconditional love, turns into a destructive relationship where you are going to fight with each other and enter into a battle that nobody wants, but that happens anyway.

As the magic threatens to disappear, you may become desperate. At all costs, you want to cling to your partner, because you once felt a sense of absolute love with that person. You are going to fight to hold on to them, and your oldest wounds, your fear of abandonment, your anger, even hatred, may come into play. It is very difficult to let go of the other person even then, because you will be driven by a reminder of how good it was when all was in harmony.

It is very important that, at this stage, you know how to let go. The moment you feel your relationship going into a downward spiral, and you are going to accuse and blame each other, is the time to step back. The risk of injuring each other badly is now much greater, precisely because you have touched each other so deeply, and that injury will be hard to heal.

So dare to take a step back when you feel that you are spinning out of control, that you are being swept away by emotions that prevent you from approaching your partner with an open heart. You may sense a deep fear of being abandoned, or just the opposite: a fear of connecting so deeply to someone that you could lose yourself in the relationship. There can be other emotions such as anger or jealousy, but what is important is that you notice how the most intense emotions are *more about you than about the relationship.* The relationship triggered the emotions, but they themselves stem from deeper causes.

What matters now is that you turn toward the hurt and neglected child within, who is the real cause of your emotional imbalance. *Doing* that is not the responsibility of your partner, but neither are you responsible for the inner child of your partner. Making someone else responsible for your pain and expecting them to heal it leads to enormous confusion in relationships.

So, how do you know whether the relationship, which was initially a loving bond, is going wrong and is getting unbalanced? Actually, there are clear signs, and one of the ways you can find out is by symbolically doing an exercise with your inner child.

Imagine you stand opposite your partner at this moment. Or take someone who is very important for you, if you currently have no partner, and allow your inner child to stand to your left. Simply imagine yourself as a child somewhere under the age of ten, and stand with that child to your left opposite your partner. Now see how the child responds to your beloved. Look at the first reaction of that child. Ask the child: "What attracted you to him or her? What did you find so irresistible? What touched your heart, what fascinated you?" And then you ask: "How do you feel now?"

Did something happen to that original quality? Can the child still feel that love? In a healing relationship, that unique quality is still very much present. It feeds you still, warms you still, while at the same time your partner has gotten a more human form, with her or his own problems and ups and downs. However, something of that original magic is still there, and because of that magic, *problems can be overcome*. If you notice that the magic is absent, if your inner child actually feels unloved or treated unfairly, then there is something going on to which you need to pay attention. Take the time to discover this with your inner child.

To clarify the situation, let go of the image of the inner child, and now imagine that you stand before the partner you have chosen and look how the energy of giving and receiving flows between you. First, see what you give the other and feel it, and it does not have to be expressed in words, as long as you sense it. Look at what flows from you toward the other, and sense how you feel in this moment. Do you become more energetic because of this giving, or do you feel empty and exhausted? Is giving inspiring, or do you become depleted by it? Hold on to that first feeling.

After looking at what you give to the other, take a look at the reverse interaction. What do you *receive* from the other? Just rely on your first feeling as it comes to you. Does what you receive feel good? Does it make your heart more open? Do you feel happier about yourself as a result of what you receive? The essence of a healing relationship is that the other gives you something that creates joy in your heart.

Finally, there is another sign of a destructive relationship. From your solar plexus – a spot close to your stomach – sense a "cord" of energy that connects you with the other. If you are sensitive, you may see the cord with your inner eye. What you are looking for is the feeling that you need to possess the other; that you panic at the thought that the other will no longer be here; that something pulls on that cord. If you sense that, then that is essentially an energetic umbilical cord that connects you with the other, and gives you the feeling: "I *need* them, I can not do without them!" That panicky feeling shows you do not operate independently, or at least you think you are not able to, and such a dependency can lead to a destructive relationship.

In a healing relationship, it is natural to miss each other if in one way or another you would be separated. It is natural to enjoy and therefore long for each other's company. You may *want* the other, but you do not *need* the other. In a destructive relationship, however, there is something malignant at work. There is a feeling that you can not do or be without the other, that you are dependent upon them for your well-being – maybe your very life! – and this substantially weakens you. There is a deep fear of possible rejection by the other, and that makes you feel small and constricted, and the whole relationship no longer has that joyful spaciousness and freedom it had in the beginning.

Try to feel these things for yourself, calmly, in your own way. And do not be afraid to make room in the relationship to allow yourself to explore this important issue. Because once you find yourself in a negative spiral in a relationship, it is often necessary that the partners distance themselves from each other, physically *and* emotionally, in order to realize where they each stand. At such a time, it is often not useful to try to talk things out. It is necessary that your energy fields first become free from each other in order to gain sufficient space to come back to the center of your heart-crystal. Descend with your awareness inside that beautiful clear crystal that is your essence. Do not depend on others to open up that experience for you; it is there for you – always. It is the whisper of God you can hear in the silence.

Feel how, from this crystal, light rays shine onto the child in you that suffers pain and who is still seeking outside itself for acceptance and love and security. Let your light rays fall on that child, and you can literally see the crystal light anchoring itself by flowing deeper and deeper down through your abdomen and all the way down through your legs into the Earth.

This is *your* light, *your* unique soul light! You are here to experience this light in a body on Earth. Your particular light is unique, it is your angel light, and if you remain connected with it, then you attract healing relationships in your life. You have no "need" for another. And you also have no need to make another into something "perfect": someone who *finally* sees you in the perspective you desire, and who *unconditionally* understands and embraces you in the way you want them to.

Unconditional acceptance and love is to be found only in your own heart – by and for yourself. Do not burden another with that duty. That absolute love is something between you and your Self. This you can only give to yourself, and when you do, you will become a fountain of love for others, because you then have become completely honest and true with yourself.

You love yourself, including the dark part: that child in you who struggles sometimes and is tormented.

When you love yourself, it is easier for you to see your partner in a true perspective. You no longer have to take so personally the sometimes offensive or hurtful things that she or he says or does. Their actions and reactions belong to them, and it becomes easier to not respond too emotionally when that happens. The other person is no longer responsible for your soul's salvation – *you are. You* are the master of your world, your reality.

You all are on this path to self-realization, and already you are touching other people with your heart-crystal: you are giving sparks of love and hope to them. I thank you for coming to Earth at this time, in this period of change and transition. I am with you and I care for you deeply. You are my brothers and sisters, and I love you all.

6. The backpack

Dear friends, I am Jeshua and I am with you. I am sitting here beside you in your circle. I have been a human being like you. I know what it is like to be part of a field of consciousness in which fear reigns and in which there is a sense of separation from the natural oneness of life. The separateness pains you and breaks your heart. People think they can not live without food and water, without oxygen from the air, but what truly makes you die, on a deeper level than the body, is being separated – and from what? Separated from Home, the Source, the primordial Oneness, the pulse of life itself.

How is it possible that you have become disconnected from this Source – lonely and wandering through the universe? Feel the fall that you made. It was a free fall and not a sinful one. To be born as an individual soul inevitably means to fall into a void in which you slowly rediscover yourself as a unique and independent consciousness. After your birth as an individual soul, you experience for the first time that *there is something outside you.* You have become an "I", and beyond is a world that feels strange and new to you, although you sometimes find yourself feeling very much at home somewhere or with someone. There are sparks of recognition as you travel throughout the universe.

Why did you embark on this journey? What motive, what primal cause lies behind your journey as an individual soul? It is the desire of Spirit itself who wanted to live *through you* as an individual, as an "I" – God wanted *to live.* That is the secret behind the diversity in Creation. The multitude of forms of life, the many unique "I's" who are growing and evolving throughout the Cosmos are all manifestations of the one Spirit. *God wanted to experience life.* And what is life but a plunge into the new, the unknown, into that which lies beyond the boundaries of what you know and have experienced already. Spirit endowed you with free will because that is the only way to create new and unpredictable ways for life to unfold.

But oh, how much sadness the journey has brought you, too! Experiences of grief, loneliness, exhaustion, have left many of you feeling broken in the depths of your soul. Did God want these "dark" experiences, too? Did

Spirit want to experience them through you, and also through you and you and you – through you all? At the moment you are able to say "yes" to that question, and can actually feel the "yes" within, you begin to understand who God is.

God is not someone who holds the reins. He, She, It did not know it all before the start of the journey. Spirit was impelled by a great desire, a love for life, and trusted you, His creations, so much that He let you be free. She trusted the flow of life so much that She let it all go freely and allowed Herself to become fragmented into an infinite number of pieces: the God particles that you are. Somewhere within, She understood that you carry inside the strength, the light to find your way back Home. But there is more to it than that, because it is not only about the return of your soul; better said, it is not at all about a return, but about pushing outward the boundaries of Creation and allowing it to expand and evolve ever deeper and wider.

Because of your path – the immense peaks and valleys that you experience – the universe expands: as you hold the extremes of light and dark within your own consciousness, you gradually develop the ability to understand yourself and others deeply, to see the light hiding within darkness, and to shine your light into the darkness. You gradually learn to *love*. Through your growing awareness, the sacred and magical reality of love enters the world. Love unites and joins, while respecting individuality, and celebrating it. The depth of your compassion, the deep inner connection that you are able to make with other living beings, is the result of your path toward individuality, which is in part a journey through darkness. You do not as yet see the significance of the human journey, but it is vast and meaningful beyond yourself.

God wants to manifest through you. You add something to Creation, something that otherwise would not have been, especially because your consciousness can hold such a wide array of experiences: from very negative to very positive. You, as souls in the flesh, are the magic makers of the universe. You are an infinite being who has received from God a spark of light in your hands to radiate in a way that is completely your own, unique and precious. *Life is not complete without you.* I wish I could make the magnificence and wonder of that evident for you. Then you would see yourself very differently, with more awe, and without those harsh judgments that you have made your own through your existence as human beings on Earth.

I have just offered a sweeping and cosmic perspective to you. Let us now descend into the ordinary, the everyday, because you want to know how you can truly experience the light, the magic of who you are, and embody it on Earth. Of course you want to know this, because it is your deepest purpose as a soul to realize yourself here, in matter, in a body of flesh and blood. And oh, what resistance you come up against: centuries of oppression, especially of the spirit. Your free, spontaneous impulses, your natural tendency to flow along with the whisperings of your soul, has been persistently suppressed in the past.

For a very long time, life on Earth has been a scene of struggle. Because what do souls do who feel deeply separated from the whole, separate from the soothing oneness they once belonged to? They feel so empty and lost that they want to feed on the energy of another in order to feel whole and complete, even if for only a moment. This creates the desire for power at the expense of another.

In this way, twisted relationships arise where you are leaning and dependent on each other. This creates struggle in the human soul. To the process of separation belongs the feeling of not being good as you are. This is often confirmed by your surroundings which are full of people who do not feel good about themselves – this feeling has become a collective legacy.

Imagine how that legacy drags on from generation to generation: a deep sense of being lost at the core of your being. A trying to survive from there by constructing defensive psychological walls, because you are afraid of the person near you, who you think wants to deprive you of something – and people often do want to do that subconsciously. They are so looking for recognition and the feeling of being Home that they will grasp from everywhere: from other people, from drugs, status, possessions. It is an act of despair to attempt to nourish yourself this way, but yet so very human. Who does not recognize themselves in this description? Who does not recognize the lost-ness inside? However, you are standing now on the threshold of a new era. A new energy mixes with the collective realm on Earth.

Imagine that, as you grow up on Earth, you carry a backpack in which you carry the energies of the past. The ideas, the energies of your parents, your family, and even your ancestors and the country and culture in which you live – these you carry around. Make a connection with that backpack. Feel how it sits on your back at this time. Observe it calmly. Are there perhaps heavy stones in that backpack? Does the weight press down on you? Perhaps you have already released some things, but there is still more that burdens you. Become aware of the weight you are wrestling with from the past. Now that you are approaching the threshold of a new consciousness, one that operates very differently than the old, the weight of the backpack becomes increasingly heavy and obvious. You are aware that it keeps you from moving forward. So I ask you now to turn toward that backpack of old energy. Take it off your back and put it on your lap and unpack it. Take the time to do this. Instead of stubbornly trying to run forward while the energy holds you back, stop, turn around and face that which is weighing you down.

Try not to think too much about it. Obsessive thinking is part of the old energy. Keep it simple. Imagine that you open the backpack and you see a stone. Touch this stone with your hands. Feel its weight, its solidity, its coldness. Connect now with the light that lives in your heart and flows through your hands. Suddenly you feel, you know: "I do not come from the past, *I come from the future*. I am not what has been made of me by the past. Those experiences do not determine who I am. I am free and grand and wondrous." With your hands you touch the stone, and with your eyes, which are not physical but are inner eyes, you go to the heart of the stone and you hear the cry that comes from inside. This stone might seem no more than a burden, a ball and chain on your leg, but it holds something that is a part of you, which has been caught in the energy of the past. It is a prisoner who needs and pleads for your help. Hear its voice.

The imprisoned consciousness has become confused, indoctrinated by the voices of fear, judgment, and separation. Can you hear it? Look at it from the fullness of your light, from the Oneness in your heart, and then tell the prisoner: "I would like to meet you. I do not want to get rid of you; I want to reassure you and set you free. You are part of my journey through the universe. You are of great value to me." And you take their hand.

See if the prisoner comes out of the stone. As they do, allow them to enter your energy-field. Receive this shadow-self of yours with arms wide open. Imagine you are a magical angel of light and, as such, you have no fear of your shadow-self. Let yourself merge with it. Feel the sadness and the despair that this prisoner has long carried for you: frustration, anger, fear. Caress this being and thus liberate it. See how it reacts to your embrace. It will change into something new that will support you and make you wiser. The energy of the past will turn into a gem once you hold it with loving awareness. It is not to be discarded; once it is transformed by love, your wisdom and love become deeper and vaster because of it.

As you connect more deeply with your shadow-self, you will start to relax, because you no longer have to struggle under the backpack that was so heavy to carry. This burden falls away from you if you no longer fight it and summon up the light of your soul. The soul has no judgment about what is in your backpack, nor about where you stand in life, what you have achieved, or where you might have failed. The soul knows that inner growth does not proceed along a straight line from A to B, or along well-defined steps and procedures. Life radiates out in all directions, wildly and unpredictably, and the darkest corner may prove to be a gateway to the brightest light.

Your soul cares about you. It wants to light up your road and ease your burdens. You do not have to perfect yourself according to some external measure; you can be who you are *and* have peace. Being human is something to be embraced, the light *and* the darkness. They belong together. It is the interplay between both that makes you unique: a human being with their own history and challenges, eventually transforming the dark parts into gems of wisdom. If you can feel the acceptance from your soul, if you can say '"yes" to life, you connect deeply with the Earth and you say "yes" to being here. Allow it to happen, say "yes" to your life.

The new Earth is created by whole, mature souls who have been honed by life, wounded by injuries as well as enlightened by profound experiences of love and healing. That is what makes you beautiful, that is the *magic* of life. I would like to invite you to say "yes" fully to who you are in your darkest, furthest corners. Darkness is allowed to be, it is part of God's plan.

When you can truly say "yes" to who you are, then you can laugh again and relax, and let life come as it will. You will be borne by life. Behind and around you works a great power: *that of your soul.* Your humanity, your human person, is actually only the outer edge, the physical manifestation of your soul. You can safely rely on the great *inner* power that wants to flow through you.

7. Levels of connection with your soul

Dear friends, I am Jeshua and I greet you all from my heart. We are here together, and by that I mean there is a merging of energies that takes place while we sit here. Imagine that the highest and most beautiful aspect of you recognizes itself in one another and increases many-fold because of that recognition. You often see in others their beauty, their inner riches, their refinement much more clearly and fully than seeing those qualities in yourself. By observing and being conscious of the other, you give that person faith and trust in themselves.

Now give this recognition to one another. Let it flow, let it happen, let your soul be touched by it. Whenever your soul is touched, it descends more fully onto Earth. When you are moved inwardly in a moment of recognition, inspiration, and emotion, your soul descends more fully into your body, because it feels more welcome and at home on Earth. An interplay happens between you and your soul.

Who are "you" then relative to your soul? I ask that question because that relationship is usually not clearly understood. Some of you conceive of the soul as something outside yourself – far away and above you. You then feel like an insignificant being who wants all kinds of things, and you experience your soul as being a power outside yourself that might – on occasion – intervene on your behalf, but you also feel you are more or less at your soul's mercy.

But you are *not* outside your soul and your soul is *not* outside you. The soul – *your* soul – is within you, here in this place, as well as everywhere you go – you are part of your soul. And although your soul is also a part of you, "you" are not your entire soul, "you" are not equivalent to your soul. There is a part of your soul incarnated in you; it lives and moves in you. But there is also a part that does not quite "fit in" here, so to speak; a part that remains behind. Or you could express that concept, from an earthly point of view, as a part that is too vast to be contained in an earthly body and personality.

So there is an interplay between you and your soul, while at the same time you are one and the same. You are of the same essence and not separate from each other. The interplay between you and your soul is about how much of your soul energy you will admit into your life on Earth. Is it an occasional spark of inspiration, getting a taste of an expanded consciousness? Or do you allow the soul to penetrate more deeply and fully, and give shape to your earthly existence in a radical and immediate way?

That is the process in which you now find yourselves: *going ever deeper;* this process of merging with your soul by way of a complete surrender to the flow of your soul. And you will be forced to do so by none other than *you.* It is a choice *you* make: to allow yourself to act upon what your soul urges you to do or be. And when do you decide to do this? You make that decision at the moment you realize it is *absolutely necessary* to do so; that this is the only way possible for you. Usually it is preceded by a period of time in which you hardly listened to the voice of your soul. You tried to do it on your own, from your head, from prevailing ideas that came to you from without: from external pressure and fear. There were many reasons why you did not listen to your soul, which caused you to become alienated from that voice – so it became a stranger to you.

That is what most of you have come to associate with being human on Earth; that you have become alienated from your roots, your cosmic origin, your soul. Then the process of incarnation becomes a very stressful, painful process. To descend into a body then means saying goodbye to who you are, your origin – essentially leaving your Home. That is a near impossible task, and then it is only natural that you will yearn for Home and want to get away from the world where you do not feel at Home.

There is a unique path on Earth for everyone, but *everyone* will experience being cut off for a long time from the voice of their soul. Until you realize: "I can't go on like this any longer; I'm totally stuck. When I live only from my head, from fear alone, from what 'should be' and 'must be', I feel dead inside." Only when you begin to experience this dilemma *very intensely* will you be open to a different voice, a reminder of who you *really* are. So then, at a certain level, you *have* to give in to your soul's urges.

The art of doing this is *to open yourself to the new and to release old notions of security,* and that is often very difficult for human beings. You associate doing this with giving up, with being at the end of your rope, and with feelings of disappointment, bitterness, and depression. But you can also see such a moment of ultimate despair, of no longer being able to continue in the old way, as if a door is set ajar to a new possibility. You can now take advantage of such an inner crisis to push through that door to another reality.

This push requires inner strength, because just at this moment of utter discouragement are you being prompted to turn around and to rely on something new that you do not yet know, something of which you still have no knowledge. It is like having a mess on the floor before you, and behind you there is a door, slightly ajar, from which a beam of light shines through. If you remain sitting with your back to the door and you stare at the mess, it causes more feelings of gloom, despair, and hopelessness. How can you then gain the certainty that this door behind you can give you the possibility of something different, something fresh? That certainty, that the door *can* open, begins to be felt when you make a connection with your soul.

You can live through pain and despair in life in two very different ways. One way is for you to be totally absorbed by it, and that means that all your energy, all that is conscious in you, is carried on the waves of fear, bitterness, even hatred. Your thinking becomes colored by it, so your emotions and your body will be also affected by it in the long term. But there is another way, a counterforce. You can, at those times, become aware of what is happening within you, and so pull back from the downward current. There is something within you that observes it closely, without judgment, from a consciousness that is greater than your earthly will, your earthly ideas, your upbringing, your fears, and everything old you know from the past. Then your soul enters into your earthly field. It often happens, to put it bluntly, that a mess *must* emerge before you feel compelled to enter into another form of consciousness. It is precisely during a time of crisis that there can be a shift in your awareness, and you can then look at yourself from a broader perspective.

The consciousness inside you then becomes very silent and still. Feel that silence for a moment; look at something in your life for which you have no answer, something you have already thought about numerous times, have looked at it from all sides, and have frequently experienced all the emotions that belong with it. Now find yourself in a still point of looking at the situation without wanting an answer. Feel how a certain peace immediately becomes present. *That* is the meaning of giving up "the fight", which does not mean that everything remains the same and nothing changes. It means you create *space* for the new, and not by thinking through what is already known and searching for answers and solutions in the past and what is behind you. The unknown, the new, the fresh, can only enter through the silence by way of that which is *not known*, and through *surrender* to the silence.

Let the silence that surrounds you flow through your body. By being still in this way, you let go of old certainties, of old ideas of how things *should* go in your life, of convictions to which you have clung. Allow them all to drift away like the dead leaves from a tree in the Fall, while the energy of your soul blows like a gentle wind through your aura. Imagine that everything that is old, everything you no longer need, everything that has been lived through and digested, blows gently away. It is just when you *do not know* any longer, that you let go more easily. In this way, a new strength gathers inside you.

The more your energy field feels empty and uncluttered, the more can it be filled by your soul. And out of the silence bubble up new ideas that are not fed from your head or by your will. The new ideas come to you from without, as it were. Something springs up, all of a sudden, and that does not have to occur immediately. What happens in this process is that inspirations and intuitions emerge freely and naturally, and feed you with new impulses.

At this point, I will explain something about the levels at which you can feel and experience your soul, and there is more than one level at which you can feel and be attuned to your soul. We spoke just now about how the soul may reveal itself through silence, through pure awareness. That experience is also a very deep feeling of being at Home, based on an ability to remain rooted, on being completely in the present, and on not being drawn in by all kinds of distractions caused by thoughts and emotions. That is one of the deepest levels at which you can have a connection with your soul: by sensing its pure Presence.

That state of silence has an immediate, positive affect on your body, your thoughts, and your emotions. *It is the healing power of silence.* When you are there, the soul is no longer something above or outside you, but is very physically tangible, in the lower half of your body, in your abdomen, and in your legs and feet. Become aware of how it feels in your body when your soul is fully connected with you, and when you are completely there with your soul. Feel the solidity of this connection, and also its tranquility and peace. This experience of peace and tranquility – *that deep stillness* – is the basis of all soul connection. If that quiet peacefulness is not there, your connection with your soul is not complete.

Why do I say this? Because there is another level from which you can connect to the soul and that level is located physically higher in your energy field. Many of you are intuitively gifted and also clairvoyant. From your sixth sense, from your energetic ability to perceive everything around you, you can pick up the moods and thoughts of others. This can happen from the third eye, or you may feel others from your heart.

Already, when I start to speak about this, you probably find that your energy is becoming somewhat more restless and ascends upward. The tranquility is gone, and you are in danger of losing your center as you tap into the many energies around you. This also happens when you connect in your heart and mind with your ideals of how you would like the Earth to be and your visions of the future. They often lift you up above yourself. There then seems to be an intuitive connection to your soul, but at the same time, that connection is not entirely grounded, and not fully making it to the silence and the stillness I spoke of earlier. You can be seized by the vision of the new era, a heart centered energy on Earth, and at the same time be very disappointed because it is not happening in your life as quickly as you desire, and because of so much resistance and opposition in the world. In this way, you feel at odds with the society around you and it seems as if you do not fit in with this world.

Although the desires and feelings that you have, the premonitions of the new Earth, are born from the connection with your soul, it is important to allow that energy of inspiration to fully descend into your energy field, your body, and your abdomen. If you have some ideas about what you desire for the future, then feel those ideas and that energy of the future in your heart. Feel, too, for the fire that lives within you and let that fire rise up to fuse the energy more solidly within you. Then allow that strengthened energy of the future to descend into your abdomen, your legs, and your feet until it becomes silent and still – until *you* become silent and still. At that moment, your soul, and the messages you receive from your soul, touch the Earth. Then a grounded, realistic flow can get underway, and you stay completely in touch with your earthly reality, while at the same time you also keep connected with your soul. *You have then built a bridge between the two.*

I see how many of you lightworkers are totally absorbed at times in visions of another world, while at the same time you lose your connection with *this* world, *here* and *now*, which is not only outside you, but also inside you. You become split, and dichotomies are created between the light and the darkness inside you and between you *and* the world outside you. Those dichotomies produce struggle and tension, both within and without.

It is now your challenge to really give up the old and to welcome the new into the depths of your earthly being, *at all levels:* head, heart, and abdomen. Your soul can only take root on Earth if you allow it to descend deeply into your being, down to the level of the abdomen and pelvis, which connect you to Earth. Feel the peace and silence when you leave thoughts (even psychic impressions) and emotions behind. *Just be there, be open to it, and the new will unfold without you knowing how.* The arrival of the New Earth, of heart-centered consciousness on Earth, depends on the presence of many people who are both spiritually evolved *and* grounded. They are the channels.

8. Making fear into a guide

Dear friends, I am Jeshua. I speak to you from the heart of the Christ energy; I speak from within you. Feel my being vibrate in your own heart, because I do not come to you from without, but from within. I am part of you.

When I was born on Earth, I was the visible representative of a much greater energy, one that had already begun to touch Earth as a wave. However, at this time, the wave has reached its full force. You who are here, and those who are touched by my energy, are part of this wave of heart energy that engulfs Earth. *You and I are one and undivided.* Connect with the voice from within that I am, the Christ energy that awakens in you at this time.

The time in which you live is a time of change, and turbulent change brings about confusion in the hearts of many people. In this day and age, people are challenged in all areas to ask themselves: "Who am I? What am I to actually do here on Earth? What is my place?" Social structures and old ideas and beliefs are crumbling. Earlier ways of relating and old traditions are collapsing. More than ever, people now have to depend on themselves. There are a multitude of traditions and cultural forms from which they can choose, with which they can identify, but still the real question remains: "Who am I amidst all of this, what is the reason my heart is beating?"

This question is all the more urgent now that the Earth itself is brought into play. She rumbles and moves from within because she also feels new tidings, the fresh wave of harmony and peace that beckons, and for which she reaches out. And humanity must come along with the Earth, whether it wants to or not. Humanity *has* to come along, because this is a time of change and a return to the ages-old unity that links all life on Earth.

I ask you to remember that unity at this moment. The unity that connects you and me, and links you with everything: the Earth, the people, and with life itself. Feel how you are linked with that age-old unity, and relax into that. You are being supported by the whole of life, and there is a logic there that transcends the intellect; it is the logic of the heart, the naturally spontaneous warmth of the heart where you are loved and received effortlessly. The energy that holds the universe together is a mother-energy. You often miss this energy in your life, the feeling of being able to breathe freely, simply being yourself without effort, to feel you are wholly accepted as you are.

This sensation of being loved is what you desire, and you can give it to yourself by remembering and trusting that you are connected with the whole. Only by sensing your connectedness can you find your way at this time: to find your path in life; to find the work of your heart: that inspiration for which you are searching. Often, you think you need to do this alone, so your mind runs full speed ahead in order to figure out how it should happen, what obstacles you have to surmount in your everyday life. But I ask you to take a deep breath, take a step back, and know you need not do it alone.

It is through the connection with the whole, with what is unconditionally supporting you, that you will find your way, that your life-path appears at your door. You need only to open the door to find it. Allow yourself to relax, have faith that you are guided and led and that you do not need to know exactly how that works. *Life is a miracle, a wonder that can not be grasped by human understanding.* Attune yourself to this miracle, and know that it speaks through you. Your body has knowledge of it; your heart is alive when you are open to the wonder of life and are willing to receive it.

You are afraid to surrender to the wondrous magical flow of life, and you have also been *made* afraid of it. In your life, you have become accustomed to excessive thinking, to wanting to bring about order and structure through thinking in order to realize your goals. But this is short-sighted and is not possible. *Authentic living is something you do from the heart.* Decisions are to be made from your whole being, not solely from your mind. And that means you must, in a certain way, release your mind and dare to trust in the unknown. Imagine making a jump into the "deep end", and see what this evokes in you, the fear of it that you feel.

I would like to say something about fear today. Fear points to that part of you where you do not surrender, where you do not dare rely on that larger whole that supports you, *that whole which is not comprehensible to the mind*. Fear points to a lack of confidence and trust in yourself. At the same time, fear is an indicator that tells you: "I have to grow around this issue, to learn from it, to become wiser". Can you, when you feel the fear inside you – that feeling of contraction that runs through your body – can you welcome that feeling as an indicator?

At the time you feel fear, you often leap back into your mind. You think: "How can I fix this, how can I eliminate the fear". You look to the future with all your might to try to see if you can master and direct all the aspects of your life. This is often your response, your reaction to fear. But in this way, you actually give the fear even more power over you, because the mind is helpless in regard to giving direction to life and the creation of the future. *Life evolves out of trust and surrender, and fear is exactly the opposite of trust and surrender.*

If you are afraid, you make yourself small, like a ball that rolls itself up and is very tense with restrained energy. The fear says to you: "I can't, I don't know, I'm too small to understand, I am nothing, I am not able to successfully live life." But take a good look at that tight ball of energy. See it before you, just as it lives in you, just as it lives in every human being. See that ball before you, the tension that you are able to feel, the mistrust, the powerlessness.

Then imagine for a moment that you put your hands around that ball. You hold that very tense ball in a gentle and loving way, and you feel the tremble in that ball of energy, the turmoil and the panic. It feels totally separated from the peaceful whole, which in truth supports you. But have respect for the fear, for this ball of restrained energy, for it is also a part of life. The fear shows you where you undervalue yourself and do not truly know yourself, where you fail to sense your own courage and strength.

Imagine that you go within that tense ball of fear with your consciousness, and imagine that your consciousness is very objective. It does not think: "What is this nasty ball I should get rid of?" It has no judgment about the fear. You, as your consciousness, enter into the ball and breathe in deeply. Let your breath fill that space, and feel then the miracle that you are *not* that ball, you are *not* the fear in you. You are the one who reaches out your hand to the fear and asks: "What is it? What makes you so afraid and tense?"

Feel the calmness that radiates from your essence in the moment that you extend your hand to the fear. Feel that you embody the opposite of the fear: peace, surrender, trust. "This is *my* fear. It is here within me and I allow it to be. It is a part of me and is *my* darkness, because I am a being of duality. In me live both darkness and light, and they are both allowed to be here because they perform a dance together, a dance that enriches the universe by allowing growth, expansion, and creativity."

The light is attracted by the darkness. The light wants to shine there, and the darkness draws attention to where the light needs to shine. In a sense, the light is infatuated with the darkness. It feels attracted by this element and it wants to enter into a dance with it. The darkness seems to be static and passive, wanting nothing, only simply resisting and persisting to hold on to the fear. But when the light turns toward the darkness and the darkness feels welcomed; when it knows it is not judged and is respected for its contribution to Creation, then the darkness opens up and is taken up into the light in a dance that opens new vistas.

You can easily recognize this in your own life when you have the courage to face your fear, and to see it as an indicator to what direction to take. When you are able say: "Okay, I'm going with you and I'm going to do the things that instill fear in me. I will go with you and take on the confrontation. I allow the fear because my fear tells me what my deepest challenge is and what I most have to conquer and discover in my life". When you are able to travel together with the fear, with that darkness in you, then you are able to uncover new areas in your life. You are able to say goodbye to your old life: to leave a job, or a relationship, or a place of residence. You are able to start something new, something uncertain, because you are willing to take a step into the unknown.

That then means you cooperate with your fear. You agree to use it as your guide, who is testing your ability to trust and stay true to yourself. As you take up the challenge, you allow yourself to be led by the unknown, by what seemed dangerous and uncertain at first, but that now has become illumined by courage and perseverance as a beautiful path, a new future, a new horizon in your life. And you know that feeling of deep joy and victory in yourself when you have reached a hand to the fear in that way; when you have widened and broadened your limits; when you have cultivated new areas in your life. Then you feel it was worth it, that the dance with the darkness is valuable, and that it brings real growth and change.

I therefore ask of you: *make peace with your fear*. It does not matter that you are afraid. More powerful still: *search out your fear*. Make it into your guide. Because whenever you feel fear, there is the opportunity for your courage and strength, now dormant, to be awakened. Your greatness can be called to life by the fear, if you are willing to face the fear and reach out to it. Do not fear the fear, trust that it leads you somewhere, *and trust your own greatness*.

The fear tells you something about your greatness. It might seem like a sign of smallness to feel fear, but it is not. The fear is the darkness that wants to play and dance with you in order to show you your greatness. You all have a heart's desire in your soul: to be who you really are, to manifest your true and unique qualities, to be able to share with the Earth and its people the light and the wisdom that blossom in your heart and soul. *Believe in that desire*, and celebrate this beautiful ideal in your heart.

When you become aware of this ideal in your heart, you may notice that fear can attack you, and sometimes forcibly. Then you are going to doubt yourself: "Can I do this, am I big enough to depart from the trodden path and direct my own path in life?" *Yes, you are big enough, you can do it.* Let the fear be your guide for the light to reach ever deeper into your being. Fear is not your enemy, and if you welcome it as a friend, it may guide you to your deepest essence.

Sometimes it is such that fear is not felt in your life. Many of you feel that you are stuck; feeling that you have lost your passion for life and are unable to connect and move with the flow of your heart. You may feel life is boring and meaningless. In fact, you then have not yet fully faced your fear. It may be that you are in your mind and trying to create order through thinking your way through life. But this will not work, and at some point you will feel restless and stressed, or feel flat and depressed, and not alive and vital.

If you feel fear, it can at first be overwhelming, but at least it is a vital emotion. Being fearful is a clear sign that *you are alive*, that you are feeling and breathing, that you are looking for direction. But many of you have closed yourselves off from their fear, and then you live, in a certain sense, an unreal existence. You feel not quite alive, or even worn out and depressed, because you have allowed your passion to be damped and your inspiration to not soar. You remain in the false security of a structure and an order that strings the days together, and this is commonly called "being in a rut".

At the moment you try to break out of this rut, and many of you want to break out, you begin to feel fear: "Can I break free? What happens to me when I no longer have things in order? Will life truly guide and support me?" It often happens, that when you make the first move to surrender to your feelings, to listen again to your heart and your passion, that the anxiety manifests itself forcefully, and then you again shrink back into your head. The solution to this reaction is: *welcome your fear*. Fear is *not* a sign that things are wrong, fear can actually be a very spiritual emotion that explains exactly where lies the road ahead to your greatness, to what and who you truly are. Trust in your fear as a signpost, beckoning you to move forward and connect with the courageous part of you.

I salute you all. You together are the Christ energy in this time. All who are touched by my words are in essence touched by their own Christ-self, now awakening. I hold you by the hand, and I greet you with reverence and respect.

9. From the head to the heart

Dear friends, it is with joy and love that I am present among you. My energy flows within this space and is felt by you all, you who are part of this wave of energy that now engulfs the world and brings new tidings on Earth.

Earth itself is taking part in this transformation in consciousness, where everything is geared toward establishing the heart energy on this planet. You all are part of this wave of consciousness that now engulfs the Earth, and you are the forerunners of this process. You are the ones who create new paths and opportunities that will be taken by others.

Creating new avenues in consciousness, new openings and opportunities, is something that happens first on the inner level. Only when an opening to more light is created on the inner level can this new consciousness manifest itself in the outer world as new forms of community, of being and doing, and of relating to one another.

Your contribution to this awakening process starts on the inner level. To become free of old prejudices and fears concerning yourself, *that is your path and that is your mission*. By doing this, you make a real difference in the world. Even though this activity is on an inner level, and therefore what you are doing is not always visible to others, what matters is that you believe in yourself and that you recognize and feel the importance of this process.

I want to take you back to the time when I was on Earth, during my incarnation as Jesus or Jeshua, because I was much like you. I was an angel who wanted to manifest my light on Earth at a time when it was necessary to plant the seeds for a new consciousness. During that time, I could only establish a latent consciousness. It is up to you – my dear ones, my brothers and sisters – to further realize and manifest this energy, which is something you have done for centuries. It is a mission in which you all participate, and in which I was but one figure, one representative of Christ consciousness.

In my life, when I was growing up as a child, I became aware that I carried in my heart a special energy. This energy was as a gift to me. There was a strong channel that I felt in my heart, through which I was connected with God, the Father, the Mother – however you name it – with The All That Is. I was acutely aware of this energy and I felt very clearly that all I had to do in my life was to keep my attention focused on this energy in my heart so that I could hold to it, firmly and clearly, while I lived in my body on Earth. To return with my consciousness to this center at all times, to this source of love and light within myself, was my task, my mission.

As soon as I was centered within this consciousness, all events around me fell into place; everything happened as it should. Everything took place spontaneously of itself. Whatever time or place was necessary for me to be present, or to be speaking, it came to me on my path. I did not have to make an effort, I was led. By doing what was in front of me, what came my way, I arrived at the right place. And this way of things happening, is the natural way of being.

This is something you all are looking for in your own life. How does one become aligned with this flow of ease and spontaneity? Imagine there is a core of light in your heart, a sun which has a magnetic effect. The more the sun's rays are allowed to radiate, the more your soul's light can manifest on Earth through you, and the easier things come your way. Then you do not need to search for them, or work hard for them, or think about what you will do. You will attract to yourself the things you need and are productive for you, or pleasant for you. This way of being is about internal work and not about seeking in an external way.

When I lived on Earth, I was overcome by despair at times by the things I saw, by what I "thought" was going wrong, by the things that did not make sense to me and seemed not to be the way they should. But every time I became mired down in that way of thinking, I knew from my heart that I had to let go and to return to the source of light and love that inspired me, to what manifested most in my heart. If I came back to that source, I could let go of outer circumstances, the things that seemed to run awry, and the disappointments and the frustrations. I could then gather patience and regain trust in the flow of life and know that it would bring me what was needed.

And this I ask of you all, to feel this confidence in your heart and to open to it, because *that is the way*. You all are working to set down your energy on Earth; to allow the highest light energy in your heart to flow through you and to give it form on Earth. This is an inner process that demands a very honest and open look at your deepest feelings, your longings, your fears, your emotions. It asks of you that you face them honestly. It demands that you send love to that which is stuck within you and is blocked. It asks of you to face these blockages and negative parts within you as honestly as possible and to transform them. That is where your inner task lies. The more you do this, the more your inner sun can radiate and spontaneously attract the events that help to anchor your light on Earth.

In the society in which you grew up, you are very much accustomed to the energies of thinking and doing. You often feel a whisper in your heart, a longing, a desire, and immediately you try to give form to this through thinking and doing. But this does not often work out in a way that is satisfactory. The key here is in postponing your thinking and doing for a bit. That you do not try to immediately put this heart consciousness into action, but that you allow it to develop by letting yourself sink deeply into it. Trust that it will become clear, that you do not have to work hard for it. Postpone the thinking and the doing for awhile.

I want to now take you to a time that is very remote from our time today, but one that still has a powerful influence on society, and on you here and now. This is the age of an ancient civilization which was called Atlantis. There is much controversy as to whether this civilization really existed. It is still not recognized by science, but this civilization *did* exist and existed for a long time. What I now want to bring to your attention is how, at that time, you habitually put the energy of thinking and doing to work.

You all are part of a group of souls, lightworkers who have experienced many incarnations on Earth, and other places in the universe. You are souls with a very long history. You have lived and worked on planets other than Earth and given form to your soul energy in a multitude of manifestations and experiments, and at a certain point, you came to Earth.

The civilization of Atlantis is an era when you manifested on Earth with a spiritual energy that was still very much from the head. Atlantis was a civilization where the energies of thought, in the broadest sense of the word, were tried and played out, together with certain psychic powers that were actively used there. The faculty of the third eye, of clairvoyance and other psychic abilities, was deeply familiar to you at that time. This idea might seem very remote and not relevant to you, but I tell you that right now you are working to transform those energies.

At the time of Atlantis, the tendency to manipulate life was carried out to the extreme, and many things got out of hand. There was a desire in you to know the secrets of life, and by that, I mean not only on a spiritual level, but also on the biological level. You experimented with biological life in various ways in order to control it, creating and manipulating life forms so they could serve your purposes. There was a type of genetic engineering based on techniques you would now call "paranormal"; it relied on concentrated mind-power rather than physical tools. You basically tried to manipulate matter by the use of your psychic powers, which were much more evolved at that time than they are now.

In fact, the true purpose of your incarnation on Earth back then was to discover and develop the energy of the heart within yourself. But before you got to that, you strongly lived from the head, and you tried to control life with your mental energy. Eventually, this caused imbalances in the energy of Earth and the result were natural disasters which ended the civilization of Atlantis. In telling you this, I am not trying to talk you into a feeling of guilt or shame about this, rather I want to sketch the development of your souls. Atlantis was one stage in a grand cycle – of which you are now in its final phase.

You have come to realize that manipulation of life through thought, through mental energy, does not fit with your true potential and who you are meant to become: an angel serving life. Through a process of many lifetimes, you have experienced both the role of offender and the role of victim on Earth. In the time of Atlantis, you were the rulers, and you subjected life, and other people, to your own will, and in that way you tried to unravel the secrets of the universe. You acted from a certain arrogance, but also from ignorance. The energy of the heart lay dormant and was not yet developed. After the demise of Atlantis, you have experienced lifetimes in which you were the victim of control, manipulation, and aggression. You came to understand what it was like to be on the other side. You experienced the karmic consequences of your actions during Atlantis, and you began to understand the true meaning of living from the heart.

The true meaning of the coming of the Christ energy on Earth, of which I was one representative, is a shift in the energy, from the head and the ego, to the heart. This shift has taken hold on Earth, and you are among the first to accomplish this change. This means you slowly let go of the energies of thought and control – the mental energies – in favor of feeling, intuition, and the heart. Surrendering to the flow of life, to the wisdom in your heart that is not trying to push, or to force, or to manipulate.

If you look at the society in which you now live, you see around you how the results of the Atlantic energy are still at work. The idea that you can master life through mental processes and from the mind is still very much alive. That you can regulate human behavior by a mind-made order, planning and scheduling, is something that almost all governments and companies seek to do. But the natural creative processes in human beings, the organic "being" of humans can not prosper in that way. There is too little room for individuality, for your own original soul's energy, in your society. You try to fit things too much into cubby-holes, making people lose themselves, so that they no longer spontaneously feel the source of light in their hearts, *and from there derive energy for their lives*.

You became acquainted with this approach early on in your life. In your childhood, there were general rules; there were standards and values of how you should live and of how you needed to control your emotional life. In fact, many spontaneous soul energies are structured and restricted early in life, so that you lose yourself in the course of your youth and your puberty. It has not been taught to you to learn to trust your heart, and to rely on your inner knowing and instincts.

The result on you of this way of life can make you feel angry, or unhappy, or frustrated, but the important thing is that if you see it in terms of that whole great cycle of the soul that you belong to, then you might realize that you have also taken part in an energy that restrained, labeled, and categorized people and life; you have indulged in this same mental energy in many past lives. So try to see from the greater perspective of your soul that you have been not only a victim of this mentality, but also its perpetrator. In your current lifetime you now have the opportunity to free yourself from this controlling energy that you helped to establish in previous times. You are liberating yourself from an earlier mistake, from a belief in mental power and control that ultimately is driven by fear and distrust. You are searching for a natural way of life where you live spontaneously from the energy of your heart, your intuition, and where thinking is only an instrument that helps you execute things, serving the heart's wisdom rather than ruling over it.

You all are searching to express your unique soul's energy. Not only in your private life, but also in the area of your work in society. The art here is for you to concentrate fully on your heart, on your true passion and intuition, and to have faith that in doing so, you are attracting what is needed in your life. Allow the thinking and doing to be the limited function they really are. The more you know how to sink down into the level of your heart, into love, into the awareness of the angel who you truly are, the more things will happen that resonate with this vibration, and the less will you have to do and the more you can simply be.

One of the errors of the Atlantis energy, of the overly mental consciousness, is that it considers being, simply being and going with the flow of what your heart tells you, as something passive, as something static. But being is the opposite of that. Being is the Divine Energy, that which permeates everything, is extraordinarily dynamic, and embodies all that is. Just being, in contrast to doing or thinking, is therefore not waiting or "doing nothing". It is an alert state of consciousness in which you welcome everything within you – all is allowed to be. Being, or surrendering to yourself, means you come Home to yourself and you welcome everything that lives within you. Then the sun can shine within you and you can accept who you are, *and that is the key*. Everything follows from that.

I invite you to feel that energy of the heart, the energy of self confidence and of being close to yourself. If there is one thing I could accomplish today then it would be this: *to awaken that energy within you and to make you trust that.* And to tell you that the only thing I came to do in my lifetime was to hold on to the energy of my heart and to let it flow on Earth. Just what the effects of that are, you can not and need not know. You only have to be focused in the consciousness of love in your heart; just see how it unfolds. Let the magic of life do its work – *trust.*

10. Embracing the dance with darkness

Dear friends, I am Jeshua who speaks to you from the heart of the Christ consciousness through which we all are connected. I speak to you on a day when the energy feels somewhat heavy and sluggish, and you are aware of this. You attune yourself constantly to the subtle energies around you. And by subtle energies, I mean the astral influences that surround you here on Earth, which feel heavy at this moment.

Do not be afraid of this energy. Once you dare to move freely and consciously in this heaviness, it no longer need affect you so much by being caught up in it. It is only when you unconsciously react to the heaviness that you get drawn into it, and you feel irritable and bad-tempered, and you no longer know who you are and what you want. When that happens, you are pulled into a lower vibration that is not of you, and having that happen is not necessary.

During a time like this, consciously align yourself with that feeling of heaviness, something that can manifest itself in your body as fatigue, or listlessness, or a feeling of discomfort and negativity. Imagine that you now journey with an open consciousness through that density or heaviness. You may perceive it as a foggy, gray atmosphere, but allow any images to come to mind that match your feelings.

Be present with the heaviness, yet completely relax into your body, and feel the freedom of doing that. You do not have to lighten the heaviness, and you do not have to fight against it. There is nothing you *have* to do! Take notice of your breath. Breathe in and feel your freedom, breathe out and feel your presence *here* and *now*. I do not ask you to overcome the darkness, but that you go into the darkness without losing yourself in it, and that you become accustomed to feeling at ease there.

Light is very often contrasted against the darkness. In that way, there is a conflict, a clash, and then a duality is created. "I am a lightworker", you think. "I am a fighter for the light; I raise my sword and will fight against the darkness". And you can succeed in doing that for a while, but then the shadow comes over you again, because you are fighting from your will and mind, from a preconceived notion about what is right. But this world is not for the overcoming of darkness, but for gaining an understanding of what darkness is and entering into a dance with it. It is for understanding the *value* of darkness. As long as you fight against darkness, either in yourself or in the world, you maintain duality and struggle.

Imagine that you now become very still inside by connecting with the silence in the universe. Everything that appears in form is enveloped by an ocean of silence, a sea of emptiness, if you prefer, but it is not an emptiness in the sense of an absence of something, rather in the sense of pure being. Feel that pure being within you, how everything is as it naturally is at this moment. Let go of all attempts to change things.

Be with yourself just as you are, and feel the relief of allowing yourself to simply be. Allow the negativity, the fears, the doubts, and your fatigue to simply be, and now look at these burdensome emotions with an open and unprejudiced eye, with interest and wonder. Reach out your hands to the darkness and say: "I want to learn from you, I want to understand you, I want to dance with you in this universe, so that together we create something new, a fresh energy, a *combined* energy. Not just light, nor darkness, but a merging of them through this dance of *both* energies, so as to create something of even greater value."

Open up your heart to your own darkest emotions and allow them to be. They are participants in this great adventure of creation; give them a face or a form so they can talk. Imagine something if nothing spontaneously comes to mind. Give it a voice, a sound, allow it to enter into a dialogue with you.

Observe the "evil" that torments you, pursues you, and look at it and reassure it – allow it to be there. You are the angel who travels through light and dark, an unperturbed living light without any judgment, so allow the image of your darkness to speak. Give it the freedom to spontaneously express itself. Let it cry, rant, and scream, and express what it will, an utterance of its deepest emotions. Do not concern yourself with the fact that it is a part of *you* that feels bad, or that it is not spiritually evolved. Spirituality lies in accepting all that is, and discovering a seed of the divine in all things, even in the deepest darkness. And then movement occurs and something stirs, because the darkness is not a fixed and static thing.

Darkness holds energy that has been suppressed or overlooked – *it is the energy of neglect* – something that should not be seen and known, and pushing it away leads to a kind of deadness – a tiredness and heaviness. When you reach out to the darkness with a totally non-judgmental gesture, and with a willingness to cooperate with what is hiding there, the imaginal figure you just created will change. Something will stir in the heart of the darkness, a "something" that has been abandoned for so long and now feels invited to open up a little and get involved again.

You think that growth in consciousness ascends from low to high, from some lowly beginning to an exalted end point in the future, but the process does not work that way. Growth of consciousness means you descend deeper and deeper into yourself, and there you meet all that is alive in you, and all that has resulted from your many, many previous incarnations and experiences in this universe. Thus, as soon as you decide to walk the path of inner growth, the path of the light, as you call it, are you going to encounter in yourself extremes of light *and* darkness, of love *and* fear. Inner growth is not just a way upward, it is just as much a way downward into the depths of the fathomless space of your soul. And the most powerful tool available to you is an open and accepting awareness, free of judgment.

You would, of course, prefer that you feel light, happy, and joyful, but this can not always be so on this path. It is when you want to be liberated from old burdens, that they emerge and want to be seen and enter into awareness. And not just so they can be eliminated as soon as possible, but so they can be welcomed and opened as if they were "gifts". In every dark part is hidden a gift; in each piece of deep negativity lies a fruit. Something that has ripened in your soul: a talent, a quality, which wants to reveal itself. If you want to bypass all those gifts, because you do not want to experience the negativity, you would be more superficial than what you are in reality, and the depth of your soul would never get a voice. Unwrapping the gifts hidden in the dark brings deep fulfillment and sense of purpose into your life.

That is why I am asking you, even though it goes against your desire for joy and lightness, to extend your hands to the darkness within you. Be open to the fearful, negative parts in yourself, and encourage them to openly join with you. And that also means that for some time, life will be intense and you will not be as exuberant and light and joyful as you would like to be. However, there is a big difference between knowingly entering into your negativity and handling it half-consciously or unconsciously. When you deal with the negativity with full awareness, and you say "yes" to it; when you know and feel that there are hidden powers and gifts hidden in the darkness, then you can maintain this process much more easily. It is about surrendering to the process. It is about giving the darkness within you the chance and the opportunity to speak, and to transform itself into positive unique qualities.

When you always run away from the darkness, oppose it because it does not feel right, then you abandon the darkness and it feels neglected once again. The result is depression or bitterness in a part of you. And it can even go so far, at an outer level in your everyday life, that things begin to work against you and nothing works out, and there is no flow in your life. But this is in fact the dark part inside you, the anxious neglected part, which in a roundabout way now knocks on your door and says: "Hey, wait a minute, we can't continue without me! I know that, but do you know that as well? Will you be prepared to turn toward me to receive me?" And as soon as you turn inward, even though it feels intense, your life will begin to flow again, and the right things arrive on your path at the right moment.

Inner growth and lightwork always call for a turning inward. This will remain so, until the end of your days, and this is not said to discourage you, rather it says something about the nature of life here on this planet. You are living in a world of duality, but there is beauty in that. For it is precisely when you consciously take on the dance with darkness will you discover so many treasures within yourself, and start using them and experience joy in doing that.

By getting in touch with your fears, your darkness, with "the wounded child within yourself", and by remaining open to it with compassion, will you become an effective and powerful lightworker. It is what you have to offer to others as your own energy deepens and softens by an inner transformational process: *the embrace of your own darkness* – and therein lies your strength. Not by overcoming the darkness, but by embracing it, and hence refashioning the whole process to a new level and energy of compassion and understanding.

That is what this world now needs, people whose heart is vast, spacious, and boundless. People who have seen the extremes of light and dark within themselves, and are therefore not likely to judge others. To have a heart as wide as the world is your goal. That is being a lightworker. Now feel the energy and greatness of your own open and compassionate heart. Feel how it says "yes" in response to every dark part in yourself: the fear, the doubt, the turmoil, the insecurity. Your heart says "yes", again and again, so that everything is allowed to be as it naturally is. And when you hold this awareness in your daily life, you will find that you no longer wildly oscillate back and forth between extremes of great joy and enthusiasm and depression *and* hopelessness.

The kind of consciousness that I speak of here is a stable, focused consciousness, a centering, you might say, on "what is". It is also a form of being grounded, which means that you do not allow yourself to be carried away by emotions, either of the light side or the dark side. There is a sustained inner peace inside yourself when you have found this awareness in your life. There is ever a balanced foundation of silence, rest, and peace; a richness and a depth that extends beyond the inner struggle between light and dark, beyond duality.

You *so* desire the light, enlightenment, joy, love, harmony, ecstasy – and I fully understand this desire, because it is in your nature to do so. Nevertheless, on Earth, it is the case that you *first* need to strive for an awareness of peace, quiet, and openness in which you allow *everything* to be as it is and you are one with *whatever* there is inside you.

From this deep acceptance and appreciation of all that is and all that you are, you will begin to experience a joy in your life, which does not have the quality about it of elation or excitement, but is more a silent joy, a feeling of profound peace deep inside your body, a relaxation *into* yourself. You no longer fight your darkness, the fear that is there, and when you allow it to be there, it does not turn against you, and you can cooperate with it.

At this moment, I ask you to feel the silence in my being, the focus I come to bring to you. It is neither good nor bad, dark nor light – this focused silence just is. *It is the open and loving consciousness of Creation itself.*

11. Illness and emotion

Dear friends, I welcome you warmly. I am overjoyed to be with you and to share my energy with you. You are courageous; you follow your path despite the resistance and the negativity you encounter in your life. You come up against negativity within yourself and from others, yet you are able to learn and to grow inwardly because of it. I have confidence in you. The power and the light of your consciousness bring change into your own life and into that of others. Even though you are still involved in your own struggles, through your focus on inner growth, you are a forerunner who supports the transformation of consciousness on Earth.

Today I speak on the subject of "illness and health". You have all been heavily influenced by the scientific, dualistic tradition that has shaped your culture. Within that tradition, the body is essentially seen as a thing, a kind of mechanism whose components can break down and which can be repaired by an expert "mechanic". When you see the body as something that is disconnected from your soul, your psyche, then you lose your authority over it. Not you, but an expert, the doctor, knows what is best for you. The medical expert has studied the body, that is to say that person has gained specialized knowledge about the mechanics involved and can apply that knowledge to your body. But in that type of doctor/patient relationship, you become a stranger to your body and the emotional connection is severed.

From our "otherworldly" perspective, the body is something completely different than a mechanism that is separate from your soul. The body is for us the most visible part of the soul. *The body is not divorced from the soul;* it is really the observable manifestation of it. The soul itself is an eternal essence of light that temporarily manifests in a body in order to gain experience and thus to be enriched inwardly. The soul speaks to you through your feelings, which form the bridge between your soul and your body. *Through your feelings your soul descends into matter.*

I encourage you, here and now, to connect with your soul. Feel how, in essence, you are independent of time, space, and form. You inhabit this body out of your own free choice. All the cells of your body are inspired by your soul's energy, but at its deepest level, the soul is free and unbound. Your soul has chosen to manifest itself in this body during this life on Earth, *and your body gives you the opportunity to communicate with your soul.*

When you live on Earth, the connection with your soul can become severed. You become immersed in the world of the senses and of human ideas, fears, and illusions. *The body is the direct gateway for keeping alive the connection with your soul.* Your body is the bearer of your unique soul energy and continually responds to it. When you get cut off from your soul, and you no longer feel her impulses, your body will eventually respond with pain and complaints, or illness.

From this point of view, you are the only real authority over your body. Illness and complaints of pain encourage you, through your body, to understand the message of your soul. Even though doctors and medics can provide you with valuable advice and resources on the physical plane, there is a deeper level at which the illness has something of value to say to you. From our point of view, the illness is not something negative; it is an attempt of the soul to restore its connection with you.

What kind of message does your body have for you? How can you come to understand the signals from your body? And how can you concretely deal with them in everyday life? To explain this, we must take one step backward. What happens before the connection with the soul becomes so powerfully blocked that illness occurs? What initially happens is that you lose the connection with your feelings, with the flow of emotions that goes through you.

In your earthly reality, your soul manifests itself most directly through your feelings and the emotions you experience on a daily basis. If you were to be continually connected with the flow of feelings inside you, and if you were to recognize and understand your emotions with openness, then no blocked energy would be created and you would not need to become ill. The chance of physical disturbance arises when certain emotions within you are systematically repressed and not seen or heard. The emotions are there, and they continue to work upon your body, but you have little or no connection with them because you reject them.

At some point, you made the choice to close yourself off from these emotions, although you may no longer remember that happening. It has been taught to you, from an early age, to restrain your emotions or to systematically rein them in. In this respect, much has changed in human society, but there is still a mistrust of the power that lies in emotions. The idea that justifies this repression is that emotions in their raw form are dangerous and uncontrollable. Sooner or later in your life, you were taught that you have to control your emotions in order to be a well-adjusted citizen.

What happens in your body and your soul when you repress your emotions or oppose them? Emotions are in their nature a dynamic, surging energy. Notice, for example, what happens if you become angry. You feel a flaming energy coursing through your abdomen, your chest, or your throat. The location where the emotion manifests physically can vary from person to person, but in any case it is a living, dynamic power with a clear message: "*No, I don't want this!*" And when this emotion surges through you, you make a choice. Simply put, you turn toward the emotion or you turn away from the emotion.

Many of you turn away from the emotion, because you have been taught that it is not good to have or to allow that emotion. It can be anger, fear, sadness, jealousy, ambition, or desire. Even the feeling of joy is often repressed for fear of standing out from the other person, or of having more than your fair share. So you repress the emotion, which creates tension within your body. That tension remains within you, because your behavior toward other people becomes based on what (you think) is expected from you, rather than on what you actually feel. This creates a controlled and tense adult, who has lost their spontaneity and who realizes less and less what they really feel. By doing this, you lose connection with your soul, because your soul talks to you through your feelings.

It is precisely those "bad" emotions, such as fear or anger, that tell you when you need to look at yourself with understanding and love. These emotions show you where the light is missing. And the positive feelings such as joy and enthusiasm are the signals from your soul that you are doing something that suits you and allows your light to shine. If you are always censoring and regulating your emotions, or keeping them under control, your soul can no longer communicate with you. You feel tired, depressed, or you become ill, and you wonder what in God's name your soul is trying to tell you. This response by you is not without irony, considering how the emotions you had originally were giving very clear signals. Some hand has forcefully restrained them, so that now they only manifest in a whisper, through illness. It is that forceful hand of denial, judgment, and repression that eventually puts into motion the process of physical illness.

An emotion in its pure form is like a surging wave that, left alone, reaches its peak and rolls out onto the beach. A wave has a beginning and an end and will naturally return to the sea. As a self-controlled tense adult, you have been taught not to ride along with the wave but to resist it and to dam the flow. Because of this restraint, the wave is interrupted in its movement and can not disperse in a natural way. The result is that the emotion continues to create havoc within the body and the life of the emotion is extended unnaturally. In addition, a chronic state of tension arises within you as you become an adult, something that you gradually consider to be normal, but is not. It becomes second nature to control your emotions and not to show what you really experience inside yourself. Because of that, your feelings become frozen; an energy that should flow naturally now has become arrested.

That frozen state of your emotions almost always goes together with "living" excessively in your head. Your mind holds all kinds of beliefs about what is good and bad. You often make judgments about your emotions from your head that ensure that you no longer take these emotions seriously and eventually no longer feel them. These judgments gradually become profound beliefs that are then embedded in your entire thinking and doing, and they keep the emotional body from *cleansing* itself. The emotional body is naturally self-cleansing; an emotion arises when something throws you off balance and at the same time shows that there is something with which you must come to terms. The emotion itself has a cleansing effect, if you really receive its message.

How can you allow the cleansing effect to take place? Consider what happens when you let an emotion disperse like a wave, without building dams in the form of judgments? Try it. Take an emotion that you have felt repeatedly, one that you do not know what to do with. Call it up within yourself and let go of all your preconceived notions about it. Let the emotion wash through you and see where it touches something within your body. Enter completely with your consciousness inside the emotion and live it out in your thoughts. For example, if you feel anger, allow the flow of anger to make itself known through your body: in your chest, stomach, or throat. Maybe you feel that you want to make a fist, or you want to stomp your feet. Maybe you want to scream, or you want to smash something. Observe it with your awareness and allow yourself to feel everything. You may imagine that you express your anger toward others, and that your emotional truth completely bursts through your usual image of the "nice" you. Make a movie out of it in your imagination. Do it exactly in the way that spontaneously arises within you, even though in your imagination you use violence or smash everything around you.

Do not be afraid to be bad. What matters is that it becomes clear to you what is going on inside you. You are *not* a bad person if you honestly face the emotions that live within you. Real evil, in the sense of doing harm to others, usually happens because of a constant suppressing of the emotions, causing a person to become so tense, they eventually explode. Consciously opening to your emotions by experiencing them inside your body, and exploring them by way of your imagination, is healing and revealing.

Through your feelings, your soul wants to make you aware of something. You can only receive the message when you release all judgment and allow the wave to completely disperse. What you notice is that the wave will peak naturally and wash out onto the beach of your consciousness. There is a natural momentum in emotions by which the emotion, when it is thoroughly felt with an open consciousness, will at some point naturally give way to peace and calm. At that moment, you can receive the message of your soul.

Think of the moment when a wave is fully dispersed onto a beach, just before the water washes back into the sea; there is a moment of rest, such as between an exhalation and an inhalation. This can be a moment of intense awareness. For example, you may suddenly realize that your anger tells you that it is time to say goodbye to a particular situation or relationship in your life, or you realize that a deep sadness lurks behind your anger because you do not truly value yourself.

It is exactly when you allow an emotion to flow through you, without trying to reason it out, and giving it the opportunity to express itself through your body and imagination, that you create a space for something *other* than that emotion, namely a moment of silence and awareness. If you want the cleansing power of the emotion to work for you, the key is to allow the emotion the necessary space to disperse until you are completely still and hear the message that is behind the emotion. At that moment, you have completed a natural process and you have gained new and positive insights.

If you are dealing with illness and physical complaints, it can be difficult to understand which frozen emotions lurk behind the problem. However, your body itself can help you explore this issue. You can start by examining, in the manner described, the emotions created by the illness and experience *them* consciously. When you are ill, you are likely to experience a variety of emotions; you may be angry and impatient because you can do less than before; you can feel resistance against the resultant dependency; you can be sad and anxious or feel lonely and desperate.

Illness casts you back upon yourself and forcefully confronts you with deep emotions. Consciously opening up to the emotions triggered by the illness can be your entrance to a deeper understanding of what lies behind the illness. Dare to completely descend with your heart and intuition into all those emotions and give them free rein; only this will relieve your body and cause it to relax. Remain confident that the process of the illness will bring you to the original emotions, those that you have long rejected or suppressed. And if you feel the emotions rise up again, consider these as healing waves that in the end will bring you the insight that you need to understand the illness from within.

Restoring connection with emotions that long ago have become frozen is something that does not usually succeed at one sitting. It asks of you to repeatedly dare to surrender to what is, with a neutral and open consciousness. Each of you is to some extent a controlled adult who, only with effort, can regain the spontaneous child within yourself.

Imagine that your emotional body stands before you in the form of a child. How does it look and what is the first emotion that you perceive in this child? Name a quality that you find particularly beautiful in that child. Ask what it needs to come to life more, to arrive at a deeper connection with you. Realize that this child is a messenger of your soul; it is the bridge that connects you with your divine essence.

Your soul speaks to you through your feelings and through your emotions. Even though emotions sometimes seem very negative and difficult, there is always a valuable message behind them. Your emotions tell you how you are experiencing something, which is not to say that your experience of something is the only correct way and that other people must experience it in exactly the same way. Nevertheless, emotions need to be seen and experienced in their totality because they reveal something about your essence, your truth.

I will describe an example to clarify this. Imagine that from the past you feel a certain bitterness regarding your father. You still blame him for a lot of things; you felt you were not seen or recognized as a child, and you still experience a lack of connection with him. Instead of allowing this bitterness to continue to fester within yourself, you can decide to go all the way to the core of your emotions. Connect with the child within you that has been hurt. Allow those emotions to spring up vividly, and let the child rant and rave, if you want, to make it clear to you what it has missed. If you dare to completely allow this, there comes a moment of silence when the storm has spent its fury. At that time, you may feel an inexplicable warmth and sympathy emerge for your father. You suddenly realize that you still love him despite everything. Or you feel deep inside that his behavior was not motivated by a negative intention, but that he was shaped by his parents and his past, and that he did the best he could. Such an insight can co-emerge with a sense of forgiveness, but it can only break through *if the entire emotional burden that you have built up in your life has been deeply felt.* Allow yourself your bitterness, anger, outrage, and sorrow. Inner healing takes place by allowing yourself to feel what is bothering you, and to give space to those feelings.

What you must learn is to rely on the cleansing power of an emotion. If you ride its wave, you will arrive on that calm place on the beach and to an understanding of the emotion. Often, you do not trust this process. You think: "Oh, I feel fear, I feel distrust, I feel bitterness, I feel disappointment. I will not surrender to that because then everything will be very black and dark, and then I will no longer be able to live and function". But the opposite is true. As long as you continue to repress these emotions, you stifle the flow of life and you can not receive the messages of your soul. You also will be barely able to enjoy what is good and beautiful in your life.

Search out those dark emotions intentionally. Dare to descend into their depth, and the more consciously you search them out, the more it becomes clear to you that if you delve into your emotions, you do not become identified with them. You can allow an emotion to completely manifest in your body and mind without being overwhelmed by it. The art of spiritual growth is observing everything with full consciousness and finding the golden kernel within it, thus allowing the emotion and you to finally be free.

12. The role of guides

Dear friends, it is a great joy to be with you and to feel your energy. You are so dear to me. I know you, and I am with you always. Today, I would like to explain about the role of guides in your lives. I want to do that chronologically, beginning with the time of your birth on Earth.

When you are born on Earth, you become immersed in a material realm of being. Everything that was clear and obvious when you were on the other side now becomes hidden. With every incarnation you jump again into the deep. However, you are not left on your own. You are accompanied by spiritual guides who, as it were, are your spiritual parents.

Every child who is born is accompanied by two guides, a female and a male. They are present, at and from its birth onward, with this human being. They are, as it were, your parents in heaven. So you are born into a network of energies: two biological parents who receive you on Earth, and two spiritual parents who escort you, and remain next to you, throughout your life, usually in an invisible way.

Who are these guides and what is their role in your life? Often they are the souls of friends whom you have known from another life and who fulfilled a valuable role for you back then. You feel an inner kinship with them and a friendship based on being equals. There is no sense of higher or lower between you and your guides, only that you now live in different dimensions from one another.

Since the guides live in a heavenly realm where they do not have to deal with the heaviness and illusions of physical reality, they can connect with you, both from the heart sharing cosmic love *and* from the abdomen, touching you emotionally. The guide loves you in a personal way, not just in an abstract universal manner – you have a personal connection. Yet the guide operates from the level of the heart, and with that energy the guide supports you in a way that is pure and wise. A guide approaches you with gentleness and has much patience with you; a guide does not judge you and offers you *unconditional* support. Although they can not solve any problems for you, they are gently present in the background with an unconditional love that envelops you.

The reason there is a male and a female guide is because these are archetypal energies. The masculine and feminine play an important role in your life and your path toward wholeness. From the male guide typically comes a different energy than from the female guide. The female guide will be more likely to send an energy to you that is enveloping, loving, and healing, while the male guide can help you choose direction and manifest yourself on Earth. These influences are often subconsciously working in you. Even though you feel no form of connection with your guides, their energy is still part of who you are.

The two guides who are with you since birth, are part of your energy "management" – they stand in your aura. They will, however, in no way impose on you or interfere in your life, yet they are part of your auric field because they are your spiritual parents.

You can also see it in this way. A child who begins its life by having a biological connection with its mother and father, who belongs for the first part of its life with these parents, is closely associated with them. It is dependent on them, physically as well as emotionally and mentally; there is a close relationship between the biological parents and the child. And this connection more or less reflects the relationship between you and your spiritual parents. Their role is necessary for you to maintain balance. It is not easy to step into an atmosphere darkened by illusions.

We do not deny there is darkness on Earth; it is difficult to find your way here. In every new incarnation you struggle to surface again after the fall into the deep and to keep your head above water; to feel and to recognize: "This is who I am; I remember where I came from". Until this moment comes, the spiritual guides help you manage the energy balance in your life. They are necessary so you can keep a connection with "above", to remember your cosmic origin.

Guides play an energetic function without you realizing it. You *can* become aware of your connection with them, although doing so is not necessary. This connection can come to you in the form of a reassurance, a sudden quiet that comes over you, a trust in life even though you are up against difficult circumstances. These are gentle feelings of positivity, of light and joy, even when outside appearances are against it. In these kinds of moments, the guides speak to you and fulfill their function of parenthood.

The guides who have entered into a covenant with you to guide you in this lifetime do not always have to stay with you throughout your entire life. A person who kindles light in themselves, who connects with their own heart energy, gradually becomes their own guide. The energy of the angel, the energy of the higher self, as you call it, awakens in such a person and radiates into his or her life. This person is going to embrace difficult emotions in themselves and take care of their inner child.

The emotions you struggled with in your early childhood accompany you until well into adulthood. When you begin to discover that you possess power to heal these emotions, to embrace yourself and the child within you, and to be the parent it needs, it is time for the guides to loosen their connection with you. They then literally take a step backward. This is for them a deep moment of satisfaction. It is the moment when you reach within your heart, when you embrace these anxious, tired, traumatized parts of yourself, when you begin to sense: "I know it; I feel it". At that time, your soul, your angel essence, your higher self, is truly born into the earthly realm. At that time, your spiritual guides take a step backward. They observe you more from a distance, and you can experience that energetically.

Some persons sense their guides are taking a step backward and that now they are facing things on their own, but they sense this in a joyful, powerful way. You now know that it is you who is setting your own course; that you have the power and understanding within you to do that and that you carry the light inside needed to find your way. Paradoxically enough, it is an achievement when you release your guides, even though this is not something you have to do consciously. It naturally happens the more you integrate your angel-self, your higher self, and your soul merges with your earthly being. This happens with many persons on Earth, with all those who knowingly engage in spiritual growth, who increasingly incarnate their essential light and soul on Earth.

When the light of the soul becomes anchored in large groups of people, major changes can occur. In the period in which you now live, both the darkness as well as the light will be strengthened. This time encourages you to begin to live from your heart and to take on your own strength, to rely on your divine inner nature and trust your inner guidance.

When your heart is awakened, it may happen that you connect with other guides, teachers, or angels from the spiritual world. These are not your personal guides. These are helpers or teachers who inspire you to bring out your heart energy into the world to the benefit of not just yourself. This is the phenomenon that you call "channeling". It does not involve connecting with your individual guides, your spiritual parents; it is about connecting with a more universal teacher energy, who helps you to convey spiritual messages which have a healing and empowering effect on people.

Some people feel the call, the urge to open themselves to this form of spiritual connection and, if it brings them joy and fulfillment, this is the way that suits them best. It is a partnership between your higher self, your heart energy, and the energy of angels, light beings, who join with you. Through this connection, you channel spiritual energy to Earth that inspires and touches others; an energy that tells them about their inner strength and their divine nature. This is the role of channeling: to visibly set down the divine inspiration, the light that belongs to every human in the earthly realm

However, if your heart awakens and your soul manifests more fully on Earth, it is not necessary that you connect with otherworldly light beings; that, in other words, you begin to channel. It is quite possible that your soul chooses to set down your light on Earth in a different way. It may be that you have a talent to do a particular work within society without making conscious use of this spiritual opening; that you radiate your light through your own words and deeds.

So you see that the function of channeling is specific. For some people, this is the way to their higher self and the way to bring it out on Earth. Other people manifest their potential in a different way, and this is no less valuable. It has always been the case that people must find within themselves the specific way to best manifest their potential: the exact form that best suits their energy. There are no prescribed laws or ways to do this. What matters is that you connect with your heart, with your deepest desires, and feel where that leads you.

There is always help available from our side. From our realm, there are numerous beings of light who can assist you. Do appeal to them and then trust that this energy is guiding you. Do not force anything, simply let the energy come to you in a natural, spontaneous way.

It is not the case that everyone on the path of spiritual growth needs to make a conscious connection with guides or has to start channeling. In some spiritual circles, this is sometimes seen as an important step forward; as an almost necessary step and a sign that you are on the "right" path and that you stand higher than the other aspirants. *This is an absolute mistake.* What spirituality is really about is that you become your *own* angel and connect with your *own* higher self, the being of light that you are. That you feel the joy of that connection and are comfortable with it; that you relax and trust your soul to know what your path is; that you are listening to your most intimate feelings and desires and are living accordingly. *This* is connecting with your soul and being your higher self.

Connecting with guides can be helpful and supportive, but do not make it out to be more than it is. One person chooses this way, another person chooses that way. It is about the heart of the matter and that is *you*, not the guides. You are on your own path. You have to deal with dark and difficult energies in your life, and more and more you learn to be your own guide, your own teacher, your own higher self.

Do you see how this develops? First, you were a child on Earth with spiritual parents by your side; guides who literally stood next to you, in your aura. As you pursued inner growth, you became your own guide. You internalized the energy of these guides in your heart and you became the parent of your own inner child. With love and joy you let go of your spiritual parents, just as you did your earthly parents. Now you go your own way; you stand on your own two feet and become your own support and prop. *Trust in who you really are.*

Guides are a means, not an end. Their greatest joy is when you are able to find your way by yourself. They have the utmost confidence in you. Feel this for a moment. This space we are now sharing is filled with energies that want to assist you. It is not only my energy, but also that of the angels and the guides who want to be with you. They all are gathered around you and look at you with reverence and respect. Experience for a moment the great respect they have for you, for the path you are taking on Earth – sometimes so lonely, so alone. They want to serve you. It is our great joy to provide you with support and encouragement. Feel the warmth and love in this little piece of heaven on Earth we are now sharing. Make that possible by opening your hearts to us. There is no greater joy for us than when a human being opens their heart. In this way, you ground the light and the love on Earth that will spread out to others. You all are human channels of divine light, your *own* divine light. *You are making a difference.*

13. The symbolism of the cross

Dear friends, we greet you in love. I, Jeshua, am not here today by myself. The energies of my mother Mary and Mary Magdalene also stand beside me. The three of us are gathered together here in this room, the male and the female components of the Christ energy. In a joining together with you all, we offer you healing in this time when it is necessary that the male and female energies bond together, and arrive at a mutual forgiveness so as to complete a long journey.

My energy feels lighter and gentler today because of this feminine influence, an influence of healing and consolation for you all. Please accept and allow this energy of gentle healing and nurturing to flow through you, through your legs and arms, through your heart, and up through your throat and jaw into your head. Allow us to share these energies with you today. We are close to you, *very* close to humankind at this birth of a new time on Earth. In this context, I would like to tell you something about my past, about the symbol of the cross and about my crucifixion.

When I lived on Earth, I was supported by the many energies around me. I was not alone in my mission, because I could not accomplish my mission entirely by myself. I was the most visible representative of the Christ message. However, protectors stood around me who made it possible that I channeled this energy in its most visible form on Earth. The women around me fulfilled an important function; their gentle nurturing and protective energies surrounded and supported me on my path. Mary and Mary Magdalene are very important representatives of the female energy. They supported the birth process of the Christ energy on Earth.

I was also supported by you all; by the lightworker souls who, at that time, either were about to incarnate on Earth or had already incarnated. Both groups had agreed to cooperate in this wave of new energy, the Christ energy that was to be born on Earth. You all were connected with me on the soul level. You knew I was coming and you prepared the way for me, which means I did not come alone to Earth. I was only the most visible part of a new wave of energy that was supported by the hearts of all lightworker souls together.

I now take you to the image of the cross. See me hanging on the cross, at once the focal point of tragedy *and* love. Imagine that you see me hanging on the cross on that hilltop, and imagine that you were present. And that was indeed so, because either in spirit, or physically present, you were deeply involved in my life. You can say that I represented you there, that I helped plant and channel your energy on Earth: your hope, your passion, your visions for the future. I was therefore more than one man; I carried many energies in me. It is hard to explain exactly who I was, except I was not above you. I pointed you in a direction, a future that lay dormant inside you as a seed, and that you knew was your own destiny.

See me hanging on the cross. What happened there? Yes, I suffered; I was in pain and my body hurt. I saw the people around me – some took pleasure in my suffering. Others wept in desperation, deeply disappointed, and in bitterness threw themselves onto the ground and no longer believed in the power of my message. Can you feel the disillusionment that the crucifixion brought? All these emotions were awakened through me.

I was not, however, the one who was crucified. My higher self, the Christ energy, remained intact. A grand stage performance took place – a drama – wherein divergent emotions were roused. I use the word "performance" not to marginalize what happened. I use it to indicate that the event of the crucifixion awakened a highly emotional response that touched the core of your soul. You were faced with emotions that ranged from disbelief, dismay, and disgust to pure knowing – like a seed in your heart – that it all made sense and that my message remained intact. There was a deep knowing that what I was doing pointed toward the direction of a new possibility, a new energy: *that I could transcend the emotions of the crucifixion.*

On some level I did not suffer. I could stay present in my heart during my trials and I was supported in that by the presence and the powerful love of the people nearest to my heart. Through them, and through the people I knew supported my mission – through the light of their souls – I could transcend the moment. I could witness my pain, my suffering, and also observe the feelings of rejection, and transcend them both with the generosity and compassion which are the core of the Christ energy. With this compassion, I was able to look quietly at my own suffering and my dying that outwardly seemed so brutal and unjust.

My coming to Earth, and the kind of awareness I introduced, created much resistance in those days, and I had known beforehand that this would happen. It called up a play between "for" and "against". I was the one who lived the possibility of being able to watch that spectacle with compassion and generosity for the benefit of both: those who were for me and those who were against me. I looked at my beloved companions and saw their struggle, their doubts, their disillusionment. I looked at my opponents, who in confusion, anger, and incomprehension, wanted to nail me to the cross and to eliminate me, and I understood both sides.

In my being, I gathered up the power of the Christ. It is this power that also flowed from your hearts toward me, and I embodied it. I was an example for you but I also was supported by your energy, the energy of the loved ones around me and of the lightworker soul family at large. You contributed to my mission, whether you know it or not.

In the image of the crucifixion, you see *extreme* suffering, which is also depicted on the faces of the people who were there. And you see the ability to rise above that suffering and to experience blessing here on Earth, as the antithesis of this great suffering. I could remain present from a spirit of silence and grace, given to me from the essence of the Christ and the powers surrounding me, and from the energies coming from you all. I could see from the "eye of the storm". I could see my opponents and my companions with the same eye of compassion and love.

Can you feel that still point in the middle of the storm? That still point that bears all and remains untouched, either by defenders or by opponents? That point *is* the center of creation, and one that preserves the unity between extremes. In my eyes, you were all equal, because you all have been both extremes.

Before you became my companion, moved and inspired by the Christ energy, you were also perpetrators, you played the role of "bad guy" as well. Our souls have played all the roles that duality has to offer during our many lifetimes, so there is no fixed division between "good and bad guys". What you are moving toward, as the Christ energy inside you is awakened, is the deep experiencing of the stillness underlying the extremes of duality. As you become aware of the Oneness of all life in the universe, and the division between good and bad evaporates, there is just a distinction between being connected to love and being disconnected from it. As you learn to deeply understand both states of being, your compassion becomes wider than the extremes of duality.

The image of the crucifixion that I sketch is a compound image. In it are energies of the greatest despair and pain, as well as the energies of enlightenment and healing. All these energies you can find in your own personal history extending over many lifetimes on Earth. *You also have been crucified* – in the sense of being rejected and persecuted because of the light that you wanted to bring forth – and now you are working to overcome the trauma it has caused: to heal the parts of you that became disconnected from love.

In the evolution of your soul, you are now at the point where you find yourself "at the edge of the stillness". You are approaching the still point in the "eye of the storm", in the center of duality and chaos. Feel yourself hanging on the cross, feel how you have been tormented. There may have been the physical pain of violence and torture in past lives, and also the mental pain of rejection, fear, and desolation – "My God, why hast thou forsaken me?"

Do you know that feeling inside? That is what I experienced, and at the same time I experienced the mercy of the powers that uplifted me, that supported me in their loving embrace. The female part of the Christ energy comforted and embraced me. They were the female energies of my mother (Mary) and my beloved (Mary Magdalene) that helped me to hold on to the compassion and the kindness, which in that circumstance was necessary, and to anchor it deeply into the Earth. They made it possible for me, at the moment of my torturing, to transcend that suffering and *to forgive*.

To choose for love in the midst of pain and struggle is what you are growing toward in your own personal journey, extending over many lifetimes. *Have respect for yourself.* Feel how you are now able to embrace yourself with awareness while *you* "hang on the cross". The last of the series of lives you have lived on Earth, especially after my arrival on Earth, have been those of the victim. A series of lives in which you have experienced what it is like to be a lightworker, bringing in heart-centered awareness, and being misunderstood and rejected for it. You have all been wounded as recipients and victims of violence and aggression. In these lives, you have become disillusioned in the same way as those who were my companions and stood by my crucifixion.

You have intensely experienced this disillusionment, and now you are at the point where you can let it go. The point at which you feel you are coming into the core of your mission, the nucleus of your own strength – into the divine stillness. The point of unity that can embrace everything, both your suffering *and* your strength, and which enables you to release your struggle with society, with "the dark". In place of struggle comes compassion.

I would like to say something today about this still point in yourself and the letting go of the cross as a symbol of suffering. Silence is something very special. We use "silence" in our everyday speech as a word that denotes the absence of sound. Silence, however, is more than that: *silence is a concentration, an intensification of your own power, your own Presence.*

Look at what happens when you are alone and are silent. There are no distractions, no radio and television, and nothing you have to do. You begin then to feel stronger. You become more aware of yourself and this goes together with a certain intensity. It happens sometimes at night, if you wake up and there is no distraction, that you feel yourself very strongly at such a time – the outer falls away.

However, it may be that this silence feels threatening, because certain unpleasant thoughts arise and create unrest. There may be nervousness or anxiety or painful emotions. When you initially engage the silence, the noise often increases within yourself. You become aware of a constant busyness in your mind, related to external pursuits and affairs that drown out the silence. So it at first becomes noisier within.

What is needed then is perseverance and to not walk away at such a time. The aim is to take a step back and to observe the thoughts and emotions as something outside yourself, like the noise of cars, the murmur of voices, the sounds of a radio. All that is needed is for you to take a small step backward and to enter into the *actual* silence, the stillness that exists in the depth of your heart.

Right there in the core of your heart is a silence that is timeless and devoid of content – pure beingness. From a stillness that belongs to the origin of who you are, you can look at yourself with compassion and wonder. *Feel this for a moment.* This silence has no fixed location and no time, yet this is who you are in your essence. From this still silence you can look within at an emotion or a thought and distance yourself from it. You can view this emotion with kindness: "There is that emotion again ... there is that thought again ...what is it doing here? ... what does it need?" Observe it with the eye of a curious spectator.

To be in the stillness is to be in a form of consciousness that is fluid, that looks at everything with openness and acceptance. The stillness says "yes" to everything; the stillness does not require anything for itself; it embraces everything and observes it with an eye of generosity and compassion.

You then suddenly know what you have to do. And if you *still* do not know what to do with a particular problem, a certain emotion, or fear, or thought that harasses you, then try again to observe it in silence. Try to feel the emotion in you from the vantage of the silence, and to welcome and embrace the problem.

How do you observe the deepest emotions within yourself and look at what are the most difficult emotions to experience? You do it by pulling back your energy from the problem and allowing it to exist in silence. In the stillness, there are no answers and there are no questions. In the stillness, you come to yourself. In the stillness, you let go of everything and you allow everything to be *as it is* and to see everything as an expression *of what is.*

Do you remember the image of my hanging on the cross and looking at the faces of my companions and my persecutors? They were all the same to me, because I did not judge. I observed them from the stillness. Now feel the beating heart, the essence of that stillness within yourself, and allow it to be. *Open your heart to more love for yourself.*

Take one part of yourself that you abhor, that is bothering you. Take the first thing that comes to your mind, the first thing that creates resistance. Look at it from the stillness in your heart and take it in your hands and see it for what it is. Is it fear or frustration, is it something old and something you want to be rid of, or does it also bring something valuable to you? Does this negative energy that bothers you carry a message within it?

Observe it, yet allow it to just be. When there is no answer, you say to the energy: "Stay where you are, it's okay, I am here in the center of my being with you. I am not you, but you are allowed to be with me. You are welcome; rest assured that I will accept you. Even though I do not know exactly who you are and what you bring, I accept that you are with me, a friend in Creation; that you will reveal to me what I need to know about you and why you are here with me."

Make peace with the energy within yourself that you abhor the most. Look at it from the silence of your heart. The solution is always in the silence and not in the hustle and bustle of the world outside yourself. When you dare to sink down into the unrest within yourself, when you dare to face the intensity and the confusion within the stillness, *everything slowly becomes clear.* Do not force it; let it slow down and unfold quietly. Silence is a model of openness, kindness, of not forcing anything. When I hung on the cross, I was not omniscient; I was in the center of the stillness. From the stillness that upheld me, I could allow everything to be.

Hold on to this image of me on the cross and see that you are on your way to achieving the same thing within yourself. You are transcending your own crucifixion, your own rejection and abandonment, and you are observing with a gentle eye everything that lives within you.

The energies of Mary and Mary Magdalene join with me at this moment and offer you our love. This love is meant to encourage you to accept what is currently in your life and to stand next to it in love and compassion, and to *let it be.* I ask you to accept our love and energy and to feel how this healing is available to you at all times.

14. You are ready

Dear beautiful people, I am Jeshua, your friend and brother. I am close to you, right at your side. I know the human condition very well, and from the inside, its valleys and peaks. Seeing you here together, giving voice to what moves you inwardly, makes me happy and fills me with awe. I kneel down before you – you heard it correctly – I kneel down before you, because you are so dear to me.

I have a message for you today, although it may sound strange to your ears. I want to tell you – *you are ready*. You are ready to receive your soul in this earthly reality. Yes, there is still resistance, due to emotional layers that want to back away from that soul energy: stubborn old pain, old trauma – it is all there. Yet this resistance is not your enemy; it belongs to the human reality of being on Earth – welcome it! Many of you are still busy fighting against your own barriers that, according to you, should not be there. You have images of perfection that do not serve you and that deter you from the beautiful, natural reality that wants to unfold in you.

In you, as humans, darkness and light come together. This is as it was meant to be: you are angels descended from bright, beautiful, unimaginable realms. You have come here voluntarily, even though you do not always believe this. There is an incredible courage and wisdom in you that knew you could accomplish letting your light shine here amidst the darkness, the fear, the loneliness, the resistance.

You all come from afar, and by that I mean your soul has long been on this path. Precisely in this time things are coming full circle, and you begin to long for that origin again that you call Home. There is a homesickness within you for the beauty, the luminosity, the harmony of the realms from where you originated and once descended as an angel. Feel that within yourself for a moment. Go back there in your imagination to who you were when you were still very fresh and new. And at a certain moment, there was a kind of separation between you and the whole. You separated from a kind of womb of Oneness to go your own way; to create your own journey through the universe. A part of you was sad to say goodbye to the familiar, inherent Oneness of which you were part. Just as a thread is part of the weave of a robe, you were part of that Oneness. Yet you felt something bubbling up within you, an enthusiasm and a desire for something new, for growth and innovation, for knowledge and understanding. You detached yourself from the cloak of Oneness and with all your light floated downward toward the Earth.

Just see before you, the ethereal tones of light and pastel colors that surrounded you when you first entered the dance of incarnation. Call up this image! Feel the angel in you, and the ease with which it had a connection with the whole. There was actually no real separation, because your heart was still connected, and there was also no doubt as to who you were, or whether you were good just as you were. But then you encountered other realms of being where separateness had already gotten a much deeper grip on consciousness. It was not just the Earth that you visited. You also have been to other places in the universe, where you gained experience. What matters, and is of importance to me, is that you see the courage in the leap that you took; the joy of life, the adventure even. Observe what happened to such a bright, high-vibration angel, still ignorant of the lower vibrations, and the resistance and fears that were there in those other realms. See what happened to such an angel when it first encountered this darker energy. Shock, bewilderment, fear – this happened to you when for the first time you experienced those strong, unpleasant vibrations.

Can you remember what that experience did to you? The fright and bewilderment at suddenly feeling rejected after leaving that Oneness, and experiencing for the first time the aloneness, fear, and sense of being trapped. You are now aware enough to empathize with the experience to which I am referring, because there is now a place within you that can witness that descending angel with deep understanding and compassion as a result of your long experience and developed maturity. You can now see that falling angel meeting up with darkness and feel in your heart what you want to say to that angel: "Beautiful angel of light, how courageous and brave you are that you have ventured to take the leap. So great is your love for life, so great is your confidence, that you have followed your heart and have taken up the dance with what lies outside the field of unity. You did not know what to expect, and although it often feels raw and rough yet, time and time again, have you descended. What is it that lured you to continually take part in this dance?"

We have talked today about stubborn old wounds and pain, but notice how stubborn your joy of life must be that you have ventured once again to take the leap, because here you are again in a body of flesh and blood. You again felt that longing – you are alive, you feel, you are here, and that is a miracle! A miracle of love and trust, which is why I kneel before you, because you have never given up. That is the true meaning of being a lightworker: that time and again you return and choose for life – and yet again! Look at what you have experienced in the way of pain and of feeling disowned by Home and Oneness, whether in this life or in previous lives, which were often even harder than it is now in the world. How is it possible that you are here once again with a beating heart, and with ideals and aspirations? Try to answer that! My answer to you is that your love, beauty, and light are inexhaustible. In reality, you have never left unity consciousness, because you are carriers of Oneness on Earth. You come here to channel this field of light – to anchor it into this reality – because you know deep within yourself that you *are* light, and that nothing or no one can estrange you from that truth – this is why you are here.

It is my deepest desire today that you see yourself from my perspective. As an angel of light you descended, and now you have become so much more: an embodied human angel who has deeply understood all human emotions, and who can also perceive that depth in another; who can look at another while he or she tells their story and feel all the range and depth of experience the other is going through. True sympathy and real compassion are the fruit of your very long path, and that is also what moves the Christ-consciousness most deeply.

Where you are still opposed to your own negativity, and where you do that unknowingly with others as well, is where there is still conflict, separation, and a lack of connectedness. That to which you are opposed is then expelled as being not good, in need of change, and not part of the field of Oneness. When you have this attitude toward that part in yourself, then it is also not allowed in another, and then the Christ-consciousness does not extend to include the other person. At that moment, a barrier arises.

How is it that you end up in this struggle? It is because of your opposition to that which does not feel good within yourself: the old pain and persistent beliefs. You have the feeling somewhere within you that they have power over you and therefore you have to resist them. You think, "I must not give up; I must continue to fight against this or it will take hold of me and totally overpower me. The underlying idea is that fighting helps and is necessary. This is a mental construct and an attempt to get a grip on the negativity – and as you all know, it does not work. You can remain occupied for a lifetime with your own negative parts – your behavior, thoughts, patterns – and investigate them from all sides by following different therapeutic techniques, and yet the negative does not seem to want to bow to your will. And why is that? Not because the enemy is so corrupted and bad, but because the dark only wants one thing from you – *that you welcome it so it may belong and be allowed into your circle of light.*

The darkness, the negative, longs so deeply for Home, and most often it does not even know that it does. It masks itself, hides itself behind all sorts of negative behavior – but take a deeper look. Imagine those dark parts in yourself, which you have carried for so long within you, like a bunch of homeless children who are standing around you – waiting. Imagine that there are two, three, four little children around you that look like beggars with clothes that are ragged, and maybe with black smudges on their faces and hair disheveled. It is clear they are homeless. Look for a moment at the expression in their eyes. Maybe there is one child in particular that stands out. Concentrate on that one in this moment and let that child step forward. Ask that child: "Who are you? What kind of feeling in me do you represent? What emotion is strongest in you?" You do not even need to put the message into words. A child can express itself well non-verbally; you often see everything in its face. Make eye contact with the child and then ask: "What do you need from me? How can I help you?"

Can you actually give to the child what it asks of you? Perhaps the child wants only to feel a reassuring hand on its shoulders, or to crawl onto your lap to be with you, or maybe a simple connection with you is sufficient. Whatever it is, let it happen naturally. And realize that the most persistent and destructive thought patterns eventually belong to an inner child like this, who searches desperately for a solution, but can not find it alone. The child feels often as if it is drowning in a certain emotion. Only you have the understanding and ability to reassure this child, to let it feel your warmth and welcome. Try to experience this type of connection with your deepest and most painful emotions; treat them as your children. If you are dealing with a violent emotion, look at it calmly and ask the emotion: "Who or what goes on here? Show me who you are in the form of a child". That will give you the correct perspective on what is going on.

If you realize that you are in fact dealing with a child that is begging for help, then you look differently at your barriers and traumas. *You are not their victim, and you are also not powerless.* You are the parent and guide to those neglected children in you. By looking at the situation from this perspective, you realize who you are and you can start to use all the resources available to you – all you have learned and acquired on those many travels through the universe. You can do it!

What then happens if you make that connection with such a child, if you console it – will all be resolved at once? Is this child then free from those annoying emotions? No, it wants to sit with you time and again, and to be included in your circle and your vibration of light. It wants to come Home to you, and not just once, but many times, and perhaps every day of your life – *that is unconditional love*. This you allow, and by doing so you also allow yourself to be completely human – an incarnated angel. And yes, an angel who also has those dark parts within. Does that make you less good and less complete? No, it does not. The goal is not that all these children should disappear and that you become devoid of emotions. What you are growing toward is that you can actually say "yes" to each of them and live together with them as a family circle. This self-acceptance will bring you a deep sense of peace and joy. Your children will still tug regularly at your coat and confront you with emotions such as fear or anger, but you will feel no need to disown and exclude them. Your love for them will make them healthy and vibrant again.

The peace you now have comes from the knowledge that you need not be overwhelmed by the voices of fear, doubt, or anger, but that you can be merciful with them and take off the rough edges through your compassion. You are the parent and guide of the dark parts in you. They are allowed to be there and have a right to speak. When you give them that freedom to express themselves, they become transformed and turn into positive energies like vitality, joy, humor, and lightness. That is the real gift of these children; their true nature is passionate, playful, and creative.

I end with what I started, and this is to tell you that you are ready – *really ready!* You think, "How can I let my light shine if I still feel pain here or experience resistance there?" But the light radiates by way of your humanity and by way of the compassion that you show to yourself and to others. That is what you have to offer, and what people need. Not perfection, not some ideal state of enlightenment, not a person who is devoid of all humanity and who has "transcended it all". Precisely in being human do you build a bridge toward one another and do you complete one another. Everyone makes his or her own unique contribution. No one is perfect. You can grow and learn from each other. The negative is not something that you have to place outside yourself; it can belong, it can feel at Home, *here* and *now*, with you on Earth.

Be at peace.

Healing Messages from Mother Mary

15. Lightwork

Dear friends, I speak to you from the heart of Christ consciousness. I am Mary, the mother of Jeshua. I speak to you with joy, and from a place of peace and connectedness with you all. I know you, my beloved sisters and brothers. We are one in spirit; there is no real separation between us. I, too, have known the extremes of being human in my life on Earth; nothing human is alien to me. And I see you all standing with a torch in your hand to bring the light to dark places on Earth. You are bold, you are brave.

Today, I am bringing affirmation and encouragement to you about who you are. Love yourself is my message today. That is the beginning and end point of all spiritual progress. Love yourself, which includes your fears and the dark places in yourself that beg for light and acceptance.

In the lightwork you want to do on Earth, you will enter into a relationship with the world around you. There are persons you want to help, or it is the Earth you want help. Whatever it is, you associate lightwork with helping someone or something outside yourself. But lightwork is a double-edged sword. In lightwork, you reach out your hand toward another, but just as importantly, and at the same time, you reach out to yourself; you go deeply within and there turn on the light. That makes your light have a solid base by being truly grounded within yourself, so you can really radiate the energy that is needed to give hope and inspiration to those around you. Lightwork is always a reaching inward, as well as a reaching outward. If you want to assist others spiritually, if you want to help them alleviate the heaviness in their lives and to come into their own strength, you will need to also look inside yourself to where *you* are on the path to enlightenment, to your own inner healing.

The one hand extends outward and the other hand inward. *That is the way it is supposed to be!* As you travel within, going deeper and deeper, you become an ever more brilliant beacon of light to others. There within, where you heal yourself and allow light to shine into your own darkness, you create a path. There within, you create your unique transformation and awakening which is what you have to share with the world outside you. What you have to share is not something exterior; not knowledge acquired from books or other people. What you have to offer is the unique insights you acquired during your personal inner journey. Where you dare to go deeply into your *own* darkness, your *own* fear and uncertainty, your *own* illusions and ignorance, there you construct a path for true lightwork. Lightwork does not come from outside, or from above, it comes from within you. It is the light that is ignited in your *own* heart, in your *own* being, which you have to share on Earth with others.

Throughout your entire life you will be involved in this inner journey. Whether you actually act as a spiritual counselor, or whether your work is of a different kind, you are always exploring your own frontiers in order to discover what still lies heavy on your heart, and where you are hampered in allowing your light to shine. Your deepest fears, uncertainties, and self-doubts are personified through your "inner child" – the part of you that has uncensored emotions. The child is the part of you that is naked and open in both its negative and its positive emotions. It holds the emotions raw and pure. Even though the inner child is innocent in its spontaneity, it may be quite confused and in pain, because this child is often disconnected from the guidance of the angel that is present in you.

To be human on Earth is to build a bridge between the angel and the child within you. The angel belongs to another dimension; it remembers Oneness: unconditional love, light and joy. The angel in you knows that you can be who you are, wherever you are, and that you cope with reality on Earth with its extremes of pain and fear on the one hand, and love and connectedness on the other hand. The angel in you surrenders to life and embraces even the big challenges. But the child in you, the earthly part that has to deal with all your human emotions, often feels cut off from its connection with Oneness. It is immersed in the day-to-day reality of Earth, which can be very heavy and suffocating. The child in you may feel very confused at times, creating the gloom and mistrust that sometimes overtake you, as you wonder why you are on Earth to begin with and whether there really is a place for you with your unique gifts. The child can become overwhelmed by sadness, disappointment, and bitterness, and the light of the angel may become temporarily veiled. Yet it is precisely in the connection with your inner child that lies the opportunity to becoming whole and for your angel to truly descend on

Earth. The inner child is your mission, which as an angel is to embrace this child part of you, and to love and understand it. *That is true lightwork; that is why you have come!* Take the child by the hand and look at it with your angel's gaze, so as to free it from its worst doubts, concerns, and regrets. As the child feels your reassurance and acceptance, it changes and becomes peaceful and radiant with life. It will be aligned with your soul, your angel self, instead of opposing it. This is when your light becomes really channeled to Earth and radiates to others as well. As your angelhood merges with your humanness, you become a wise and grounded teacher to others: an Earth angel!

I ask you to now form an image in your mind of your own inner child; allow its appearance to spontaneously arise in your mind. Imagine that it is walking toward you. Look at the expression on its face. Make it welcome! Keep it in your gaze and reach out to it with your hands. Tell the child: "I am your mother/father/guide and I am your helper. Do not worry, you are safe with me". Take the child into your heart and into your abdomen. Do this for yourself, and know the child loves you. *This is the beginning and the end point of all spiritual evolution.* By doing this you make a loving connection with yourself, with *all of you*, and your soul becomes more fully embodied here.

All of you reading this desire to embody your light on Earth, and to pass that light on to others. This is a true and authentic desire. It is sincere, because it comes from your soul. You want to help create a greater sense of unity and connectedness on Earth. As you heal your inner child, and feel more aligned with your soul, the next step will be to enter into the world more fully, becoming more visible in your true colors. Yet this step may bring another layer of fear and insecurity to the surface. "Who do I think I am? Am I so arrogant and deluded to think I can do that? Won't I lose my friends, alienate my family or lose my job if I truly show who I am?" All these fears that come knocking at your door stem from the frightened inner child. It expresses its doubts, while the angel in you *knows* that you are meant to be *who you are* and to radiate your light without shame into the world. You need to *dare to be great*, and let go of what does not belong to you any more, even if it means you have to start anew in several areas of your life.

Believe in what your heart tells you; it is the voice of your soul, who wants what is right for you. The soul is your bigger You who urges you to stand up and embody your greatness, your purity, your love. And then there is the frightened child, who asks, "Do I dare do this? Would it not be safer to stay small and do what I am told?" Now, when that child cries out with emotions of fear, insecurity, or reluctance, do not push it away. Respect it. Embrace it and assure the child that you want to work together with it, helping it to feel safe and happy. The child always gives you the emotional cues that are important. Are you afraid? Are you uncertain? Then face him or her. This is the inner lightwork that is the basis for everything you do in the outside world. And know that the relationship you develop with your inner child will be there throughout your entire life.

It is not true that you must first heal your inner child completely to become a lightworker or teacher. In entering into a relationship with the outside world, whatever you do or whomever you are with, the vulnerable parts of you may always be triggered. But if you turn to them with loving awareness, this need not impede you. As you do your lightwork, you are involved in a triangular relationship. You are entering into a relationship with other people in the world, and at the same time, a relationship with the child within you who will still need your care and healing presence. This is a beautiful, three-way reciprocal process; this is what genuine inner growth is about. You are always both student and teacher, ever growing toward more love, both for yourself and for others.

As you heal your inner child, it becomes a source of joy and fulfillment. Just think of times in your life when you overcame your fear, when you said what you wanted to say, when you radiated what you wanted to radiate; moments when you showed your love, your integrity, your light. Think of the times when you overcame your fear and then persevered, and how happy and fulfilled you felt afterward; proud of your own courage and bravery. Then the child feels elated and beaming with joy like only a child can. It is your purpose on Earth to face your inner darkness and to transform it into all the positive qualities that a healthy child possesses: joy, creativity, love, and zest for life. The power to transform what lives in the dark is what you have to pass on to others.

If you take that inner journey upon you time and again, your vibration will change, and what you have to offer to the world will evolve naturally. When you are ready, you will feel a clear impetus in your soul, in your heart, to let go of a particular work and to begin a new work, to practice and to experiment with it. Always stay connected with the child within and you will go into the world step by step and share your light with others. We praise your bravery and courage to be here on Earth at this time. For many of you, this is a life in which you are integrating and releasing old trauma and pain, not just stemming from this life but from previous lives as well. Many of you carry a heavy burden, so have patience with yourself on this path. You are supported from our side; *we are with you!* We ask you to have patience with this process that is very intense and deep, and to accept our help. Feel my energy and the energy of your own higher self, your angel self. Feel how we are connected in one channel of light that, here and now, connects with the Earth and with you.

16. The Wizard - Allowing abundance

Dear friends, I greet you all on this bright and clear day in the heart of winter. I am Mary, reaching out to you from a crystal-clear realm that is truly your home. Feel the light around you, the light that touches the Earth from my realm, but which also pours directly from your hearts.

We are gathered here today with such a beautiful intent, namely to allow your soul to shine forth on Earth. You all are united by this intent, and that makes you beautiful and pure. Look at yourself through our eyes, observe yourself at some distance: *you are brave angels in a human form of flesh and blood.* Feel our love and appreciation for the path you travel.

Sometimes it seems very lonely and dark, but your light is *undeniable* – it is so brightly visible to us! Feel it glow in your heart, enfold yourself with it. Allow your light to flow in unison with the light from our side, and shower yourself with it from your crown to your feet. There is healing energy available to you all at this very moment, in whatever form you need. Receive it because you are beautiful and pure in your intent.

Many of you feel called to accommodate others on their path of life, and receiving is something you find difficult. Many of you easily carry your light to others, and spring into action whenever there is pain or suffering, but when it comes to giving to yourself, you are often reluctant. Why is that? Why do you deny yourself so much? You are afraid to receive, and so you make yourself small. It has been taught to you to be of service and submissive to others from a long tradition of authorities and rulers, both secular and religious.

That time is now over. You have come here, in this century, to stand up for your *own* heart, your *own* truth, your *own* light. No more listening to what others prescribe for you, but to be a beacon of light from which others can warm themselves. The world is full of fears and commandments based on those fears; norms and values that do not serve you. You have come here to claim mastery over your own life and break free from the past. You are here to be a flaming angel of light, through your *own* inspiration! Take a moment to feel the power flowing through you, pulsating like a cosmic heart. This is you! Allow your true greatness to show and dare to stand and be seen.

You have come to the end of a long road of many lives. The emotions and the deep feelings with which you are now struggling are not only from this life. You have been spreading your light for many incarnations; trying to anchor it here in a reality that has become quite darkened and dense. You all are courageous and bold. You have persevered, otherwise you would not be sitting here now, at this time. Recognize your own strength and dignity as the spiritual warrior that you are. Be proud of who you are and what you have achieved!

Descending upon Earth always requires that you leave a part of your highest light and knowledge behind. You submerge yourself in ignorance, and from there, bit by bit, facet by facet, you rediscover your light. That is the real lightwork you have come to do; to take your plunge into ignorance and to rediscover your true self. That is something extraordinary we can not duplicate from heaven. We radiate light, love, peace, and confidence, because we are in a realm of unity that enables us to do so. But you are immersed in a dense reality, where it takes effort and strength to recognize your own light and to feel the truth when it manifests within you. Because of that, you are very bold and courageous.

In this time, a great transformation process is unfolding on Earth and you all play a role in it. All people on Earth play a role in this, but you are among those who fulfill a pioneering role. You already sense the new and more harmonious reality that desires to reveal itself on Earth; one that you know from our side and that you have wanted to bring to Earth for so long. You are therefore not untrained and young as you start to fulfill this pioneering role. You have so much that you bring with you in the way of inner wisdom, warmth, and compassion in your heart. And yet you hesitate to fulfill this role, to stand up and assume the leadership role that belongs to you at this time.

Why do you hesitate? From where emerges that fear and uncertainty that you feel? It is there partly because of personal experiences of rejection, and partly because of the massive presence of fear on Earth, a collective fear. Humanity is in a sense lost, and wanders about not knowing what to hold onto. Truly, the world has gone crazy! But now, at this time when there is crisis in many areas – economic, political, environmental – precisely in this time is there a need for new voices and a new energy.

You are so modest, often hiding yourself behind your own doubts and fears, but it is you the world is waiting for – you and people like you. Can you believe this? Shed your false modesty! You came here on Earth with a pure and beautiful intent – believe in your strength! Feel it flow throughout your body. Many times you have felt rejected on Earth because of who you are, because you were different, because you came to bring something for which the time did not seem ripe. Yet there are sprouts growing that have germinated from the tiny seeds that you have sown during your many lifetimes. You have helped make possible this time of transformation.

What is of concern to you now is to find a balance between your personal self and your task as a lightworker, that which you want to convey to the world. If there is one commandment that you should obey, it is this: *take care of yourself!* Put yourself as number one! Enfold yourself with warmth and compassion, just as you do for others. *You* are the channel, the instrument through which a new awareness wants to manifest! How can this channel function properly if you do not take it seriously and do not nurture it? What does it need the most from you now? Let the most spontaneous part of you speak. Feel the child within you cry out. There is something you are holding in that you want the most – allow it to manifest.

Perhaps it is peace and space for yourself. Maybe it is that you let go of all those self-critical thoughts that you "dump" on yourself. Maybe you want to discuss your unresolved emotions with someone and express your feelings to them. Allow the child within you to tell you what it needs most from you, what you can do for it. Believe what that child tells you, for it is the most honest and spontaneous part of you.

Being good to yourself especially implies that you take your own feelings seriously. You must *not* be guided by "ought" and "should" from the outside, but by the inner voice, the longing that speaks through your heart and your abdomen. *That* is the truth for you, and *that* is the course which will bring you to exactly where you want to be. Take your feelings seriously and you will see that your external reality responds to it.

In many of you lives the fear that if you were to actually choose what you *really* want in this life, you would lack money and material abundance. You doubt whether there truly is a place for you in this world. And this doubt translates into a fear of lacking financial resources. But the core of this anxiety is not about money, but revolves around the question of whether you may *really* be who you are. Can you believe that you have the freedom and means to do what really inspires you? Do you trust your soul's whispers? What holds you back is not the world outside you, but your own reservations about truly embracing yourself and receiving whatever you need to flourish and find joy.

Look inside yourself. Imagine you are sitting in a beautiful spot in nature. Spring has begun, the greenery is budding, and the sun shines on your skin. You sit in a clearing in the woods and suddenly there appears a wizard who comes toward you. He comes to you, and out of his sleeve he conjures up gold coins that he smilingly tosses to you. "How many do you want, just say it," he asks. Look at your response. What is your first reaction to that offer? Can you receive it? Can you tell him exactly what you need? Or do you feel something blocking it in your heart? Do you ask, "Am I allowed to have this? Can I ask for this much?" Do you need to think about it and do you have doubts? Simply register your first reaction.

Then take one of the gold coins and hold it in your hand. Feel its energy. See or feel what is inside that money. In that gold coin is a promise of abundance on Earth, whether it is a nice home in which to live, a pleasant workplace, or enough money for living expenses. It is really about the freedom to explore and discover and create, the feeling of being secure and safe – everything you associate with earthly abundance. Experience the warm golden energy in that coin and see if you can feel it flow through your arms toward your heart – see if you can receive it. Ask the wizard: "How can I better learn to receive?" Or keep it simple and playful and ask him: "Can you teach me this trick?" Let the wizard show you with a word or a gesture how the key to earthly abundance lies within you.

The key to abundance lies within you all. In this phase of your life, the time has come for a stronger manifestation of your higher self, your soul. You secured this intention for yourself when you started this life long ago, and even before that. You have carried this intention with you for a long cycle of lives. Trust then that there is a path ready for you with whatever supports and helps you to maintain it. By constantly listening to what you truly desire, and what nurtures you inside, you keep on course and the path finds you. You do not have to strive for it or fight for it, the path will find you.

17. The fire of your soul

Dear friends, I am Mary. I was the mother of Jeshua on Earth, and that is how you remember me. In my heart, I am connected with the Christ energy, and I am also connected with you. I greet you all, heart to heart. I recognize you, I understand you, and I know who you are. Together, we will go over the threshold of a new time and that does not happen without a few bumps.

Feel in your heart for a moment what this process of change, in which you find yourself, does to you. More and more, you let go of who you thought you were. The identity you have built in this earthly life partly crumbles. In that identity are layers that are authentic, and layers that are *not* authentic and, at times, they are inextricably intertwined. Sometimes you do not know what is real and what is unreal in yourself. There is a process of rebirth that takes place within you: your soul is manifesting ever more deeply into the material reality of Earth. But in this material reality, you already have a personality constructed by your genes and by outside influences: your education, and the culture and society in which you have grown up. These constitute a whole array of influences which have contributed to your personality. You are the carrier of the past, of traditional influences and, at the same time, you are the carrier of a future that diverges from the past, a future that takes a new path. Your soul holds the promise of a New Earth.

How do I know that? How do I know there is a new future? I see it in you. I see there is a light born within you that is not fed by the limiting influences of the past, but that has its roots directly in your soul, in that which is greater than the external influences which have shaped your personality. There is a light within you that is stronger, more all-encompassing than your earthly personality. It is like a fire that crackles and sputters, and the flames surround the old and consume it. What does not belong to you is burned away by the fire of your soul. That causes pain for your personality – sometimes a lot of pain. Yet this is the only way forward, because you can not step over the threshold of the new age with all those heavy burdens from the past. The fire is cleansing, even though you often do not experience it that way.

Allow yourself to be warmed for a moment by the fire of your soul. *Feel it in your body right now.* Everything that you are – your body, your thoughts, your feelings – are in the end formed by your inner fire; they are a mirroring of that fire, a manifestation. The fire is the element of the soul, so connect with the fire within you. Look intently for a moment at what you see before you. Do you see a large blaze, or a torch, or a small flame? Allow the fire to manifest itself in an image that fits you.

Then feel the warmth of this fire, of these flames. Take it into you, and look to see through what part of your body it moves the most freely. When you imagine that you accept the fire of your soul, look at where it wants to go in your body. That is where you need the power of your soul the most. Imagine how it burns there, gives you your strength and nourishes you inwardly. By nourishment, I mean inspiration, confidence, and strength. Allow the fire to flow through your legs toward the Earth, to connect with the ground through your feet.

The people who have gathered here today have chosen to become able channelers. You are taking this course because you have the desire to channel the energy of your true self, the fire of your soul, from heaven to Earth. I would like to say something about the meaning of channeling. Channeling means creating a bridge between the world of your soul and the world of Earth as it is today. Your soul belongs to a different reality, not bound by time and space. Your soul is free, unlimited, and chooses to be on Earth, here and now. It is a joy for the soul when it can truly descend into earthly form, into your body, and into your mind, your thoughts and feelings, your attitude toward life. There is no greater joy for the soul than to emerge from that dimension of the One and to descend into material form, to manifest itself here. Then the soul is truly tangible, visible, and concrete in her being.

It is not, as some of you think, the process of taking form that upsets the soul. It is when the earthly personality is not open to the soul, is not receptive to her fire, that life here feels scary, that your being feels imprisoned in the body and in the reality of Earth. But this is not how it has to be. The soul *wants* to enter into a dance with material reality; she *wants* to express in bodily form in order to gather experiences, interact with other souls, and live through the adventure of Creation.

The soul, *your soul*, wants to be here. Channeling means nothing more than that you make your earthly personality receptive to the fire of your soul. Channeling means that you open to what wants to flow through you as an earthly human being. Channeling is therefore mainly a movement from top to bottom, not like some of you think, from bottom to top. The intention of channeling is not to transcend the earthly, to leave it behind because it feels too heavy. That way you create a duality between being connected with Earth and being connected with the otherworldly. And it is precisely this duality, the gap that occurs whereby the soul feels less at home here on Earth that causes you as an earthly creature to feel cut off from your soul. Therefore, channeling is about building the bridge, enabling the movement from top to bottom.

You do not need to work more on becoming your soul; you already *are* your soul. It is about receiving the soul energy as effortlessly as possible into your earthly being that has been formed by so many influences. To allow the fire of your soul to flow through to where it is blocked the most. *That* is where your attention needs to go. In everyone's personality, there are blind spots, fears, and judgments in which the light of the soul can not fully take root or breathe. There are shutters on the windows through which it can still not shine.

Channeling in the true sense of the word means you allow the light to fall on those dark spots where the light has not been allowed to flow, where it has been blocked. Channeling is therefore not about leaving or transcending the Earth's darkness, but is about fully turning toward those places within yourself where the light is not allowed. Again, it is a movement downward, a descending to what most needs the light.

Therefore, channeling is in the service of becoming whole: becoming whole within yourself; integrating the cosmic and the earthly; carrying your fire into earthly reality. That is where all spiritual exercises or disciplines should eventually lead. Those are the true disciplines, the right methods. They are not aimed at transcending the earthly reality, but at fully descending into it and channeling your light here.

Being here fully from the heart, allowing your light to shine brightly, is the fulfillment of your soul's mission. It makes you into a joyful, creative person, *and may that be!* You are not here to suffer, to merely be tried and tested. You are here to live and to enjoy the earthly. In the end, that is what your soul wants: *to enter into a magnificent dance with the material realm.* There is deep knowing in the soul how beautiful and enriching that can be.

You struggle with a past on Earth that contains a lot of pain, several lifetimes in which you even experienced violence and rejection. Let us now look at it through the light. Each of you knows there are aspects to your personality that make it difficult to surrender to the light, hard to trust in life on Earth, to trust in people, to trust in the life plan that your soul drew up for you before you descended here, and to say "yes" to all there is. Now see for yourself what aspect blocks you the most, keeps you from saying "yes", keeps you from allowing your light and your soul energy to completely incarnate.

I ask you to give this most troublesome aspect the face of a child. That way, you will be able to penetrate to the most difficult and blocked aspect of yourself. Allow this child to appear to you. Is it a very despondent child, a frightened child, an angry child? Give it sufficient space to be seen completely. It shows you where is your greatest hesitation, your biggest resistance to being on Earth. This child carries your old burdens with it. Let it enter this circle of you and me where it is safe. This child most needs your light, and you can help him or her by reaching out your hand to it. Behind all the dark aspects within you hides the face of a child. This child suffers and does not know why. If feels misunderstood, oppressed, stepped on, humiliated, but it does not understand why this is happening to it. And that is at the heart of suffering – *there appears to be no meaning.*

This misunderstood, pained part of you can sometimes be violently opposed to life on Earth, no longer wanting anything except to close itself off. It is the child within you that cries out in fear, "Do nothing; do not cross that threshold; keep yourself small; seek cover and hide yourself from view." And what you can give this child is understanding. You can surround the pain of this child with your understanding. That begins by saying to the child, "I understand how you feel, and you don't need to explain it to me – come to me". By channeling the energy of

understanding and gentleness to this child, something begins to thaw –
there will be hope in the eyes of the child. It does not know exactly what
is happening, but it feels good. It is as if an angel appears to the child
who says, "Come with me, I will bring you to a better place".

So you bring the highest within you together with the most painful,
rejected part of you, and in this way you pave the road for your soul to be
here on Earth. I ask you to actually kneel down before the child within
you and to have respect for it. This child carries all the experiences from
the past which have not yet been exposed to the light of your
understanding. It is the traumatized part within you. It asks for patience,
for your allowing this child to come to you, to build trust again, to open
itself to you. And each step that you take forward over the threshold of
the new time, each step that you take to set down your soul more fully,
becomes possible when you put out your hand to that child within you.

If you want to move forward without the child, if you abandon it, this
neglected part of you is going to resist behind your back and you will
have a duality within you – a part that wants to move forward and a part
that wants to hold back. Therefore, kneel down to the darkest part within
you. That is how you pave the way, how you make it possible for the star
light of your soul to radiate here on Earth.

Finally, I ask you to feel the energy of us all together, the circle of people
who are here, and all the people who are reading this at a later point in
time. Imagine that we gather all our inner children on the inside of this
big circle, so they are protected by us. Allow these inner children to
receive the reassurance and comfort present in our circle. Each receives
what it can handle, what it needs, very gently and quietly – no forcing.

The power of love is immeasurably great – it can and will reach
everything. It penetrates into the deepest darkness because it says "yes" to
everything and does not resist what is. Let the love flow through us.
Receive it in yourself – *you are so worth it*. Feel how grounded and real
the love is. It does not ascend but connects itself to what is stubborn,
reluctant, and wants to hide. Love is compassionate and patient. It will
wait and stay present until the last child has returned Home. Such is the
power of love.

18. The Oasis

Dear friends, I am Mary who speaks. I am here with you today to remind you of the legacy you carry within your soul. You are old and have travelled a long way, and you are now here on Earth to become truly yourself, to show all your treasures, and to share them with others from a deep balance within yourself. You are ready for your mission; you are ready to do lightwork, which from your soul is what you wanted to do in this life.

You are here on Earth for a reason. This is a time of great change and major turbulence. Many people live in uncertainty these days. There is a financial crisis going on in the world, which confuses some people to their marrow, and strips and robs them of their certainties. This is now quite palpable in the atmosphere of the Earth, and many of you feel it. You feel a restlessness, an imbalance in the collective mindset around the Earth. This affects you, too, because you are sensitive souls whose heart is open, and that is why you are here. You follow this path to discover who you are, and to see how you can rekindle your light in this world. You are ready for this, yet still there are fears and hesitations in you that hold you back from this work

Along with doing this work, there is the need to acknowledge your greatness. You are a beautiful angel of light, whose energy reaches up to heaven itself, as well as down into the Earth beneath your feet. You do not believe in your greatness and so you limit the scope and the extent of your light. Imagine that you are not your bodily form, but a sphere of light, and see how far you radiate. Can you see yourself, how you radiate out light several yards from the center of your being? Can you feel the divine fire you carry within yourself?

Light up your environment – let it shine! And this is not something you accomplish by using your will-power, it is something that naturally happens when you let go of your smallness, the constriction and containment. The light radiates effortlessly. Allow the light, the fire in you to flow through your being, through your legs into the Earth, through your heart to other people, to nature and the animals.

yes, connect with the world! Effortlessly, in one breath, your light extends to the far ends of the world. This is not something you need to work hard to achieve. The fact is, you are *already* one with all the world. Where there is light, there is no separation. Feel the light that holds together the world and the Cosmos, and feel yourself as a connecting link in that holding.

You are always connected with the whole of Creation. Feel how there is no separation, no isolation. This is merely an illusion in your mind. You are one with all other beings. Feel the power of this, and also feel how your greatness serves the world. The greater you allow yourself to be, the more light flows through you to others. So do not fear your greatness. The greater you dare to be, the more you have to share with the world.

How can you hold on to this notion of greatness in your everyday life, and make it something you practice in your daily life? I want to tell you something by way of a story. Imagine that you are alone in a huge desert, with sand under your feet, a hot sun in the open sky. Feel for a moment how the elements of the Earth are present there in the extreme and how they challenge you. It can be unbearably hot in the desert during the day and freezing cold at night. Your body is tested and so is your spirit. There, in the desert, what is demanded of you is an intense concentration of being totally present and aligning with nature and the elements around you, so that you, at the right time and in the right place, will have what you need. There, in the desert, it is a matter of life or death.

Now imagine that in such circumstances you do not contract into your smallness, into your fear of survival as a human being, but that you choose for your greatness. That you feel one with the desert and the elements there: the sun, the sky, the wind, the water. That you know: "I will be nourished by these elements if I am attuned to them. When I say "yes" to my own intuition and divine power, I will know what to do and how to find my path here." In your heart beats an infallible intuitive awareness, a knowing about what is good for you to do in every moment of your life.

Imagine that you love the desert, and every day you manage to find your way there, because there is where you are completely present in your body. You keep a connection with the ground beneath your feet, and you listen to what nature around you has to tell you: the Sun, the sky, the plants, the animals. It becomes easier to live and be there, because you feel at one with nature, and you accept your greatness.

Whenever you are in the *now*, you become attuned. Can you feel how this demands a certain discipline? It asks of you to always stay attuned to yourself, to your body, and to your capacity for intuitive awareness. It asks of you to be present in the *now*.

Imagine that you are now walking through that desert. You have been on your way for months on a long journey – a mystical journey, and you now no longer feel lonely or afraid. You feel a deep unity between yourself and this world, and one evening you miraculously end up at a small oasis. Suddenly it appears from out of nowhere behind a hill. You did not know of this oasis, but you had a feeling that everything would be okay, even when you were thirsty and tired.

You now sit on the bank beside this oasis and you take the precious water in your palms. You feel the coolness, and you wash your dusty face with it, and then you drink it. The water tastes delicious, even divine, and you feel nourished on multiple levels. Your body uses this liquid for its life processes, and you feel gratitude, deeply supported within your soul by the knowledge that the Earth gives you precisely what you need.

You put your head down to rest, and your mind drifts off to sleep and you have a dream. In that dream, a circle of people appear around you who want to ask your help. You stand in the middle of that desert. The sand is dry and hot, the sun burns unmercifully, and the people who come to you suffer from it. They are thirsty, they are hungry, they fear evil, they fear death, and they are insecure and afraid. They say to you: "We have heard that you know where the oases are, that you know the hidden corners in this desert. Lead us there!"

Feel their call for help, and see how that affects you. Can you keep your balance even when these people tug on you as they do and ask for your help? What is your first impulse? Do you want to take them to the place that you have discovered in the desert, take them to the oasis where you are sleeping in your dream? Something is restraining you. If you had still been in your fear, in your smallness, you would have thought: "Yes, I have to help these people with my skills; I have to lead them to the solutions that I have found in the desert. I have to draw them a map so they can find these places." But now that you have come to stand in your greatness and have experienced the mystical unity between you and the world, and you know that the world provides your every need, you realize that this can not be the way in which you help people.

You are aware that if you did this, within a short time people would come in droves to the places that have quenched your thirst with water and given you shade and rest. These places would become overcrowded and exhausted. The sources would dry up, the shade would be insufficient. This can not be the way to help these people.

In the dream, you realize that you do not have to let them share in your resources; that these resources are there for you. What you have to give them is not something external, not anything out there in the world: no map, no signpost, no oasis or hiding place, but that intuitive awareness in your heart: your inner knowing, your greatness. That is the gift you have that you can share with that group of people who seek your help.

So you tell them: "I can not give you anything to drink, or to eat, and I can not give you shelter, but I can tell you how you can find all these things yourself. I can point out the light in your own heart, the flame of your intuition, the inner knowing." And feel what it is like to give that to these people.

In this fantasy, you now wake up from your dream. You are back at the oasis and you feel that the oasis is a mirror for your own inner wealth. The oasis reflects *your* faith in life, the source of light in *you*. You feel that with this knowledge and this wealth, you can go out into the world and connect with people.

Imagine that what you take from this fantasy is a jar. A jar filled with water formed of living energy. The jar is the symbol for a source that takes care of *your* needs, through nature and the Earth that are at your service. The jar is the symbol of your inner balance, the ability to attune to your own knowing, your own needs, and to remain true to that.

I invite you to feel this jar of living water in your own heart, and to protect it with your angel's wings. This is yours; you have acquired it throughout many lifetimes; it embodies your greatness. Feel free to drink from it whenever you feel the need, and realize that what people need from you is not the water from *your* jar, but to make the connection with their own jar of living water.

With this your mission stands or falls. The realization of your own greatness; the continued attunement to yourself and your connection with heaven and Earth; the cherishing of the jar that you carry within to quench your thirst whenever you need to, and whenever you need to distance yourself from the world and all the stimuli that you receive there.

This is your power source. For everyone who wants, as their life path, to be a guide to others, it is absolutely necessary to achieve this. You do not help others by giving of yourself until empty, or by wanting to resolve or remove their problems. Those are all superficial solutions. What is important is to ignite the light in *their* depths; that is your task when being a lightworker; that is your job as a guide and helper. Remember this, because many of you are so sensitive to the suffering of others, that you are drawn to help and give away your resources, and even lower your energy in order to serve another.

It is not the purpose of lightwork to diminish or deplete yourself. The purpose is to remain completely convinced that other people have their *own* resources, and that those resources are ever at their disposal, even though they do not see that. Being a lightworker has strongly to do with maintaining and standing firmly in one's own strength. Always keep the connection with your own core, your own greatness.

Can you remain standing in a world that tugs at you as soon as you allow your light to shine? The world is not there to be saved by you, the world is there to discover the light within themselves. Remember this when you meet people as a helper and counselor: *the solution lies within themselves*.

119

Enjoy watching people discover this, and honor the balance between giving and receiving.

This is what I wish to convey to you today, because it is the first step toward being a healer and guide to others. Staying true to your intuitive awareness, and being good to yourself is fundamental here. *Remember your own greatness.* Do not be afraid to distance yourself from others in order to fully experience the light within yourself. It is only from the greatness of your soul that you can reach out your hand to another.

19. Peace with yourself

Dear friends, I am here, deeply moved with love for you all. I am Mary and I have been the mother of Jeshua on Earth. I enacted that role two thousand years ago, yet this is not only who I am. It was one role, and I learned a lot from it. In that life, I experienced intense feelings, and I return to you here in order to reach out my hand to you and to tell you of the inner peace that is available to you all at this moment.

The life in which I became known as Mary was a difficult one; however, it also was a life that opened the doorway to a light for which I was searching diligently. The most shocking and appalling event of that lifetime, the crucifixion of my son, was something my soul had consented to experience. Watching my son die shattered me as a mother, yet it also made me aware of Jeshua's essence, the part of him that could not die and which remained with us after he left the physical plane. His death opened up a gateway for me, beckoning me to enter into my own essence and feel my true strength.

My life as the mother of Jeshua evolved around the issue of faith, trust, and surrender to life. There was a guiding hand that led and carried me during that life. It enabled me, through my grief, to hold on to the light even though life seemed unbearably heavy at times. I have now transcended that heaviness and I am in a place of inner peace and freedom, yet with a deep commitment to you who are my sisters and brothers.

Only when you are in state of inner peace and freedom can you make a complete commitment to another; can you be involved with another, while at the same time stand next to that person fully in your own freedom. This I had to learn in the relationship with my son, Jeshua. I had to learn how to see him as a mature soul with his own mission; a mission that was so all-embracing that I had trouble containing it in my mind and with the heart of a mother. My emotions and thinking as a mother lagged behind the reality of the situation and this caused me much conflict and struggle. Eventually, what saved me was a sense of trust in the deeper wisdom behind the outer events, even though they seemed brutal and unjust.

Whenever I trusted, I could feel myself being lifted to another plane of existence, from which everything that took place gained a depth and meaning that I could not fathom with my human mind. It is of this level that I wish to speak today; it is the plane on which your guides reside and from where they want to reach out to you. It is their most sincere wish to make you aware of the peace, the love, and the light that is always available to you. However, you hold the key to that plane of existence and the key is *peace with yourself*. Making peace with yourself, accepting yourself as you are, surrendering to life as it is, opens the gate to joy, healing, and true change.

You struggle with yourself a lot. This is apparent to me as I look at you, at the people on Earth. Many of you are embroiled in a deep and intense struggle within yourself. People get worked up about world events, about the discord that takes place outwardly between people, or between people and nature. However, in this fierce battle that rages inwardly, so much energy is scattered and wasted that you have no energy remaining to truly stand in the world, to allow your light to shine there. For that reason, it is necessary that you are able to say "yes", first deeply within yourself to all that you are – including the dark parts.

To do this, you have to first accept that you *are* in conflict with yourself; that you do not find it easy to say "yes" to who you are; that you do not see it as a simple matter to trust your own true nature, to believe in it. To participate fully and truthfully in the process in which the Earth and humanity find itself, requires a deep introspection and an observing and feeling where you are in conflict with yourself, where you condemn yourself, and where you do not accept yourself as you are.

Where this attitude of struggle resides within your mind and being, you are divided within yourself, and you can not radiate to the world, because you deny yourself the light. Therefore, I now ask you to feel the energy of peace. Feel the energy of peace from within. Imagine having peace with who you are – *now*, at this moment. No judgment, no standards from outside – just being who you are. This is the greatest gift you can give to yourself – any time of the day.

Stop the battle, and say: "Yes, I have these emotions. I have difficulty with this or that. There are things I want to achieve and I am uncertain how to do them". Allow all this to be there fully and freely: this confusion, this fight, this inner judgment – let it be. Feel that there is a consciousness that lives within you that can observe without identifying with the problem.

Peace does not mean doing, it means *being*. Allow all the emotions that live within you – the confusion, the disillusionment, the fear – simply *to be*. By allowing them *to be as they are*, a space opens within you that allows all these emotions to flow through you and eventually dissipate, because you no longer feed them. By accepting who you are, and not doing anything to change yourself, you create a basis for peace within yourself.

Be yourself, be true to yourself, observe yourself, and feel that *you are good as you are*. Trust your own true nature. You are so often engaged in measuring or comparing yourself against certain ideals that were presented to you from society during your upbringing. This is a source of a lot of struggle. If you feel you must be different than you are, you are going to fight with yourself and you create turmoil. The key is to let go of this struggle and to discover who *you* are, *your* true nature hidden beneath all those images, ideals, and standards that cling to you.

By way of an exercise, a playful exercise, I would like to invite you to go with me to a beautiful garden. Imagine you are walking on a path and in the distance you see an iron gate, or an entrance that is bordered by flowers and plants of whatever kind you want. With a feeling of elation, you walk toward that gate. You know that behind the gate lies a beautiful garden, which is all yours.

You go through the gate and you smell all the flowers. Look at the first flowers you see. What color are they? How does it feel to be in the garden? Does the sun shine, or is there just shadow? Is it sheltered or open?

Then you find a place to go to and sit down, a bench, or on the ground, whatever you like. You relax the muscles of your body. You sit on a lovely spot. You smell and breathe in the garden around you. You feel: "This is my true nature, this is who I am. Everything grows and thrives in its own rhythm, at its own pace – just like me. I grow and flower in my own rhythm and at my own pace. I trust in this rhythm that reflects itself in the garden around me".

There are flowers that are in full bloom. There are also budding ones, and there are wilted flowers. There are leaves that lie dead on the ground and turn into compost. Every part of the cycle is present in your garden. You are confident that everything finds its own way, and feeds the rest by its own means. *This is your true nature*. Feel the well-being of the garden; this is who you are. The life energy goes its own way. There is a momentum in your life that you do not need to control or worry about; this is done for you. Right now, you have to only be at a spot in the garden that attracts you. Is it a light or a dark spot? What kind of plants are there? Are there any animals or birds? When you feel a connection with one of the living beings around you, an animal, plant or flower, then pose the question: "What would you like to tell me?" The response need not be in the form of words. It can be a flow of energy or a feeling or a simple realization. Allow the message to gently come to you.

Take pleasure in your garden. Admire its effortless connection with the elements: the earth, the sun, the rain, the wind, and the seasons. Feel that all you need to do is to walk around and to go where you feel drawn. Trust the messages of your inner garden. They will guide you to a path of happiness and peace on Earth. Let go of external judgments. They have nothing to do with you; you have your own rhythm. The sequence of events in your life have their own meaning. By relinquishing external judgments, you are less embroiled in an inner battle and you can surrender more easily to the dynamics of *your* garden, of *your* life.

Now, I would like to tell you about the connection you seek with guides or higher energies in your life. Do this according to your own nature. Do not impose anything upon yourself; do not force yourself to *do* anything. When I invite you to sit in your garden, then you probably get spontaneous images of the plants or flowers that grow there, the type of weather there is, and of the environment of the garden. You feel you are free to fantasize. However, when it comes to making contact with guides or angels, you often feel restricted by rules from outside yourself, by tradition, literature, or by what people say. That is a pity, because it can be so easy! Just as you are wondering what flower speaks to you the most, you may ask: "What is the most helpful energy for me now?" *Follow your own nature*. In small things, this happens spontaneously and easily, so try the same approach with something bigger. Often there is a whispering voice in your heart that knows exactly what you need in your life at this moment.

When you seek connection with a guide, an angel, or a loved one from the other side, allow that connection to come to you just as easily. Do not concern yourself about the form in which it appears to you. You essentially have no fixed shape either. You think you are a well-defined identity, that you are as other people see you: female or male, big or small, rich or poor, sick or healthy. All these visible properties make you who you are in the outer reality, but in the inner reality, those are only roles, only images and labels. In your core, your essence, you are free and formless and that is the place where you find inner peace.

In the formless, you are free; you are who you are. You can enact all kinds of roles. At one time, you hold a red rose, and at another time, a daffodil. At one time, you ask for guidance and a guide appears before your inner eye in the form of a figure with a magnificent robe. At another time, a child might come to you who says something quite simple. It also can be a physical child from your immediate surroundings, or a book that you open to a page that gives you exactly the message you need. Do not let the form dictate as to whether or not you consider the message as genuine. Search for connection with a spiritual helper in a way that appeals to you.

When you are looking for connection with a guide, imagine once again that you are in your garden and ask yourself what kind of guide you would like to see exactly as you did with the flower. Make a game of it. What would the ideal guide be for me, now? The energy of the guide will adapt to you. Guides are not so interested in form, but rather in the energy they want to offer you.

Play around with it. When you think you see something, a figure, a face, or a presence of someone, try not to force yourself to see this very accurately. Join in the feeling and let it take the form that suits you. That is sufficient; that is enough. Know that in your essence, you are without a form and so is your guide.

I, too, am without a form. In the past, I manifested as the woman who bore Jeshua as a child, and that has been one of my roles; a role through which I experienced much and felt intensely. But I am not that only; Mary is one aspect of my entire Self. In my essence, I am *One* and formless, and you are that, too. Beyond the forms and roles lies the inner peace that you all desire so deeply. Do not allow yourself to be distracted by forms, definitions, and rules that are imposed upon you from without. *You* are the master; *you* create your reality. The forms will adapt to that.

I embrace you with the serenity and peace of heaven and I am telling you that it is available for you all, right now. You are like a garden that is under development. It is perfect as it is, reflecting the seasons of life. Some plants and flowers will wilt and die, and become nutrition for a new life cycle. Let them go, have faith and confidence. Look at your life as would a benevolent gardener. Occasionally a plant needs water, some attention, some help. But, especially, appreciate and enjoy your garden. This makes the garden grow and flourish abundantly. Be at peace with yourself; this ignites the light within and allows it to shine into the world, pure and bright.

20. Circles of light

Dear friends, I am Mary, mother of Jeshua on Earth. It is such a joy for me to be among you, to be in your circle of light. I wish to celebrate with you this morning, and to envelop you in a mantle of sweet love, very light and gentle – feel it.

Your hearts are in need of light. For you all, this is a heavy place to be. Your natural state of being is joy, playfulness, creativity. Your often feel smothered by the heavy energies on Earth, and you feel disconnected from Home. I want to bring the energies of Home, the original source, to you today. So breathe it in and remember who you are. I want you to bathe in the light of your soul and the connection between our souls.

Imagine that the light of reconnection and oneness is flowing throughout your body. Make sure this flow visits every part of your body, especially the parts in need of healing. Let it flow all the way down to your feet. There is now a halo of light around us all. Feel how you can relax and be safe within this halo of light, even though you may sense that some parts of yourself are tired and feel heavy. That is okay – let everything be as it is.

You all carry a very precious light in your soul. When you are connected to this light you feel one with the universe. This is the divine experience for which you are looking. You are not yet aware of this inner light when you start out as a young soul on your journeys, so you look for it outside yourself, in the external world. You are truly like a child looking for guidance, but your real mission is to find the guidance within, and doing that becomes the birth of your Divinity.

Most souls spend many lifetimes throughout the ages trying to find light outside themselves, and that is part of growing up. But you are now becoming a mature soul. You are aware of the need to go within, because you have tried all the other ways. You have tried to find the light by gaining worldly power or possessions. You have tried to find the light by creating a big ego and gaining recognition from the world. And you have tried to find the light by losing yourself in romantic relationships; by trying to merge with another soul. These are really the stages that every soul goes through on its evolutionary journey.

But at some point, the soul discovers that those things do not work, and then the soul goes through a deep inner crisis. As it is maturing, it discovers deep emotions of loneliness, separation, and fear, and there is a growing awareness that nothing outside itself can fill the void. This stage of a soul's journey can be called "the dark night of the soul". The soul can not lose itself any more in anything external, and yet it does not know *how* to nurture itself, *how* to go within. This is when loneliness can hit you hardest, and when you are at this point, as often happens in relationships, you realize you can not find outside yourself what you are really seeking. So there is no other road to follow than the road that leads to your heart.

You are the only one who can acknowledge, and thereby ignite, your own fire, and you often wonder: "How do I do this?" That is your perpetual question: "How do I become enlightened; how do I enlighten myself?" And the answer is that it is not you who is doing it. The "you" who has been searching, who has felt lonely, who despairs, is not the one who is becoming enlightened. Essentially, enlightenment occurs when you give up the "you" part of yourself by releasing it. You completely kneel down within yourself and you give up. Your ego bows down, because it acknowledges the fact that it does not know a way out – it does not have the answers. Therefore, not knowing the answers, and being in the "dark night of the soul", is often the heralding of enlightenment. It is when you give up that you become open to something new, something you are not able to control. This "something" – the energy of your soul – has been knocking on your door for a very long time. In truth, you have been afraid of your own divine love and light, because from a human perspective you can not control it, and so you have resisted your own light and source of joy. This is very paradoxical for us to see from our side, because the most precious thing you seek is already present within you! And therein lies the answer to your emotions of despair and loneliness.

When you stop trying to change yourself, when you stop trying to make your life "work", you are opening to a greater force that wants to carry you with lightness and joy. Once you are in this flow of lightness, you will connect with others who are in the same flow and your heart will be filled with joy. Meeting with your spiritual family on Earth will be one of the deepest sources of happiness and fulfillment for you. But before this happens you have to let go. You have to entrust yourself to the flow of your heart. Do not try to manipulate and control life so much. Life becomes much easier and lighter when you live it from the heart.

The most difficult step is to acknowledge that you do not know the way. Every human ego contains pride, which often shuts you off from the flow of love, so you have to let go of your pride. This is what you do when you connect with the wounded and vulnerable child within yourself, and that is a deeply spiritual thing to do. By recognizing the core of your vulnerability, you are actually coming closer to other people. By becoming aware of the wounded child within, you are also seeing it in the eyes of other people. Truly embracing your own darkness, your own vulnerability, builds a bridge between you and other people. It naturally creates compassion and understanding in your heart.

When you are inside the ego, you tend to judge and criticize other people. You need to do this to maintain your identity. But when you look at them with eyes that see their inner child, you recognize that they are wounded humans, just like you, and so it becomes easier to reach out to them. And it also becomes easier to receive support and love from other humans. This is what it means to create a circle of light; to acknowledge your vulnerability, to release the need for control, and to release your pride. To the ego, this seems to be a very high price to pay, but it is actually small compared to the loneliness and despair you have to suffer when you are clinging to the ego.

At this time, many people are yearning for connecting from the heart. My message is especially meant for people who are ready to take the leap: to let go of your judgments, of your criticism – especially of yourself. Open fully to the immense source of light available to you. You have built a prison around yourself, and I am inviting you to step out of it. You can do it now, you are ready. All you have to do is simply to ask. You do not have to fight or struggle to get out of the prison. You can simply ask Spirit, or whatever you call the endless source of this universe. Or you may do it by way of prayer: "Release me, I want to be Home again".

Home is within you all, and when you open the doors of your heart, the light will shine *so* brightly! Your light will bring joy to others, and you will joyfully connect with other people, but you will also be at peace when you are alone. You will not *need* other people to be fulfilled, but it will be an experience of enrichment and abundance to meet them, especially soul mates.

I would like to end by asking you to imagine that we are planting a seed today. See it as a small seed of light that each one of you is holding. Imagine that you are putting that seed into the Earth and you wish it well from your heart. You entrust this ray of light to Earth, and then you let it go. You release all control, or desire to manipulate, or to know. *Just see what happens.* The Earth will someday return this energy to you in the form of a small miracle entering your life. You will ask yourself: "Why did this happen to me?" And maybe you will want to ask a psychic or medium about that, and I would tell you: "Do not analyze it with your head, just receive the gifts given by the universe".

So let us now for a few moments enjoy the halo of light that is still around us and has expanded by now. The light, at this moment, is warm and golden. Please know that you are always connected to your soul family. We from the other side are always next to you. Accept our love.

Teachings from Mary Magdalene

21. Power and powerlessness in the soul of women

I am Mary Magdalene. I salute you with joy in my heart! You are so familiar to me. We are related through a shared past and a common goal. You and I are walking the same path. *And oh*, how long and arduous that path can be, and how it leads us through deep valleys before we reach the Promised Land!

I would like to address the depth of those valleys. I prefer it when we speak openly about the darkness that befalls us now and then, because honesty and openness bring clarity and peace of mind. Only this will lead us out of the valley and into the Promised Land, the New Earth that you and I have been dreaming of. The Promised Land is not a place, but a state of mind, vibrating inner peace, joy and abundance. If enough people vibrate this way, the New Earth will be born as a physical reality. The vision of a New Earth is deeply etched in the hearts of us all, and because of that promise, I am here today. I am your sister in spirit, and since I know what it is like to be human, I understand the depths and heights you are going through.

Why is it all so difficult? And why must we descend so deeply? It might disappoint you a bit, but *I am not here with the definitive answers!* For one, I have not yet reached the finish line from where I can teach you by way of spiritual discourse. I am just as much on the path as are you, although I now see things from a much wider perspective than when I lived as a human being. I have had several awakening experiences in my lives on Earth, but I am still on the journey, and therein lies part of the answer, and also part of the liberation and the relief: *you do not have to know it all!* You are allowed to be on the journey, and you do not have to understand everything with your mind. It is the way of the human being to understand through *experience*; to experience life with its many highs and lows, and from there to stumble upon fragments of truth, moments of deep insight and understanding – precious jewels that can *not* be acquired by the mind or the intellect. That is why I am not here to preach to you about intellectual truths. It is the "way of experience", the road from within, which fascinates me and makes my journey one in common with yours.

As I speak of darkness and the depth of the valleys we go through, I can not but address the wounds that have been inflicted on the feminine energy, on *your* feminine energy, whether you are female or male. These wounds account for much of the darkness that people experience in their lives. The feminine energy is about intuition, feeling, flowing with the rhythm of nature, being receptive and open, providing care and emotional safety. No one can live life with joy without those qualities. Now, to be sure, much has changed during the last century on Earth regarding the rights of women and the way women are treated. Women now have virtually the same rights as men, at least in the West. Women in the modern world can realize themselves just as freely as men: take dominant positions, build a career and amass wealth. Does that mean however that there is a true balance between the masculine and feminine energies?

When women fight for equality in the area of work and career, they often embrace the old masculine energy of dominance and power and now use it for their own benefit. It can be liberating for women to claim their independence and autonomy in this way, but the question remains whether the rebirth of the feminine energy is about an equal distribution of power between men and women. Is it about women amassing power, becoming more *like men*, or is it about a new understanding of masculine and feminine energy, beyond definitions in terms of power and powerlessness?

The true meaning of the rebirth of the feminine energy is that the feminine qualities of intuition, connection and care are recognized as a vital part of creation, and as necessary qualities both for individual men and women and society at large to function harmoniously. The return of those primal qualities to everyday life will not change women only, but men as well. Not only women have been robbed of their basic sense of worthiness as a woman, men also have suffered as they became alienated from their female, intuitive side. The wound of the feminine energy concerns us all and its true rebirth is about emotionally healing this wound, and thereby changing our definition of masculinity as well.

What is the female wound in its essence? It is a deep sense of unworthiness in the psyche of women, caused by centuries of sexual violence and continuous denigration of the typical female qualities of intuition and feeling. The feminine energy was disempowered in ways I do not need to describe in detail, for women all know that subjugation from the inside. What I would like to focus on now is how the wound looks like energetically; how it manifests in the female energy field.

The female wound: a hole in the belly

Individual people have an energy field surrounding them, which reflects their moods, thoughts and emotions. It is called the aura. There is also such a thing as the collective human energy field or aura; it reflects the way in which humanity generally vibrates. Within the collective human aura, one can distinguish between the archetypical female aura, and the archetypical male aura. If one looks at the female aura on a global scale, one notices that in the area of the belly or abdomen, a hole has been driven into the feminine energy. The energy centers which are the earthly foundation of the aura, i.e. the bottom of the spine (the tailbone) and the centers at the navel and the solar plexus, have become disempowered and robbed of life energy. There exists in many women, sometimes without them even being aware of it, a deep sense of unworthiness, inferiority and insecurity. Reliance on the female abdominal strength has become uncommon, because that abdominal strength is really something quite powerful. It is *not* a gentle, kitten-like energy, but a strong, knowing wisdom; one that has deep roots in the Earth, and one that tolerates no pussyfooting!

In order to allow that strength, that power, into your belly – after long centuries of being raped, harassed and tortured – is a leap into the abyss! What happens when you have been humiliated, rejected and violated in your deepest core, and when this has been going on for centuries for many women? You push your energy upwards and you pull back from that place in the abdomen, which is also the place of emotions, of intimacy, sexuality and reproduction. Your pelvis, which is so naturally connected with the Earth forces, becomes empty. You pull back from that area of your body, because it feels scary and dangerous to be there and to express your power from there. And what happens in that movement of retreat? There arises a kind of gap between above and below; between the energy of the heart and above, and the energy of your solar plexus and below: that energy in the abdomen.

Now, how does one bridge the gap and heal the female wound? How will women feel safe again in the energy centers which are connected with intimacy, sexuality, pregnancy and child birth? How do they own their power in this most precious and sacred space in their bellies? Political rights alone will not heal the female wound. Spiritual, inner healing is needed here. How does one heal from within? How does one become an empowered woman who can truly embrace herself with a sense of dignity and self worth?

What women need is a spirituality that comes from the heart but has a keen eye for the belly. Here, I would like to point out that dedicating yourself to the spiritual path should fill the hole in your belly, not entice you to "rise above it". Many sensitive women run into the pitfall of being very caring, giving and empathetic toward other people in their lives, while not being able to really stand up for themselves and their truest desires. This kind of giving is not the "rebirth of the feminine energy" that we are looking for, it is a way of escaping the dark instead of facing it.

The moment you develop your spiritual awareness, your heart opens. When you connect with your deepest feelings, when you start to get glimpses of your soul, when you no longer identify solely with the 3D person that you are, your intuitive and psychic abilities are awakened and you become much more sensitive to energies around you. With your heart open, you become sensitive to the energies of others, *and* you may become depleted, because you feel so much for others. As your mind has opened up to new ideas and your heart has opened and become much more sensitive to outside energies, what has happened, in the meantime, to the area of the belly that has been sucked empty by old trauma? Even if you have not been treated badly or aggressively as a girl, or as a woman, in this life, an essential part of the feminine energy still contains deeply ingrained patterns that continue to live on in every woman; images of humiliation and pain. It is not easy for any woman to let the powerful energy of her belly flow naturally.

Paradoxically, it is precisely when you start on the spiritual path that, sooner or later, confronting this situation will be necessary. There is much talk about the heart, and about opening the heart and connecting your heart with the whole, but here lurks a trap, especially for women, but for all persons in whom the feminine energy is strongly developed. If you connect with others, *without* being present in your belly – in this center where you can remain in contact with *your* needs and *your* truth – then your connection with others can lead to a loss of self, to exhaustion, and to an unending giving to others. This, in fact, is what happens very often to highly sensitive women. And it certainly happens to highly sensitive lightworkers, who already feel a strong inner drive for a New Earth, where more harmony can exist between people, and more freedom and love. *But oh, how easy it is to go under*, when you are not able to integrate fully the energy of your soul and your heart into the level of your belly, and thus to truly sink deeply into the cavity of the pelvis, which symbolizes the power of the feminine energy. But when you *do* live from that area of primal strength, you can feel that everything in nature can only survive when there is balance between giving and receiving; between being with yourself and being with the other; between connecting and letting go.

It is because of this necessary balance that I want to make a strong appeal to women; to highly sensitive people; to spiritually motivated people: *take care of that abdominal strength and make it your own.* Dare to stand up for yourself, and to develop a healthy sense of boundaries! Often you associate spirituality with love, light and connection, and you crave for those energies, but a truly balanced connection stands or falls with the ability to create boundaries, to own your individual space and to fully experience your own strength and dignity.

I lived in a time when free expression by women was not accepted and not valued. I felt a deep connection with the message of Jeshua Ben Joseph, and with the essence of the Christ energy. I was touched by his words, his charisma, and I experienced all of that in my own way. At the same time, there lived in me a rage, with regard to the ruling powers who prohibited me from being who I was: independent, powerful and strong willed. I was regularly thrown back on myself in that life, and I struggled with my own feelings of powerlessness and rage. My belly was seized by the energy of frustration, and underneath lay dormant a sense of inferiority for not being seen as fully human. At the same time, I also could be taken over by the ecstasy of feeling connected with friends and soul mates. There, I felt a power and a recognition that supported me, which reminded me of Home. Still, it was my inner work to come to terms with my own feelings of inferiority and insecurity. I had to face my inner darkness, and not escape it by giving myself away in a relationship or losing myself in a communal goal. I had to bring peace to the area of my belly all on my own.

It is precisely because women have learned to feel powerless from that space in their belly that they are inclined to give too much from the heart, to give of themselves until deplete, or to lose themselves completely in relationships with others, with a loved one or with a child, parent, or friend. The losing of oneself in the other, too often shows that you do not feel at home in yourself, and safe in your own ground. If there is a feeling of emptiness or alienation that prevails, it is tempting to reach out to another, seemingly in love, but there is another motive lurking there: you need the other in order to make *you* feel good, to make *you* feel at home, and to help *you* feel accepted.

To distinguish between proper and improper giving was my inner work, and here is an invitation to you to determine for yourself how you connect with the world around you, with your beloved, your friends, your children and parents. Take one particular relationship to focus on now and see how it feels on the level of the belly. How much space is there for you? Can your belly relax in this relationship? Do you feel nourished, grounded and accepted in this relationship just as you are? Or do you feel you have to make an effort, and that you lose your energy to the other when you do? These are signs that something gnaws at you, that you are giving too much, or that you are working too hard to get the approval of others, because somewhere deeply hidden away in your belly lives a fear, a pain, a void.

Let us now approach that void and let us join together. I would like to invite you all to descend with me into that area of the belly: so battered, traumatized and burdened with the past. From each of you I ask, man or woman, to descend with me into this area of collective pain. See before you the collective female aura and let us approach the hole in her belly.

Take a torch along and do not be afraid. You are stronger than the pain, and your presence brings light to the darkness. Sow light in this forgotten area and invite the power of the feminine energy to manifest again on Earth: *The power of the Earth and the forces of nature...the power of feeling and intuition, and the power of Mystery...the rhythm of sowing and harvesting and of the seasons... the quiet light of the moon...may these elements come to fruition during our lifetimes, that the feminine may shine again... not only from the heart, but from the deep source of wisdom that is in your belly.*

22. A bridge to the male energy

Dear brothers and sisters, I greet you all from my heart. I am thankful to be here with all of us present. This is a new time. You are in the middle of the birth of a new consciousness that has already taken root on Earth. From very deep inside your soul, you know and sense it. Before your birth, you were planning to dance along with the flow of consciousness now awakening on Earth. What kind of consciousness is this?

You are carrying an old past with you and not only from this life, but from many lifetimes before. The energy and vibration on Earth was dominated by fear and struggle and by the battle to survive, and not only physically, but also emotionally and spiritually. You have often felt abandoned and lost on this Earth that is now slowly making way for the new Earth, which is being born through *you*. You have been here on the old Earth many times and you have tried to bring in the new – cautiously through the small openings for change that existed before – but the consciousness on Earth has been very, very stuck. There was a dominant male energy, both inwardly and outwardly, which was holding life in its grip. This form of male energy has caught you in its spell and has kept you suppressed. Inwardly, you have absorbed this energy, both consciously and unconsciously, and it has become part of you.

This dominant male energy was born from fear in the past. When the male energy becomes separated from the female energy, the natural balance and dance between both sexes becomes distorted and the male energy moves and operates independently of the female energy. It loses its connection with feeling and the rhythm of nature, and thereby loses its respect for the Earth and the living creatures here. The male energy then operates from distrust and a need to control, and a desire to master its environment by exercising mental and physical coercion. That tendency you see repeated in the many religions on Earth, and certainly in Christianity. The Christ energy has been appropriated by a male hierarchy through which the living core, the source that was its basis, became weakened and hidden.

You are the ones who retain knowledge in your heart of the source of the Christ energy from when it was still flowing and fluid: the living energy, the living truth that wanted to be brought to Earth. I, Mary Magdalene, was one of those persons who was touched by the source of the living Christ energy. You could say that I fell in love with the spirit, the energy, the radiance of the Christ energy. This has also happened to you; your hearts were also touched. It may have been by being alive on Earth at the time of the birth of the Christ energy, or right before or right after. But however it happened, your lives have been touched by this energy, just as was mine.

I lived at a time when women dared not bring their inner knowing outward; their feelings, their hearts, their independence, and their strength, and the culture of that time deemed them not even capable of doing so. Still, I was driven by a passion, an energy through which I refused to be bound by the existing order. I closed ranks with the one that you call Jeshua. He was for me a friend and a teacher. I felt deeply and dearly connected with him. It is true that I was ridiculed and scorned by the existing order and even by men who lived around Jeshua, because I was not considered fully worthy. But Jeshua and I had a bond that was completely equal and by which I felt fully seen and accepted as a woman by him for my understanding of spirituality, my inner knowing and the wisdom that I carried in my heart through the city streets. Meeting him has healed me inwardly.

Nevertheless, I was a separate human being, independent of him and I led my own life. The wounds that I have experienced in the area of the female energy, of not being allowed to be who I was, have for a long time occupied me at the soul level. I, too, have lived several lives on Earth and I see in you the same struggle, the same wounds, which were present also in me as an earthly woman. And I want to tell you: "Something fundamental is changing during this time on Earth".

First, I want to say something about the balance between male and female and the dominance of a mentally focused, authoritarian male energy. Not only women have suffered and been victims of this energy, men have as well. Of course, the rights of women have been trampled upon and women have been left with a deep sense of inferiority because of this oppressive tradition, but look what it has done to men. Men also have female energy in their being, just as women possess male energy, and sensitive men were often misjudged by this authoritarian tradition. There emerged a very one-sided definition of masculinity that has hurt not only women, but has also affected men deeply in their hearts and damaged them. They were no longer allowed to live from the heart, feel intuitively, and connect with others, which was seen as not manly. The definition, the image of masculinity, was eroded to a rigid, one-sided energy that essentially does not at all express true maleness. It is a warped and destructive version of the male energy that does no justice to how masculinity could be if it emerges from the soul. So when we are meeting here to discuss the rebirth of the female energy, I want to stress very strongly that this rebirth also has to take place in men in order to restore balance on Earth.

How do we do that? How does that happen? It is important that there is a bridge between the male and the female energies. In the past, many women have been so hurt through what has been done to them to cause feelings of inferiority, that hostility toward the male has arisen. Many women have of necessity built a kind of protective wall around themselves when it comes to commitment with a man, especially from the abdomen, which is the area of sensuality and intimacy. When there is this kind of mistrust in women regarding men, they also put the male energy *in themselves* at a distance. They have a hard time making use of the male energy that is necessary to act with freedom and independence as a human being, to act as a self-conscious woman in the world.

Many women have learned to be giving, caring, and connecting toward others. But in doing that in a one-sided way, they can lose themselves whenever there is a need for male energy; a strength you need in order to connect from the heart while keeping your boundaries intact. In the new spirituality, there is a consciousness from the heart, and that is certainly fundamental, but for women, it is extremely important that they also dare to take possession again of their abdomen and their emotions, their self worth and self respect. Only when they find that foundation within themselves, can they give and receive in a balanced way from the heart. With merely an open heart, you can become unbalanced and stand unsteadily on the Earth. The male energy gives you the protection and safety and the foundation you need to be present and open in your female energy.

Now I ask you to focus on your male energy, the energy that allows you to separate yourself from others and experience yourself as an independent being. Can you experience your own foundation, your own anchor in this earthly body connected to the Earth? Allow your consciousness to descend quietly into your abdomen, your tailbone, and even into your legs. Experience there your earthly being. Feel your physicality and ask yourself: "Do I allow my needs sufficient opportunity for expression and fulfillment? Do I take good care of myself and allow myself to receive as well as give?" Because taking care of yourself is just as important as connecting with the world around you from the heart and from the third eye. Always come back to the foundation in your abdomen.

It is precisely through this care-of-self, and this setting of your boundaries that the essential male energy becomes your protector, the knight who stands beside you to protect your female energy. That is the balance you are looking for. The female energy feels and connects, the male energy guards, protects and disconnects whenever it is necessary. The male energy anchors you in yourself and teaches you how to say "no" when necessary and to be true to yourself. Feel the depth and importance of that. Feel how appropriate the male energy is in its true form as a protector, a knight. Allow this energy completely into your body. Imagine that a beautiful woman lives in your heart with a man standing beside her holding her lovingly, one who lets her be free completely, but at the same time gives her strength and tranquility. Try to allow that man into your heart. Imagine that you are leaning against him and notice how that feels for you. Can you do that? Can you allow it? Can you be that relaxed in the presence of your own male energy?

You are within yourself this combination of male and female energies; both are part of your soul. The purpose of my message today is to create in the world some balance between men and women. This must first be done inwardly and, for women especially, that means to make peace with the male energy. To let go of old images wherein the male was equated with aggressive and suppressive power, abuse, and control, and to create a new image of masculinity. Please be aware when you experience resistance against male energy to ask yourself: "What kind of male energy sparks resistance in me?" Know there is also a male energy that is loving, warm, and powerful. You need that energy for yourself; it is part of your being.

During this time, the rebirth of the female energy also brings about the rebirth of the male energy. From a spiritual perspective, inner changes always precede changes in the outer world. If men and women bridge the gap between their inner male and female energy, then this eventually becomes visible in the world as well.

23. Lust and love

Dear men and women, I salute you all. I am here in your midst as a soul, as a woman, as a sister. I am one with you, and having been human, I know from within all the feelings you have today. They are not foreign to me.

What strikes me most, now that I am looking at life on Earth from this side, is the preciousness of life on Earth. The vulnerability of being human, the pain and the wounds that you sustain while on Earth, and conversely, your incredible courage, your persistent desire for light and love, your perseverance and joyous victories. That for me now characterizes life on Earth. I see you as courageous angels who take that experience, that adventure upon yourself.

When you descend into the earthly life, you almost always come from a realm which vibrates at a higher level than human society now does on Earth. Somewhere deep within, you say "yes" to encountering this Earth energy. You make the decision: "I'm going to take this on": the dance with life on Earth, which is in part a dance with darkness, with fear, resistance, loneliness, and the feeling of being lost. You take that risk, and I can now see why. Despite all the suffering, the effort, the heaviness, there is no place else so deep, so rich, and so intense as when you are embodied in matter, in form.

Often, though, you want to sever yourself from form and move beyond it, to merge with something grander, something higher. You seek to be released from the confines of earthly life. But I see the beauty of you *as you are*, as earthly humans: man, woman, child, or adult. In that specific form that you have, you radiate the light of Creation. Many spiritual traditions have been focused on the transcendence of the human form: "the body is no good, it is not a messenger of truth; the emotions are suspect, passions out of the question; sexuality is a source of temptation, yes even poisonous." The entire earthly existence was actually weakened and robbed of its sacredness by this type of thinking and this has happened out of a desire for control.

There have been powers on Earth that wanted control over life. And to exercise control over people, over life, you achieve that best by way of the mind: through ideas and images that you disseminate, that you use to indoctrinate. Mental control is far more all-encompassing than manipulation by physical power. You can touch people deeply in their souls and change them when you put before them certain images about who they are, about their worthiness or unworthiness, and the goodness or "badness" (evil) of their natural impulses.

You have been affected very deeply in that way, and because of that conditioning you began to see life on Earth as unworthy in many ways. This has been taught to you, and unconsciously you still carry these impressions with you. They still have an influence on how you think about yourself, feel about your body, your lusts, desires, emotions, and your passion.

Nowadays, things start to loosen up; old ideas are on the verge of collapsing. This is because more and more people are waking up, feeling the desire to be true to themselves. This new wave of energy is awakening people individually, one by one, and as it grows, it will affect society as a whole. It is a movement back to Earth, you might say, and back to your natural self, as you are *part* of the Earth. Your *body* is part of the Earth: your sexuality, your instincts, the language of your body are part of the Earth. Your earthly nature can not be denied indefinitely; it is a viable part of Creation.

And how do things stand with you in that connection, between the lower and higher? Traditionally, you were told that spirituality had to do with "the higher", and often also with servitude to an ideal – you in the service of something higher – such as putting yourself in the service of your neighbor and of your community. And the lower was equated with what is ego-oriented, focusing on yourself, pursuing your own desires. If you followed your own inclinations, you got "off track"; the ego-oriented was laden with sin and judgment.

Now, however, you are in the midst of a transformation in thinking about spirituality. You feel that call for change from your entire being, and you have come here to support the awakening of consciousness on Earth.

Before you took the leap into your current lifetime, you felt the potential of a fundamental shift taking place at this time. Your soul felt the pull of this and you decided: "I want to part of this, so here I go again." The dominance of the old consciousness has, as it were, been stretched to the limit. Things *should* be different now. Even the continued survival of humankind, nature, and harmony with the Earth depends on it.

This process of awakening and transformation asks that you turn toward the so-called lower in yourself and to assign to it a completely different value. And what does that turning to the lower mean? *Making connection with your body, with your belly, with your feelings – recognizing your own animal nature.* As human beings, you have lived in your mind for so long that you have lost the connection with what I would call your "animalism", the animal, instinctual part of you. That term immediately evokes certain associations, but what is "animalism" really? Animals have no mental energy such as do people. They live from instinct, but that instinct is much more sophisticated, a much finer tool than is generally thought by people. *Instinct is in your belly.* Instinct helps you sense directly how something feels to you: if it feels good or if it feels repulsive; if it brings you something desirable or if you prefer for it to go away. But what is difficult for people to do is to rely on their instinct, and sometimes they can no longer feel it. So strongly have you lived from your head that you have lost connection with your instinct, the wisdom of your animal nature.

Your troubled relationship with your own animalism, the animal inside of you, shows itself clearly in the area of sexuality. What happens when people take on an intimate, sexual relationship with another? In a friendship, where there is no sexuality, you can to some extent remain outside the area of the instinctive, the animal nature. You may connect from the head, and when the connection deepens, also from the heart. But once the area of sexuality is opened up between two people, there are other forces at play. There is an instinctual attraction on the physical level, an attraction between opposites, that has little to do with the head and not necessarily with the heart, either. The power of their sexual passion often frightens people and they may react in two ways. The attraction can instill such a fear of losing control, of losing *yourself,* that you shut down and withdraw. Or you go with the flow of the attraction, but you keep focused on the sensations of lust that you have in the body and you do not open up to the profound intimacy that sexuality can initiate you into. It is seldom that two people can be intimate and experience connection at both the levels of their animal nature and of their heart.

This is such a shame, for sexuality can truly be the gateway to a profound mixture of spiritual and human love. Why is it so difficult for men and women to experience the sacred and healing aspect of sexuality? When it comes to the physical, the sexual instincts, you have grown up with all sorts of taboos and prohibitions. That has started to change for a few decades, but there is still no *real* freedom in that area. Can you feel at ease with the sensations of lust that you experience? Can you enjoy them? Or is it actually something disturbing that you want to get rid of, either by having physical sex (which makes sex into "scratching where it itches"), or by shutting yourself off from it through the force of the mind? It is still difficult for people to playfully and joyfully embrace their own sexual desires. What happens is that they either get stuck in judgments or fears about it, going into the head. Or they submerge into their lust in a guilty, secretive way, making sexuality into something that happens in the dark. In both cases, there can be no connection between the heart and the beast, between the higher and the lower, between lust and love. Not being able to value the animal part, shuts you off from the loving and spiritual part, too.

How can you reconnect what was separated and feel more free with your own animal and sexual nature? First of all, honor the body and let go of old judgments about lust and sexuality. Lust is a natural flow of energy generated by the body. It is innocent and not inherently dangerous or destructive. Try to welcome it with joy and pleasure. Whenever you feel lust, enjoy the tingling sensations in your body, see it as enjoyable in itself, without having to act on it. There is a basic sensuality to your body that exists as an undercurrent, and it enables you to enjoy different kinds of bodily sensations, such as eating, drinking, touching, dancing, bathing, or walking in the sun. Sexuality, having sex with someone else, is one expression of this basic sensuality that belongs to you as a human being. Do not be ashamed of it, enjoy it. Your sensual nature is something precious and delicious. If you embrace your own sensual nature and welcome sensations of lust with an open mind, you would have fun with it! You could share it with another person and if there is a deeper connection between the two of you, you will notice how the flow of lust will actually bring you closer to them, allowing your hearts to open up to each other and merge, not just on the physical level, but on the emotional and spiritual level as well.

Lust can lead into love and genuine intimacy. What I like to stress is that lust is not the opposite of sacred and serene love between two people. Lust and love can go together and lust can actually help you reach a deep state of intimacy with another, if you surrender to it without shame or reserve. You have this deep-seated notion that if you let go, if you ride the wave of your emotions or passions, things will get out of hand. But it is often just the other way around. If you try to curb or control something like sexual passion, you are working against a natural force that is so powerful that you will lose anyway. By curbing it, you elicit twisted and even perverted expressions of sexuality. Demeaning forms of sexuality always go together with sick and rigid judgments about human nature. That is why religious fervor and sexual perversity often go hand in hand.

Feeling safe with your own sexual nature, is the first step toward an intimate connection with another. You appreciate your own body and the kind of experiences it wants to offer you. Of course, to connect intimately with another person requires more than just this. You are dealing with another being, shaped and molded by a different background and history. For you both to feel safe and secure, your hearts will need to open up to each other. Both of you will have built defenses to protect yourself against surrender to another, against trust. You all carry within old emotional wounds. Each of you have such defenses, and it is important to recognize them in yourself. Emotional intimacy arises when you are willing to face your own fears and when you are truly willing to understand each other's pain. As you are willing to do so, there is joy in your hearts and there will be a flow of healing between you. You will come closer, both on the level of the body and on the level of the soul. This delicate process of coming together is what the art of love making is really about. It involves devotion, patience, honesty, and courage. It is both passionate and highly spiritual.

When I initially talked about the preciousness of the human experience on Earth, I was also referring to the art of love making. As a soul, you are not bound to a form. You are not, at your essence, a man or a woman, a child or an adult, sick or healthy – these are all temporary manifestations. Nonetheless, those impermanent forms offer a variety of experiences that are potentially exquisite and profoundly spiritual. Being a woman or a man offers to you the possibility of experiencing human love making, and to enjoy it physically, emotionally, and spiritually.

There is much confusion about sexuality in human society. In the encounter between man and woman, there can be an opening into a sacred communion, a space in which you feel lifted up into a wholeness that transcends you both as human beings. You can call it the soul, or God, but the remarkable thing is that this sacred experience does not at all look like lust, although lust – exploring each other physically – forms the entry into it. Your earthly nature is not base or vile; sexuality and spirituality can be partners. That is why I encourage you to feel at ease with your own passion, your bodily desires, your sexuality. Explore it at your own pace and in your own rhythm. In fact, I would like to invite you now to allow your awareness to descend into your belly. Your awareness is nothing else than a focus, so now direct that focus toward your belly. Experience how that area feels, and sink even deeper into the region of your sexual organs and the tailbone (root) chakra – your pelvis. Descend downward to that region of your body with your attention being objective and neutral. This is a wonderful part of your body, and sense here the source of the life force – you may see or feel a color. Experience how you can allow that flow of the life force, of sensuality and physicality, to descend through your legs and make connection with the Earth. Feel how beneficial and natural it is to experience this flow of the body.

Observe, if you can, whether your body needs something now, whether you are allowing your body to experience all that it likes to experience. Perhaps there is something that your body would like to experience more often in your everyday life? It may be a simple thing, something you bypass with your head. Take those needs seriously; the body wants to bring you Home. *The body is not in opposition to the soul, it is the soul in material form.* It is your head, rather than your body, that banishes you from your soul. Make peace with your body and enjoy its many offerings.

24. Living from your heart

Dear friends, I am Mary Magdalene who is speaking. I connect with you and I am in your midst. I do not want to talk to you as if from some pulpit, I am one of you and one *with* you. I want you to recognize yourself in me just as I recognize myself in you. We share in the human adventure, and to see it in all its multifaceted beauty is the challenge for humans on Earth. Not to transcend it, or to look down on it from above, or to manipulate it from there, or even to change it. That is not the purpose of spiritual growth, but instead to descend and to surrender to the reality of being human, of being embodied here on the Earth. To dare to entrust yourself to that process *is* the art of living on Earth. Wanting to be above it, wanting to make yourself free of it, is an attempt to control life and to recreate yourself into an ideal image that you have.

Observe for a moment how in every era of history there have been idealized images and they are all different. Many of those idealized images come from religious traditions; images of how an ideal human is supposed to be, which often meant ridding yourself of all kinds of human characteristics that were assessed as bad, or even as evil. In this day and age, old traditions are being discarded. However, there are many new idealized images being presented to you for which you are supposed to strive and to which you are supposed to compare yourself; images into which to change yourself and with which you need to align. Do you feel the compulsion that hides behind all this? The wanting to push and to direct life? That compulsion stands in opposition to surrender and to entrusting yourself to the earthly life as it flows naturally in and around and through you and all people in the world. This element of flow and surrender is the true art of living on Earth.

Feel what happens when I connect with you. I open my heart in acknowledgment, in friendship – I embrace you. Do not worship me as an all-knowing teacher or master. Let go of that idea. Do you feel how you move away from a real connection if you take that attitude towards another human being, whether that being is on this side or on Earth? Feel the power of the connection, the open flow from one heart to another. When you dare to stand next to me or any master and dare to connect in equality, then the gates open to a different, more joyful reality on Earth.

This can only happen when people acknowledge their own deepest wisdom, their own knowing. Not by transcending the earthly or by wanting to teach others, but by recognizing and affirming their own greatness, while simultaneously maintaining their connection with others. Not to put yourself above someone else, but also not beneath someone else. No more looking up to spiritual masters, but also not looking down on those who "are not so far advanced." This hierarchical thinking breaks the connection.

Remaining in your heart, embracing your own worth and beauty, being there in openness with others – these bring a new path full of surprises and wonders. Judgment gives way to openness and curiosity. Imagine what it would be like if you were to approach life in this way every day? To get up in the morning and make that connection with your heart, the access point to your soul.

Often, it is during the night that you have more connection with your soul, your inner self, than during the day, when your attention is drawn away by all sorts of external stimuli. You are, as it were, drawn out to the periphery of yourself and before you know it, you react to stimuli from outside, from people who behave from old patterns of fear or mistrust, and you lose the connection with your heart, and thus also the connection with the hearts of the persons around you.

Imagine that every morning before you start your day, you go inward and feel your body from within. Outwardly all kinds of things have to happen with your body. It needs to be washed, fed, and dressed, and it will have to encounter more of those every-day occurrences. But take some time for the inner self, for going within to feel who you are: flowing, living consciousness. Appreciate your body from within; feel and experience it as the beautiful instrument it is. Connect with your heart: "I am open to life, I don't build walls any more, I let go of judgments, I allow life to come as it may"; and then you enter a new way of life, a new reality.

You might say that you, as human beings, generally resist life based on fear and distrust fed to you from the past. You get up in the morning and the battle starts – you dig in your heels. You try to exercise control over what you want from life. You stand ready to act, to react, to survive. Do you realize how this way of being is without connection? When you resist something, you oppose it and refuse to accept it. And rarely is your heart touched by something exceptionally beautiful: the loving gaze of another, or by a deep understanding, or by humor and laughter, or by emotion or crying. That ability to be touched is what wants to penetrate through the fortress wall you build around yourself when you put up resistance against life.

This way of life is taught to you from a past in which fear reigned: fear of life, of feeling, of being human, and all the deep emotions which that produces. Religious belief systems have certainly contributed to this resistance against life. By holding on to those rigid dogmas and prejudices taught to you, you knew exactly how to deal with these pre-judged emotions, passions, and urges that make life unpredictable and intense.

However, at this time, many people desire to break free from this ancient prison, because when you are without connection, after awhile something dies inside and there will be emptiness, loneliness, and a sense of futility. Almost every human being on Earth has to deal with that. It makes people desperate, and so they display desperate behavior, such as running around madly seeking assurance and gratification, and trying to get it from things that can not truly fulfill them: excitement and stimulation, addictions, being busy and never stopping to make time for silence and space for yourself. All this behavior originates from a deep inner void that people experience; the lack of connection, most specifically with oneself and everything that lives inside as feeling and emotion.

If you want to join in the wave of light that currently engulfs Earth and that announces new tidings, then it necessitates doing this one thing: connecting from an open heart with everything there is. It is not to be better than what you are – a more loving, more perfect human being – it is precisely the opposite: the letting go of all the images that sooner or later become a prison. And really daring *to be*, naked and vulnerable, and at the same time, strong and indestructible in that choice for openness.

Feel how I am here with you. I have been a human being; you can sense in me all my vulnerability, the emotions that I have experienced, the seeking and finding, the trial and error. Now I can see that this constitutes the beauty of life as a human being. Dare to entrust yourself to this adventure; dare to trust this beauty in yourself and also to recognize that beauty and innocence in another. Not to repress anything and not to judge anything brings deep, quiet understanding and joy to your life.

Just see how it feels for you. Imagine that you very calmly and quietly descend into the area of your heart. Experience your heart as an open space, which extends inwards as well as outwards. If you follow the thread within experience then you see there is no end to the space within your heart. It is not bound by your body, not encapsulated by your skin. The space within your heart points to another dimension, the dimension of the infinite.

Feel the infinite space within your heart, how it is part of an infinite source of life. You have adopted many different forms before you came to inhabit this body – *and you were there in all of them.* During all those experiences in many different forms, you gathered more and more inner richness: knowledge and understanding from having seen and experienced life. And that richness is now part of the interior space of your heart.

Imagine that you enter the outside world from within that interior space. Then you will look at things not so much from the outside, but you will feel more from your heart as you encounter certain situations. When people say things to you that, for example, frighten or hurt you, you do not immediately become defensive. You return to the center of your heart, the big and quiet space within, and you look at what effect it has when people say something against you. You look at your own hurt and pain, and you let it be. You do not react against it.

It is part of being human that you are a being who has emotions and you do not have to change that. The attitude I am suggesting is very different from the one that you are used to. Your first impulse in such an experience of pain or of being hurt is that it has to go away, that your reaction must be transformed, that you need to work on yourself so you do not feel the pain the next time. But imagine that you just allow it, let that pain echo through you without shutting down the space in your heart.

You could put a hand out to the tormented part in you, to touch it or to caress it gently – but no more than that.

You can go one step further and take a quiet look from the heart at the person who is hurting or frightening you. Feel what is behind their behavior towards you. Is it about you, or are they responding to pain within themselves, that was there before they even met you? Let go of judgment, connect directly to the heart of the other person and do not be afraid of their emotional energy, even when it is aggressive. From an open heart you look at those energies, and again, you need not change anything. You need not attack the other to defend yourself. Nor do you need to pity, fix or heal the other. You let everything be.

What happens if you live that way? You may wonder: "Is this not being just passive, withdrawing from life and not changing it for the better?" In reality, to live this way requires a high level of consciousness. It is more difficult to *not* react to something that emotionally triggers you than to react with judgment and emotion and act accordingly. The latter happens almost instantaneously. To not react in this way requires that you acknowledge your own pain and take care of it yourself. You do not lash out or try to "fix" the other person. You turn within, consciously recognize the hurt inside, and gently embrace it with your consciousness. Your pain will subside, and you know you are the master of yourself, and not at the hands of outside triggers. This is what living from the heart means, it is a highly active and composed state of being. When you live like this, there will at times be a clear impulse from your heart to act, to say or to do something, but this type of action will not be defensive or aimed at defeating others. Heart-based action comes from an impulse of joy.

When you meet others from an open heart, you bring a lot of spaciousness to the encounter. In releasing your expectations, your hopes and dreams about the relation you have with that person, you are actually giving something deeply valuable to them. Your presence radiates compassion and quiet love. This is the most beneficial energy in the universe.

157

25. The Gate

Dear friends, I am Mary Magdalene. You know me, my figure and face have become part of your history, and thereby have become distorted and marred. But you know my origin, because we live from the same source – the space within the heart, the Home of the soul. You have been moved by the same desire that possessed me during my life on Earth. A longing, a desire for truth, for what is real, for the essence. A desire to live from your soul, from inspiration, from your core – that is what matters for you.

To live in this way can hurt. It brings you to the darkest parts in yourself, because to live from your inner core means that everything must be seen. The light needs to shine on everything, so you can become one and complete unto yourself. Many people are engaged in a struggle with themselves, and this is painful to see. People often live by images, pictures, and idealized sets of rules of how to be a successful human being who is recognized and respected by the world. Then before you know it, you are carried away by the opinions and demands of the mainstream of society. You feel you need to adjust to their way of thinking, so you can appear attractive and good in the eyes of the world. This takes you away from your inner core, and in this way, you disconnect from yourself. But still there is a voice that says: "go inside, discover who you are". In that open space of no judgment, you *can* discover who you are: the light and the dark parts, the impetus behind your feelings, thoughts and reactions.

To love yourself is to allow that open space within yourself, and to be with yourself and observe what is there. Yet again comes that voice from the outside, all too often the voice of fear, that says: "be good, be obedient, and adjust to the norm; do not appear different or strange in the eyes of other people", and you again lose the inner dialogue with yourself and that open space. You force yourself into shackles; you judge according to the standards of the outside world, society, and by doing so you hurt yourself. So you are pulled back and forth between the call of the world, which so often is the voice of fear, *and* the cry of the soul, which would lead you inward, to the core of who you are. And how can you deal with that battle, that tug-of-war between inside and outside, between the core and the external?

159

Listen to the voice of your heart. Choose for yourself; choose the way you want to go in this life. Decide to do it with all your strength, *unconditionally!* Take the plunge into the deep, where real love prevails. But know in that deep space there is no bottom, and it can feel like a leap into the abyss, into the void. You will no longer be supported by the approval, compliments, and recognition of others; you will stand alone.

Feel, for awhile, the immense space in the center of your heart, where there is no judgment, and no idealized images of where you should go. Only Being is present there, pure Being. Can you stand that much freedom, or would you prefer to stay on the leash of norms and values provided by others? Can you take that dive into the depths? *Can you truly live?*

Life challenges you to take a leap into the unknown, which is scary. However, to restrict yourself to the narrow path of the known, and not live fully, is worse. You then become a slave to impulses from outside yourself, and you lose "you" and no longer feel happy. Finding true satisfaction in life can come only from going with the current of your heart. Your heartbeat, which is unique in the universe, alone knows the road. And sometimes, if you get lost, there needs to be a dark time, to bring you back to yourself, to help you remember who you are in your deepest core. All outer certainties fall away, and insofar as you were living according to exterior standards and ideals, you have the feeling that everything is lost, that you have fallen into a deep, black hole – and this feels awful! It is called "the dark night of the soul", yet it is but a passage. You are being taken to a gate, one that opens to something beyond, something greater; a vista that your usual sight, conditioned by fears and old ideas, can not envision.

Imagine you are in a dark tunnel. You can not even see the walls of this tunnel, and you feel surrounded by nothingness. There is nothing wrong with nothingness. In its essence, nothingness is neither bad nor evil; it is absolute openness without any preconceptions or expectations on which to rely. Yet nothingness evokes fear in you, as if it will destroy you. What nothingness does destroy are old identities which you thought were part of you. But know that who you *really* are can not be destroyed, can not disappear. It is eternal, and as limitless as the space in your heart of which

I spoke earlier. That space is there – always. Imagine that you accept nothingness and the lack of certainties, and at the same time, you feel your strength and independence. You then are not bound to this world; you are free in the depths of your being!

Continue to imagine you are going through that dark tunnel and suddenly a gate appears in front of you. Look at what that image does for you: are you afraid of the gate, or do you want to go through it? Are the doors heavy and closed, or is one door ajar and is there light that shines through from the other side? Just take it in; you do not have to do anything. Imagine now that you stand before that gate and put your hand against it. Allow the energy of the gate to flow through you. The gate is the threshold beyond which lies the new, that which your soul wants to show you – when you are ready to see it. By placing your hand on the gate, you become acquainted with the new, and with what wants to flow into your life – at a rhythm that suits you. See if you can receive it; the energy of the new, the energy of Home and of your soul. Allow it to flow through your hand and into and throughout your entire body, in a way that feels good – not too little and not too much. The energy flows around and through your head, your shoulders, and your heart; and goes even deeper: into your stomach, your pelvis, your tailbone, and through your legs to your feet. And be aware, if you are in the dark night of the soul, there is something new awaiting you beyond the gate, although it still can not be seen with the eyes you have now. With new eyes, you will see that reality on the other side of the gate, and you will develop these new eyes by letting go of the old way of life; when you grasp no more onto certainties and survival patterns to which you clung before.

How do you recognize when you are ready to let go of the old? Often it is through feelings of discontent, anger, dissatisfaction, or despair and hopelessness, which indicate that you no longer want things to be the way they have been. You could then be thinking: "I don't want to be here any more; I don't want to live on Earth", but actually what you are saying is: "I no longer want the old way; I don't want things as they have been". However, your mind, formed as it is by the past, may not have yet imagined that there *are* other ways, and therefore the dark night of the soul becomes desperate and intense. As the old falls away, but the new has not yet arrived, being on that borderline and in that dark tunnel forces you to choose. Either you continue to follow the voice of your heart and remain faithful to yourself, or you retreat back into the voices from outside: that of fear, of the familiar, of the past. So I entreat you: if you are now experiencing the dark night of the soul in your life, stay with it, keep going inward, and feel what is there. If there is fear, uncertainty, sadness, or despair, do not judge it; stay with it and do not retreat from it.

Your light is stronger than all those emotions, which are not the end point, but a halting place along the way. *See the gate in the distance, which is already there!* Connect with the energy of the new, by way of that gate. And one day the doors of that gate will open wide – see it before you. Maybe it is too much to feel it all now, but observe it for awhile from a distance. How will it be when that gate opens wide, and you walk through it? What awaits you there? What feelings does it call up in you? You do not have go beyond the gate yet, it will come – everything comes in its time. But feel the promise of it now: the beauty of the light there; the delight, joy and comfort of being there. Feel the serenity of life there and rejoice, because this road you are travelling on now – the one that feels like a dark night which boosts your fear – *leads there!*

Keep that perspective before your eyes, and your path becomes easier. I hold you by the hand; feel my presence. Every time a gate opens, it makes us happy and we feel more deeply united with you all. We are all connected to each other, and every step each individual takes, carries something of all of us to the Whole.

26. The polarity game between men and women

Dear friends, I am here and with you. I am Mary Magdalene. I am the woman who once lived on Earth alongside Jeshua. I loved him; we were both touched by the same inspiration and this created a bond between us. I was that woman on Earth, living as Mary Magdalene, but I am more than that individual person; that was only one expression of me. Beyond the earthly, beyond the body: male or female, there is the soul, and there is no time or form in that dimension. You are part of a unity that is inexpressible, that can not be captured in words, and I want to speak to you from that field of unity. Feel it here in this space. It can be here because all of you have opened your heart to that deep unity in your soul – *remember that unity.*

At one time, your identity was not as delimited, as separated, as it is now. You did not experience yourself so strongly as one ego opposite the whole. You flowed more easily with your surroundings, and you were more part of the whole; more like an arm is part of a body. An arm is an entity in itself, but functions as part of a whole body. Being an individual, yet strongly linked with the whole, is what distinguishes the graceful and free feeling of being on the New Earth. That feeling gives you a sense of security and belonging, while at the same time you sense yourself as a separate individual.

Feel your connection with the whole as female, and sense your individuality as male. Both aspects are necessary to play the game of creation. If you are complete in your own being, when your individuality meets another individuality, that meeting can be a source of wonder, attraction, and interest. This is the true purpose of the game between men and women.

In female and male, there is an opposite, a polarity. Opposites attract each other and can also complement each other. Feel the tension for a moment: the excitement, the wonder, and the curiosity in the polarity. It is what makes a man fascinating to a woman, and what makes a woman fascinating to a man. Powerful forces, desires, and feelings can generate in such relationships, and they can be very contradictory forces, because in being attracted to each other, there is a craving for fusion, to become completely one. Yet, paradoxically, the game of attraction can exist only if you are different from one another, if there *are* opposite poles: a sense of unity contrasted by the feeling of being different, of being "me". Both poles are necessary, because it is only through this contrast that we can discover one another. Both elements are required for a fulfilling relationship where we experience each other as complementary and renewing.

However, if you play only the game of male and female, only the game of polarity, then this could eventually erode the relationship. There is admittedly great attraction, and the possibility of great passion, especially in the beginning. But eventually the feeling of unity and fusion can be only experienced when you feel deeply connected at the soul level, which is a level that goes beyond the polarity of man-woman. When you have that soul connection in a relationship, then something moves along in the game of man and woman that infinitely deepens and empowers the relationship. It begins with the attraction of man-woman on the physical level, based on the polarity of the male and female energies, but only when this attraction is complemented by an encounter at the level of the soul does the dance between man and woman receive its true beauty and joy.

Of what then constitutes that attunement at the soul level, that unity that can be experienced there? It feels like a miracle, and is impossible to describe or put into words. Some of you know that experience as a mysterious feeling of deep familiarity with another that is inexplicable to the rational mind. You do not need to express much or to explain yourself to one another. There is a natural connection, somewhat like you might feel with "family", although not based on biological ties, but rather on an inexplicable inner bond.

On the level of soul there *are* families. Very far back there was a field of unity from which you were born, from which you as a soul separated yourself and went on your soul journey of incarnation. Not only on Earth, but on a multitude of places in the universe: the universe being rich and very large, there is much to experience – feel the greatness of it. You can imagine that each of you gained many diverse experiences in all your travels and explorations. Yet early in the journey of the soul there is a kinship with other souls with whom you have travelled for quite awhile, and with whom you shared certain interests. From those common travels in the past emerged a kind of family bonding, and this bonding now causes you to recognize someone, as it were, and to make contact with the soul behind the earthly person, which can bring enormous joy and peace to your heart. It can raise you to heights in yourself of which you were not aware.

Now that we are on our way to the new Earth, and the new Earth is awakening around you, relationships based on a soul connection are taking on a much more important role. Much less is determined by your earthly background in this life, and by your biology or your upbringing. More and more people want to open their hearts and seek for depth in their relationships; they long for a sense of unity that transcends opposites, and includes not only the outer game of man-woman – romantic love and passion.

I ask you, if you have a partner in your life, to verify this for yourself. Imagine that he or she stands before you, and if you have no partner, just allow someone to appear. It might be someone you know, or an imaginary person, or the inner man or woman who comes from your own soul – let your imagination run free. Now imagine you stand facing one another, and slowly release your human form, let it fall away from you. See or feel each other from soul to soul. Maybe you see yourself or the other as a figure of light, or of different colors, or maybe more as a feeling; you might see yourself and the other as an angel, without a specific gender. Is your relationship beyond the limitation of the earthly form, the polarities, the opposites of man–woman? Look what flows between you, and feel now the basis of your relationship. What gives you joy, and what does the other give to you and you give to him or her?

Think about the symbol of infinity, the symbol that is like a figure eight lying horizontally. The two halves of the eight meet at the joining point, forming two equal ovals that lie against each other. Imagine the line that forms the symbol being drawn around you and your partner: you in one oval and your partner in the other oval. At a certain level you are separate beings, but on a deeper, more profound level, that continuous line forms one energy flow. Sense if you can feel the flow of this energy between you both within the form of the symbol of infinity. By being aware of this energy flow, you sense a return into the field of unity from which you both were born, and you allow that energy to awaken in your relationship.

By experiencing this field of unity between yourselves, your relationship becomes richer and more profound, because you feel you are part of a greater whole. It is very joyful and fulfilling to experience that greater whole which connects you at the soul level, yet at the same time to see the other as a different and unique being. Because of that difference, the other remains a source of wonder, mystery, and attraction. The other is never fully to be known, so there will always be something new to discover in every human being. By making contact with the deepest bond between the two of you, you get a sense of the unity between your souls. This makes the game between man and woman lighter and easier, and more a journey of discovery than a battle ground.

So much fighting and suffering takes place in relationships between men and women; so much misunderstanding, and so much polarization. Both sexes have experienced power and oppression in history. The female energy has once occupied positions of power, too, so it is not only the man who has been in the role of offender and the woman the victim. There were cultures in which the roles were reversed. This is something you can feel deeply in yourself, because you have been both male and female in previous lives. You know deep inside how both women and men can abuse power. (Pamela: see chapter "The dignity of the female energy" in Heart Centered Living for elucidation of this point).

In this time, there is the desire in both the male and female to transcend the old pain, to heal the old wounds and traumas, in order to come back to each other. Inwardly, women are going through the process of regaining their strength; to allow their masculine energy to flow together with their feminine side, so that in a self-conscious and powerful way, they dare to step into the world with their intuitive gifts, their vision, and their capacity to connect. And men are on the way to connecting again with their hearts and to being open to their feelings; to show their affection and to express their emotional warmth towards women and children, and to *all* fellow human beings. There is a movement on its way that can transform all the old suffering and misunderstanding, and the fastest way is through the field of unity. Unity allows you to recognize that, although you are a man or a woman in the earthly life, there is another connection between you; a connection that allows you to recognize each other at a much deeper level, and to have understanding for each other's way in a manner that is not comprehensible by the mind. It can, however, be understood by the fact *that you are connected at the level of the soul.* You are not *only* this particular man or woman, but a much larger being; a soul that has experienced and explored all sorts of aspects of creation.

In this time you will see, increasingly, more and more relationships arising that are born from a soul recognition. Those relationships give the chance, the opportunity, for deep inner healing. And the beauty of such encounters between individual persons, *between individual souls,* is that these also have an effect on the collective male and female energies. As soon as a man or a woman experiences healing and fulfillment in a relationship at the soul level, then something happens with the collective energy as well. Something is healed and released that becomes open again, and there is more trust between men and women. And the more individual human beings realize this healing in their own relationship, the more this benefit becomes available to humanity as a whole. For all of you, your relationships hold the invitation and opportunity to make room for the dimension of the soul. Of course, you can still be the earthly man and woman, who play this game of polarity with one another. But by connecting at the level of the soul, this game acquires more lightness, more joy, and more glow, and that is what I wish for you. We empathize with you, we stand beside you, and we are deeply connected to you.

27. Awakening your ability to channel

This channeling was received in the context of a workshop on channeling. Most people attending the workshop were spiritual therapists desiring to enhance their channeling skills and rise above a lack of self-trust in this area.

Dear sister and brothers, I greet you all from my heart. I am Mary Magdalene and I am not alone; I am here with many others. Today we will speak about the art of channeling. Many of you desire to channel but feel locked into self-doubt and anxiety about it. Some of you already channel but you dare not express it publicly. Today I would like to offer a different perspective on the question of whether you can or should channel. I am telling you that channeling is not new to you at all; you have done it under different names in many lifetimes before this one. It is not such a big deal! Opening up to channeling is not about learning something new for you, it is about awakening skills that are familiar, even innate to you.

You all have been on this planet before and have expressed your inner gifts on Earth in previous lives: the gifts of intuition, of channeling, of the third eye. Your previous lives were often marked by those gifts, and they are still here today. Each of you is surrounded by personalities that you once were, who in one form or another gave a hearing to that inner voice, the voice of the soul, and passed it on to other people on Earth. You were a bridge between this world and the other, the world of the soul from which you originate. This has been your soul's calling for a long time. Try to sense, if you can, those personalities around you. They are a part of your soul, like a ray of the sun is part of the sun. Not the whole, but still an inalienable part of it. Maybe you see or feel some of these past life figures around you now. Take a moment to feel that, calmly and clearly.

Channeling is not new to you. You have already done it many times before, in different ways and in different forms, and it was something familiar that came naturally for you. I ask you to now make connection with that familiar and natural way of channeling that you knew in previous lives, or call it "other lives" – these things are not as bound to time as you might think. Allow one of the individuals that you once were to approach you and to flow through you. Just observe who steps forward and do not go into it too much with your head; just let it happen naturally from a feeling. You do not even need to see any person, you can simply sense them. And sometimes it just takes time before you feel anything. This woman or man, whom you feel near you and who is part of your soul, wants to now give you something.

Previous lives are like all lives, a mixture of the beautiful and the less beautiful: light and dark; good and evil, if you like. That person, who is now with you, comes to give you their light, and the beautiful flowing part of him or herself that felt a connection to, and formed a bridge with, the other world from which they channeled love, encouragement, and hope to people around them. Remember this connection, not through your mind, but through your cells and your feelings. Get a sense again of what that bridge to the other world was like.

Allow yourself to be helped with this process by considering the person from that other life as your guide. Imagine a time when channeling went well and you were able to share the flow of your soul with others. You do not have to imagine the details of what happened. It is about the flow and the safety of it, and also the familiarity and self-evidence of it. In fact, none of you have to learn how to channel, because channeling is something you can do already. The key is to re-establish the way it is done: to re-connect with that part of yourself that does this so easily. Although there exist fears and pains built up in you that are resistant, by reminding yourself how easy channeling used to flow, you remove some of that resistance.

The time has now come when there is really an opportunity on Earth for what you have to give. There are people waiting for that energy to flow out through you and through your lightworker sisters and brothers – *the world is waiting for you!* Where in past lives, and in former times, you often had to be very circumspect and to operate almost surreptitiously and in secret, there is now a need and an opportunity and openness to receive your gifts. The female power of the inner eye and of intuition is once again welcome – and that is actually an understatement. *It is not only welcome, it is desperately needed!* Humanity is in distress; there is a crisis going on all over the world: an economic crisis, as well as an environmental crisis. It is a deep crisis in that it raises fundamental questions about how you relate to yourselves and with your world and the Earth.

There are many people on Earth caught in fears, in struggle, in illusion. People have lost themselves, and there is a deep loneliness in the hearts of human beings. From that loneliness comes a desperate search for a beacon outside yourself on which to hold. But that guiding light is not outside you, and you will not find it in another, or in an institution or organization. In this time, it becomes clear there are no certainties that lie outside you: not in a job or a house, and not even in a personal relationship or a circle of friends. You are led ever more deeply within by everything that is happening without, and this can be very frightening for many people.

What is your role in all this: your task, your path? The answer lies in your inner reality. It is always about staying close to yourself, because you know the "way" lies within. You are already familiar with this inner world, with the peace and calm that you can find there. For this reason, you are at this time to be guides or teachers for others and to be that in the most free, gentle sense of the word. Not like those who are leaders in the traditional sense, but to be a living example of how to make a deep connection within yourself, with what transcends the earthly life, with what transcends outer certainties, and with what is independent of these – *a connection with your soul.* To radiate this connection to others is in a sense your life's mission. It brings you directly into the core of who you are, and in this way, you also touch others and invite them to do the same.

Direct yourself again to that small circle of past life personalities around you, who are part of you. You share qualities and traits with them, yet they lived in very different times and surroundings; but in essence, it is the same heart. Tell them, those who had to operate in the dark and in secret, that the way is now open: "I may now reveal all the qualities you have developed in the past; I can now radiate my own light; I am welcome on Earth." In some of those personalities, you can feel there are painful memories of being rejected, of being condemned for what you were, and for which there was no opportunity to share the reality you had to give. It is now time to heal that old pain. It must be seen, remembered, and honored, so that it may be released to give way for a new joy, a new lightness, a way of effortlessly being yourself.

These old personalities can remind you of your gifts, your natural connections, your soul. That is their gift to you: qualities you were ever building up and developing very carefully in other times, through experience, practice, and training. But you also have a gift for them in return. Tell them they can now let go of their old burdens and can release the feeling of not being welcome, that pain from the past. Not to feel welcome, and not to live what was natural for you, *was* a deep pain for you. Yet your wisdom has grown because of that experience; your understanding of human nature and of light and dark. Accept this past and let those old lives go free again, no longer bound to old pains or traumas, let them all go their way. Take what is wise and beautiful about them into your heart. Thank them for it – *really do so from the heart!* Thank them for the gifts they are leaving for you, and then release them to be free, so they can finally put to rest their painful connection with Earth. In this way, the past is healed.

Everything that is good and durable from the past stays with you; it is not lost even though it has long been surrounded by pain, uncertainty, fear, and frustration. You can set it free and bring a diamond from out of that past. It is now in this life that this diamond can shine and radiate into the world and give you happiness, the happiness of simply being yourself and no longer having to hide. *That is the key to everything.* If you can experience this beautiful diamond in yourself, then everything else in your life happens almost by itself. You attract relationships and living and work surroundings that belong to the diamond. Feel the presence of this brilliant energy in you. *So much strength and wisdom bundled up in you from so many centuries and the many persons you have been.* Feel the depth, the mystery and wonder of it. Have respect for who you are and stop looking down upon yourself with contempt and criticism.

Feel how you are a channel, here and now; feel the diamond that you are. See if there is a place within your body where you can feel this jewel and allow its radiant energy to flow through your entire body so you are bathed in its light. I am here as your equal; I am not a teacher who stands above you. I am exactly like you and so I feel very close to you, equal to you in my heart. When you have doubts, which arise easily in the reality of human beings, I am with you to appeal to your strength and remind you of the dazzling diamond that you are already, *here and now*.

28. The battle of the sexes

Dear brothers and sisters, I am full of joy to be here with you. My heart truly opens up, because I love you so. I am now free from earthly burdens, so I can easily see your beauty and your courage as you move on in your life on Earth, and I wish you could see it for yourself. You are so often caught up in self-judgment and in belittling yourself, that it makes it difficult for you to receive all that is given to you. I can see that your energy is often tied in knots: your eyes are closed and you are imprisoned in your own negative judgments. And it is to be expected that you all have to deal with this sense of unworthiness when you are born on Earth; it is part of being on Earth. In fact, Earth is covered, on the energy level, with a sense of self-belittlement and judgment that is passed on from generation to generation. Some people are blessed in childhood to have experienced the sense of innocence and spontaneity that is natural to life. But when you incarnate on Earth as a human being, your consciousness often gets easily clouded over by the negativity and fear that is here.

I am here to remind you of your true nature and to help you awaken to it in your everyday life. Because even if the energy of Earth can be very dense and heavy, I know your soul's strength. You are truly warriors of light, even if you seem to have forgotten that fact. I sometimes feel grief and a kind of sadness seeing you feeling so lost, because I still have human feelings, you know, and I am connected to you from my heart.

Today, I would like to tell you a story about what happened between the sexes, between men and women, because much of the dark energy, and the deep sense of unworthiness you experience, has to do with this history, which is the history of the area of sexuality. As you know, sexuality should be a source of light, of love and a genuine meeting of souls. In a true sexual encounter, you are open from the heart, and it is an experience of bliss and ecstasy to meet a person on that level. But tragically, few people on Earth can experience sexual union in this way. There is so much deep pain in the hearts of both men and women in this area, because it is in the area of sexuality that you are most vulnerable as a human being.

You all are aware of recent history, and by recent I mean the last four to five thousand years. During this period of time, the female energy was devalued and humiliated by an aggressive male energy. In the female being, this has created a wound on a very deep level, but it has also hurt men. Because of this aggressive male energy that was present throughout this era, men were not able to develop their sensitive, feminine side. It became difficult for men to connect to other people from the heart and to show their emotions. Women, on the other hand, lost touch with their sense of self worth and empowerment, and as a result, men and women became estranged and alienated from one another. And the area of sexuality, which is the most sacred relationship between man and woman, became violated. Instead of blissful, it became an area of great pain. I want to now go one step further back and to tell you about a part of history which is older than is known to you.

There have been times in which women seized power and exerted power over men, and women can sense this ability within themselves. Even if they have been a victim of male aggression in many lifetimes, they can also sense this ability to manipulate energy in men. I am saying this not in any way to make you feel guilty or ashamed, but because I want to go to the essence of the wound in men and women. And so I ask you to now feel within yourself whether you recognize the wound of which I am speaking. Is it possible for you to feel true love in a relationship with the other sex? Can you be a woman or man without shame, and with no reservation toward the other sex?

I am telling you that the sense of unworthiness you all are struggling with is closely related to the sexual wound in both men and women, and now is the time to heal that wound. I ask women, especially, to rise above the issues of anger and distrust they experience toward men. You, both men and women, have been both victim and perpetrator in this long history of the battle of the sexes.

Imagine with me that you are in front of your lover, and if you do not have one, just imagine someone standing there. First take a look at the flow of giving: what are you giving to this other person, and what are you *able* to give? And take a good look at your own body as you give this energy. How does it feel in your heart, how does it feel inside your belly?

And if you notice that the flow of giving is interrupted in some area, do not judge it, or to now try to change it, just observe it. Now look at the flow of receiving. What are you receiving from your partner, and what are you *capable* of receiving?

You will probably notice there are areas in both the flows of giving and receiving that feel blocked within you, and I want you to know that these blocks are not just your personal blocks. You have inherited them from history, so do not judge yourself for having them. What you are invited to do in this time is to heal this pain, and in doing so you will help to heal the collective pain in humankind as well. You are much stronger than you perceive yourself to be.

I invite you to do a little healing exercise with me. Now, I am *not* asking you to heal the pain or the blocks you perceive in yourself, but I am asking you to look at the pain or blocks *in your partner*. Keep it very simple, and just ask your partner: "What would you like to receive from me? What would serve you best? What would help to empower you in your life?" And then give that to him or her on the energy level.

I would like you to have an understanding of your partner, especially to understand the specific pain of the opposite sex, because the wound or pain is different in men and in women. Men have become estranged from their feeling side, their own feminine nature, and so they long for more true connection. And women need to again connect with their own power and self worth, and men can help women do this by showing them their true beauty and strength. Women can help men by forgiving them and taking responsibility for themselves. And when this healing happens, there can be such a beautiful interaction between men and women.

Although the spiritual path is basically about healing yourself, it is now time to join hands and to build bridges between men and women. It is by having true compassion and understanding for each other that you also truly heal yourself. You rise above the old battle and once again allow the area of sexuality to become one of true joy and companionship.

As you struggle with inner darkness and a sense of unworthiness, I ask you to consider to what extent this is due to your wounds as a man or as a woman. By being aware of this aspect of yourself, you become more understanding of yourself and allow more light into your life. On the New Earth that is being born in these times, men and women will again join in harmony, and their energies will naturally complement each other. It is in the area of sexuality that your soul, your spiritual energy, truly comes down to Earth, from the highest energy center to the lowest one. When there is sexual union from heart to heart, you are back in the center of paradise. You feel one with Spirit for a moment, and in that moment of togetherness, you channel the purest energy to Earth.

Sexuality is originally such a precious gift. The fact that it has become clouded over with dark and painful energy is a big burden to you all. It is the cause of so much of your emotions of loneliness and despair, but there are many signs of hope in this time. Men and women are genuinely seeking to establish a true connection with one another. There is a heavy burden on you all, but also a great potential for healing.

Again, I invite you to see yourselves as I do from the other side of the veil. I ask you to now be one with me and to look at yourselves through my eyes. Can you see yourself as the beautiful and courageous souls that you are? *There is nothing wrong with you – nothing!* You are perfect beings. I wish you could accept that from me.

29. The Tree and the Rose

Dear friends, I greet you affectionately. I am Mary Magdalene. I represent one aspect of the Christ energy that is being born through all of you on a grand scale on Earth. Not only I, but many guides and angels are here with me; those who belong with you and who want to support you on your path. Feel them around you in this room. They are here for you; guides and angels of light, whose highest joy is to hear you laugh and see your eyes shine.

You are not here to feel pain and suffering, but to experience the joy of channeling your soul's energy to Earth. To feel you are an angel who is truly incarnated here, and to know that your inner life, your inner fire, will manifest itself in flesh and blood on Earth, brings you great happiness. You are here to channel your soul's energy into material form, and you do this every time you come to Earth to undertake this great adventure. You have amassed a great store of wisdom that you bring with you into every subsequent life.

Your current lifetime holds great potential for change. Humanity and Earth have been engaged in a long process of evolution, a cycle whose completion is now in sight. Heart consciousness is now awakening on Earth, and you are the first to embody this type of consciousness. Through many lives, you have been inspired by the Christ energy, and you sought to bring of a torch of light to Earth. You have anticipated, through many lives, what it would be like to live from the heart, from a connection with all that lives, instead of being involved in a struggle with your environment.

For a long time, a consciousness of discord and strife existed on Earth, but now there is an awakening to more unity. Therefore, many angels and guides now feel an attraction to Earth, because they want to support this process – and you work together with them, hand in hand, when you go on this path. I wish to convince you that you are doing beautiful work here while you live and are active on Earth. You sometimes get discouraged by setbacks, by the resistance that the old reality seems to bring to the new vision that you offer, but this is only an illusion. The New Reality is already active.

The collective consciousness of humanity is changing; you have done your work well. Everyone in his or her own way has contributed to this process, and we here thank you for this. Feel our gratitude at this time; we are touched by your bravery and perseverance. We would like you to know how much admiration and respect we have for you when you take upon yourself the heaviness of the earthly life, and continue to try to find ways to let your angel light flow. You construct a bridge between heaven and Earth, and you also build a bridge from the inside to the outside. When you live as a human on Earth, you are also in a relationship with heaven. This relationship between Earth and heaven runs through you in a vertical alignment, from above to below. And alongside that, a horizontal alignment runs through you in a relationship from inside to outside, between you and your fellow human beings, and between you and the society around you.

There is then both a relationship between above and below and between inside and outside. That is the force field you live in as a human being. But what actually happens from your birth, because of the way you are educated and trained, is that the emphasis comes to lie more on the relationship between you and the world. So the outside world becomes the standard for comparison with all else. You, when you are born as a little child, are viewed as a tabula rasa, a blank slate, on which can be written the ideas from the traditions of your culture and your environment. If you, as a once empty vessel, become filled with the energy of the world, the result will be that your relationship with the world will become completely affected by the old energy that comes from that tradition.

It is not yet fully recognized in your society that you begin earthly life as a mature soul with a great store of wisdom that is not of the Earth, but which comes from a whole different sphere. You are not a blank slate. When this is not acknowledged, then the relationship between inside and outside is imbalanced, with the share the world gets being much too large. So it happens that the consciousness of children is slowly immersed in a series of illusions, beliefs and fears that are handed down from generation to generation. What happens is that your original relationship with the heavens becomes clouded over. Your soul no longer speaks very clearly to you as you grow up, and you become smothered under the judgments and beliefs of a very limited worldview.

You, here, are pioneers; innovators who bring change to Earth. You have done that in your own life, at a particular time, by withdrawing internally from the world. You still remain involved in the world, but at some point in your life there springs up a profound doubt about the things you were taught by your parents, school, and work environment – and then something breaks open in your consciousness. You feel for the first time that something is not right and that what is true remains hidden from your view. It is your soul's consciousness that awakens. You are, as it were, souls that are pre-programmed to search for Truth. You have come into this life with the intention to awaken, to feel that doubt, and to shift the emphasis to your inner life, to what your intuition and deepest feelings tell you. And in that way, to recover the relationship between the outer and the inner, between Earth and heaven, and to feel your cosmic roots. This has been your soul's intention.

All the misery you have experienced, if you want to call it that – the doubt, the fear, the feeling that one does not belong – has, in a certain way, been self-imposed from a higher knowing. *You have taken this on to yourself from your own soul!* Understand, then, why we praise you so highly for your courage! You walk this lonely road on Earth so you can again ignite the light in yourself, and through yourself, in others and in the world around you. You are the innovators, the bringers of light to Earth! Now, at this moment, the completion of the cycle approaches, and it is the time for you to start doing the work of your heart. That is what you so desire! It is actually your desire to *just* be yourself, and to experience the joy of being conscious of your *feeling* self. To do that, it is necessary to strengthen your cosmic roots even more than they are now, and to put the relationship between you and the world "on hold", as it were. To take the world less seriously, and to really *feel* from inside, the relationship between you and your cosmic source – heaven.

Who are you and where do you come from? You are a being with infinite possibilities; a huge potential and strength are at your disposal. To allow you to feel this more clearly, I would like to invite you to a garden; a garden in your mind. A garden you create in your imagination, and one which lets you go easily into the light. Take the first image that comes to mind. Imagine that you walk with bare feet on the Earth, and feel the soft, spongy soil beneath your feet. Remember how pleasant nature is and what a wonderful feeling it is for your toes and the bottom of your feet to feel the Earth beneath you. When you touch Earth in this way, you sense a heavy load of stress slipping from your shoulders: the stress of having to struggle, the many "shoulds", the competition for position and possessions, and the worries and thoughts that race at high speed through your head – *let everything go.*

Concentrate on your bare feet that stand on the Earth, and let your consciousness sink into your feet. Simply notice where your feet are taking you. Imagine you are in a big beautiful garden with flowers and plants and trees; whatever comes up in your vision is good. Soon, you see a big old tree with thick roots that stick out partially above ground, but also grow deeply into Earth. You go to the foot of the tree. Maybe there is moss around the tree, deliciously soft to the touch, and you find a pleasant spot to sit down. You rest softly and easily with your tailbone on the Earth and your feet flat on the ground.

You are now leaning backwards against the tree and you feel the gentle, yet enormously great power of the tree flowing through you – you are one with the tree. Rest your hands on those roots that grow downwards into the Earth. Look up now along the trunk and see the branches and the foliage. You realize that the tree is so high you can not see the top of its crown. The top of the tree is in heaven, reaching far above the clouds into the sky. If you see the top in your mind, you might feel a tingle in the crown of your head. At the very top of the tree, the energy is so refined and ethereal, it is no longer of the Earth. Feel how you perceive this in your body. The top of the tree is represented in your body by the crown chakra on the top of your head, which lets you make contact with your deepest inner knowing; your cosmic roots.

You then move your attention farther down the tree. Imagine the balmy foliage, the soft warmth of the green of the tree, and feel how your consciousness descends into your heart. Feel the life force in the tree, the sap that flows through all the branches and into the leaves. Maybe there are even blossoms – just look. You feel strength flowing into your heart. You feel yourself included in this cosmic stream. It is your connection to the heavens.

You attention now goes lower down the tree to its trunk, where you feel its primal strength; the endless patience with which the layers of the trunk have built up through the many centuries; the unshakable power of it, and that silent, but great strength. You feel this strength as it flows downward from your stomach, your third chakra, through your belly to your tailbone, thighs and knees, and then on through your calves and feet. You look again to your bare feet that rest upon Earth. You let go of all your earthly worries, because you are here with your tree, that source of your strength. You feel refreshed and you remember that you are not of Earth, that you are here visiting. You came here to bring something very precious – a gift – and now you feel this gift in your hand. You imagine it as a beautiful rose. You feel this gift grow in your hand and you see the color of the rose. It can be one color, or perhaps multiple colors. Maybe they are colors you can barely name. Smell that rose and feel her ethereal beauty. You then stand up, and you feel recharged with energy.

We are now going to visit Earth to find out your connection here. Imagine you have carried the rose in your heart. Take her now in your hands and allow the rose to flow now from your heart to your hands where you hold it. Let us see how this gift from your heart is welcomed on Earth and how the rose can best come into her rightful place. Let us go first to where you live on Earth, and to the people with whom you relate most closely. It can be your partner, or your children, or a parent. Choose someone who is very important to you and give the rose to that person. View how the rose is received, and see if that person is happy about receiving it. Also, observe any feeling *you* experience when you hand the rose over to that person.

Now take the rose back in your hand and with it look closely at the area of your work, that aspect of the flow of your creative energy, and ask the rose where it wants to go. Trust the answer you get. It might be something very concrete, or it might be something that is not so easy to describe; a sense about what makes you happy in life and what is your destiny. Wherever you find joy and love, that is where you are destined to be, so let the rose take you there.

You all have a destiny on Earth; your soul's purpose. The way you find out whether you fulfill your purpose is to attune yourself to your heart's energy, which has been given to you in the form of this rose. And that, in the end, is the fruit of your relationship with the heavens; your deepest inner self, the angel in you, or your higher self, however you want to name it. It is that vertical relationship, from heaven to Earth, which is the source of your creative activity on Earth. Therefore, only that which feeds from this source can give you true satisfaction. Look closely to see if the work you do now fits with that; if your rose will be received there, or if you see it wither and die in those circumstances. Put out your hand with the rose in it and see how it reacts in that context. In this way, you discover what really suits you and what does not.

You have assimilated all kinds of beliefs and convictions from the past about what you should do and be in the world, what your responsibilities are, and your obligations. Therefore, it is very important to create time and space in your life to get in touch with your *own* inner flow; that flow from above to below we have identified as the Tree of Life that grows in and around you. It is necessary to be receptive to the new energy you all want to bring to birth on Earth. Feel free to take the time and space for doing that. Do not be afraid to do nothing, or to not be productive, because the real work lies precisely in the maintaining of that inner relationship with your source, with your soul. *That is the main work you are to do here on Earth!*

If the relationship with your soul flows well, it then naturally produces outer work that suits you on your path. So the most important thing is that inner alignment with your soul. Do everything you can to help maintain this inner flow in yourself, and the rest will come to you quite naturally. In making that inner attunement, you do the lightwork for which you have come, and for what you planned to do on Earth. Free yourself from social prejudices and beliefs about what you should do or should accomplish, about usefulness and functionality – *let it go*! You have come here to help overcome outdated ideas and to really start living from your heart. Not from any "should", but from a sincere desire and yearning to experience joy, and *that* is true creativity!

30. Feeling at home on Earth

Dear friends, dear men and women, it fills me with joy to be with you on this clear morning. We are old friends. Our paths have crossed in time and space many times before. Feel our old friendship; we are part of the same family. Cherish for a moment this feeling of familiarity, of coming Home. Simply relax and let go of all tension inside yourself. Visualize how the tension flows into the Earth and is neutralized. Feel how your body relaxes and becomes heavier. Receive the healing energy returning from Mother Earth and let it encircle your feet and your legs and flow into your waist and belly. Feel supported by Earth; you are safe.

Feel the rhythm of Earth; it is slow and steady. This is the rhythm you seek. Your soul comes from a different realm, and when it descends it has to adjust to the rhythm of Earth. Your soul has to dwell in a body and has to learn how to use a mind, and it can become confused because of that. The soul is on a learning path. It is not just you as a human who is learning, your soul is learning and growing as well.

In your soul, you carry painful memories about being on Earth and, therefore, it is not evident to you that you can trust Earth and surrender yourself to it. There can be a blockage in your body preventing you from relaxing and feeling safe here. This blockage is an energy, it is not something just physical. In reality, this blockage was not caused by Earth, but by what happened to you in the human world: the negativity you experienced here, the pain of rejection and not fitting in. This has made it difficult for you to feel at home here.

I want to remind you of the true nature of Mother Earth. She is an angel herself. Think of the beauty of the forests, the oceans, the flowers. That is the true nature of Earth, and you are part of this majestic reality. You are like a flower yourself, but a flower can not open unless it is firmly rooted. You have to feel at home on Earth in order to be able to express yourself, your light. So I now invite you to connect to Earth, the angel that she is. Feel her energy deep within your body; you are her child and you can relax.

Imagine you are now walking in a beautiful place in nature. It can be a forest, or near the ocean, or in the desert, and make this vision very real and alive for yourself. Feel the elements of nature, the wind, the sun, the air. Feel the ground beneath your feet. Then sit down and put your hands on the ground. Allow Earth to affect you, to heal you, and to remind you of your partnership with her. Your soul wants to be here, even though your soul has been wounded on Earth, especially by the fear and the struggle that pervades human society. But as a human being, you are also connected to nature and to the harmony and the rhythm that is there. And if you embrace nature, both without and within, you can clearly hear the message of your soul.

So you are still sitting on Earth. Feel how an energy comes to you from above. You are very well able to receive it, because you are now connected to Earth and her energy. These two energies are meant to be together. Let this energy from your soul now shine on you like a sun. Just enjoy it for a moment. Often, when you connect, or try to connect to your soul, your mind interferes. You want to have concrete, practical information about your life. But to receive real information, you have to first shift your consciousness, because the need for information, the need to know what to do often arises from fear. You first have to relax completely and be in a state of alert fantasizing or imagining. So go into that state now.

Imagine you are completely free, not bound by the laws of human society. You are an angel, and like a butterfly you go from flower to flower. Ask yourself: "What gives me joy in my life?" Do not think of the results it brings to you, just focus on the feeling of joy and inspiration. You can receive inspiration from very simple things like taking a walk or having a quiet moment for yourself. It is important that you recognize the language of your soul. It does not speak in an obvious voice that you are used to. You are used to speaking very sternly to yourself; you criticize yourself a lot. You have a mental picture of how you should be and you constantly compare yourself with it and feel that you are failing. But it is in fact the judging that is the real problem. This type of judging, or this tone of voice, does not come from nature.

The language of your soul is very different; it is very gentle. It offers suggestions, but never wants to force you to do anything. So simply ask your soul: "What is it I need right now?" And you might receive the answer as an energy and not necessarily in words. Let go of all expectations. As a human, your problems are often caused by the fact that you have a blind spot. You have some persistent beliefs of which you are not really aware and your soul wants you to step out of those beliefs. This means you have to let go of your deepest convictions and be open to something entirely new. You have to let yourself be surprised by your soul.

So whenever you have a quiet moment and you long to connect with your soul, let go of your mind and connect in a spontaneous, playful way. That is the way of nature. You can see it in all the animals and plants that live on Earth. They joyfully go along with the rhythm that is theirs. They do not think of the future, yet they are perfectly aligned. You, too, can be perfectly aligned, because you are part of Earth and part of nature.

31. Love completes the cycle

Dear friends, dear sisters and brothers. It is with such joy that I am here with you today. I see you as eternal beings living temporarily on Earth. I see you focused on the finite, fearful parts of yourself, and sometimes I feel concerned about that. This is a time of great opportunity on Earth. You all are old souls. You have visited Earth many times in many lifetimes. Feel how far back your story goes. It is not just about this lifetime and this personality you have now. Feel how much you have experienced, how old you are and how mature you have become.

Feel now your soul joining you. Your channel is already open. Many of you, in fact all of you present here, were born with the deep desire to know who you are, to rejoin with your soul this time on Earth. You did not want to be distracted by anything else; you were focused. That is why you felt different from many around you. It is like you knew from early on: "I have something to do, something of ultimate importance" and this very important thing was to know yourself as eternal beings. You have had many lifetimes, especially in the beginning of your cycle on Earth, in which you became a part of life on Earth, a part of society, exploring all the energies here. In fact, you took a deep plunge into duality. On the soul level this was okay, because this was your purpose. You *wanted* to experience and to understand the extremes of duality, although you became lost in certain emotions, such as fear and ignorance.

And now, in this time, you are reaching the end of your cycle of lifetimes on Earth. You took a plunge into the depths of duality and now a turning point has been reached and you want to move upward, and *you want it with all of your being*. You have experienced pain, loneliness, and rejection within duality, and many of you felt great resistance when you entered this incarnation. When you were born, you knew on a subconscious level there was only one thing you wanted: to move beyond duality, to recognize yourself on the soul level.

I would like you to see and appreciate your own courage. When you started this incarnation, you had doubts and felt insecurity about coming to Earth again. You knew you were going to be confronted with old pain and fear that were not resolved in past lifetimes, yet somewhere deep down inside yourself, you decided to take that burden upon yourself. You were very courageous for taking this leap and I want you to recognize your courage and determination. You are warriors of light.

Living on Earth is often difficult, and the energies, the negativity, can be overpowering. Terrible fears can come to the surface of your awareness, especially when you decide: "I want to express my soul's light on Earth". But I want to tell you that this is alright, because now is the time for healing these fears. It is now possible to do so and I want you to feel this for yourself.

I ask you to connect profoundly with the Spirit of Earth, of Gaia. She is your host and she is your dwelling place in this life. Connect with her from the heart. Feel her energy beneath your feet. Feel how she cares for you, how she welcomes you. You are like a child on her lap. Feel safe again within your mother's embrace.

You are now here, in this lifetime, to cure yourself, to heal yourself. I want to state this very clearly. Some of you feel burdened, or even guilty, for not completely expressing your light yet. You become angry or frustrated with yourself. I see this with tears in my eyes. Do you not realize that you have suffered so much? You have been here on Earth in earlier times; you have experienced how it was when your soul's energy was not welcome. You are healing from those old traumas, those old wounds, and you have to treat yourself with the utmost care and patience. I encourage you to be truly tender with yourself. The most traumatized part of you will not be healed by impatience or judgment, and only by the softest possible energy, the energy of love, will it recover. And that is also the purpose of your long journey through duality; that you *become* the living reality of love.

Throughout your journey, there were times when your third eye was highly developed. You had acquired a great amount of knowledge and there were cultures in which it was easier to speak with the other planes of existence. But even though you had this wisdom and knowledge from the third eye, your light had to descend deeper into your heart. And that is exactly what the Christ energy is about and what Christ came to tell you on Earth: to connect from human to human from the heart, from a sense of oneness. So it is not your spiritual knowledge that will help you complete your cycle on Earth, it is your *ability to love*, and first of all to love yourself, especially the hurt parts of you.

Whenever you feel impatient or frustrated with your own progress, remember that these energies contain judgment and these energies are the ones that need to be transformed. Completing your cycle of lives on Earth asks of you to really bow down to yourself, and by that I mean to honor all parts of you, especially the hurt child inside. Perhaps your mind, or your third eye, holds a lot of knowledge which you want to act upon, but the child inside feels blocked and resists. I ask you to now see this child within, the child who feels so burdened by the past. Please welcome it and let it be in our midst. Imagine that you are holding it carefully, tenderly, and encourage it to look around and see the faces of the people present here so that she or he can feel how welcome it is.

When you see this little child, this vulnerable child in another person, you want to reach out to and tell the child how beautiful it is. Now, could you do this for yourself, for your own child as well? As a matter of fact, to be so loving and kind toward yourself, you have to go against tradition. Much of your tradition tells you that the emotional impulses of a child have to be restricted, so the child becomes more or less imprisoned in a mental cage of do's and don'ts. I invite you to free this child, to see its spontaneity and its innocence. See how it responds to your touch, to your caress. *It loves to be loved by you.* In fact, you are its parent, you are the perfect guide for this child. I ask you to take good care of her or him. As soon as it feels welcome in your heart and in your arms, you, as a complete being, will relax and feel at ease with yourself, and that is the real aim of your life: to become at peace with yourself and your life. Feel this peace now. Welcome the child and just relax.

The only way to become whole and to manifest your soul on Earth is to work *with* this child and not against it. By loving your child, you embrace your humanness, and your light becomes a guide for others. You all are meant to shine your light on Earth, but I ask you to not feel pressured by this. You can do it in a calm and peaceful way. When you judge yourself for not doing things right, you are alienating the child within. *See what you have already accomplished.* By simply coming here again into this incarnation, you have already shown your courage. Celebrate every step you take. If you think you are expressing only, let us say, half of your potential, tell yourself how incredible that is, that in spite of all the negativity and the pain, you are doing it – and doing it well!

I would like to end this channeling by celebrating the presence in this room of your inner children. Just imagine them creating a second circle at our feet. Hear their voices, their excitement. They feel so happy at being recognized by you, and notice how even though they have been hurt so deeply, there is so much light in their eyes. They are like Spring coming back every year, full of new life. Embrace your child and receive its gift.

The Wisdom of Earth

32. A time of choice

I am the voice of Earth. I am the angel Gaia, who speaks to you and is present within you. I am in the blood that flows through your veins and your body cells are part of me. I am the angel who inspires planet Earth, and who is embodied by Earth. I speak to you from the deepest core of Earth, and I would like to tell you of the transformation that is taking place within us both.

So much is changing on Earth. An awareness is penetrating into people that things can no longer continue on Earth the way they have for centuries. Humanity is waking up and is gradually remembering where it comes from and who it is and what is its destiny. Humanity is a bridge between heaven and Earth; a channel between these two realms of being. Humanity carries a star-light that can touch and inspire Earth: the star-light for which I have been waiting, so we can truly work and create together.

You form that channel between heaven and Earth. The star-light that burns in you wants to take shape here, in the same way that the life force takes form on Earth by way of the light of the Sun. I, planet Earth, receive the light and the warmth of the Sun and, because of that, life flourishes in and on me. These forces are also present in you; a sun lives within you. Every soul is a star of light, a sun in and of itself, and this sun wants to manifest, wants to take form in matter. And why? Because the nature of Creation *is* creativity. It wants to take individual form and become visible, and at the same time, it wants that individual form to be connected with all the other forms in Creation.

The essence of the Sun is an angel like me, not a mere "thing". That essence radiates to me as the light of the Sun and becomes manifest and tangible on the surface of this planet as its many living beings: from stone, to plant, to animal, to human. In that way, a dance is visible between the essence of the Sun and I, Gaia, the angel of Earth. This dance also takes place inside you.

To make this dance a thing of beauty, a dance of joy and connectedness, it is necessary that you first embrace both elements in yourself: your star-light as well as your roots in the Earth. And the latter has been difficult for you, partly due to the history of which you are a part: a history of the negation of Earth in many of its aspects. Earth has represented the "lower" in many of your traditional beliefs and religions. Earth also stands for nature, your instincts, the natural impulses that are present in the plant and animal kingdoms, and equally so in human beings. To understand and relate to these impulses has been a difficult challenge for humankind.

Humanity has fallen in love, as it were, with one aspect of its creative power. The fire in human beings, which originally comes from their star-light, their internal sun, has taken on a life of its own and has in some respects become a raging fire that is consuming and destroying life on Earth. When the fire stands by itself and does not connect with the elements of Earth, then it becomes consuming and destructive. In the human being, this fire is represented by the will. The will is located in the solar plexus, which is also where the energy toward action is located, converting inner impulses into the energy of doing and manifesting.

Humanity has fallen in love with the possibilities that emerge from the solar plexus: doing, creating, and manipulating reality by use of the intellect, analyzing by means of thinking, and putting that analysis into action. In this way, you get a sense that you have power over the reality in which you live, over nature of which you are a part. By this attitude, humanity has actually come to stand in opposition to nature, as an acting and thinking being who believes it is able to acquire power over nature, and to shape nature to its own ends.

This has been an illusion, a dream from which you are now slowly awakening, because it has become a nightmare. You can not rule over Earth, because Earth is what carries you, what makes you possible. It is only in connecting your star-light with the energy of Earth that you can really create something that is beautiful, harmonious, and viable.

You are standing in a tradition where the balance between your Sun energy and your Earth energy has become unbalanced. The fire has come to stand by itself, and this has had a consuming effect on the life of the planet. Even now, many of you are possessed by the fire of thinking, the fire of doing. I mean that your consciousness in everyday life is mostly occupied with thinking about what you have to do, how you can bring order and structure to your life. You feel driven to control life and to make it follow a certain direction.

You see this very clearly at the level of your leaders in world politics; their attempts during this time to avert impending doom through thinking, analyzing, and organizing. Much of this thinking is driven by fear. In fact, the thinking and the doing that stands isolated, that is not rooted in Earth forces and operates from a void, sooner or later manifests itself in a sense of loneliness, of being shaken loose from your roots, and as fear. And this feeling of emptiness, futility, and fear is something that holds the world and humanity captive.

Therefore, it is now truly important that there are people who dare to again trust in the power of Earth; to see her and to understand her as the positive energy that she essentially is. Not as the lower, the instinctive, that needs to be curbed and controlled, but as life itself that speaks through nature. Life that is naturally seeking a balance, a balance between all that lives on Earth and a balance between heaven and Earth.

I, Gaia, long for this balance, and you who are present here also feel that same longing. You are, in a sense, the pioneers. On this great wave of change upon which humanity finds itself, you can be a source of inspiration for others, those who are searching for more balance in their lives. When many people respond to their natural desire for grounding, for connectedness, for meaning in relationships with others – this call of the heart – you will manifest a new reality on Earth.

The time for change has come. You see it on the television news, in magazines, in the newspapers, that this time is crying out for change. It is now time to make a choice for light, joy, connectedness, rootedness, and nurturing yourself from the core of your being. It is a time to release the cosmic loneliness that humanity has known for so long a time. Humanity has lost its roots, and it is now pressed from all sides to return to those roots. The current financial crisis forces humankind to return to the basics, and to not be fixated on money. To discover what real abundance is and means, and to discover that true abundance can only flourish in a network of connectedness among human beings.

Abundance and connection belong together. You are not happy through money alone. Money is functional and can be a means to realize abundance, but at the core, abundance is found in the sense of fulfilling your destiny on Earth. This sense can be found only in connection: the linking of the star-light within you with the energy of Earth. And also in the linking between you and the world, and with the people around you. Recognize in people both the star-light and the Earth light. Dare to mingle among people and to speak your truth, your inspiration. This is the abundance that humanity is now looking for: to get back to its foundation, its roots.

I want to tell you how you can realize this abundance in your everyday life. Many of you pursue a dream or an ideal; you seek to fulfill here on Earth the deep longings of your soul, whatever those may be. All who are present here are seeking your spirituality, your inner knowing, the heart beat of who you are, and to pass that on to others: to be the channel you are meant to be. At this moment, it is important to embrace the Earth element, the place where you and I merge and where you are a part of Gaia; to embrace that element in yourself and to let go of thinking, worrying, over-analyzing, excessive doing, structuring, and regulating – to let that all go. *I ask you to trust me.*

I, Mother Earth, flow through you. I can help you to find your destiny, if only you have trust in me! And how do you do that? By listening to your body. Your body is part of my soul. Hear your body speak; let it tell you what it needs. The body is not simply a means or an instrument, it is much more than that. It is a part of God itself, a part of the living Creation. If your body tells you that it needs rest, or more freedom, or more fun, or warmth, or nurturing, pay attention to what it is saying. The soul of Earth *speaks* through your body, and the connection with me is a prerequisite to being who you really are, right here. Embrace again the spontaneity that shows up in your bodily sensations, in your emotions. It is there where I, Earth, speaks within you.

What gives you joy? What gives you inspiration, a sense of passion and awe? Where do you feel your creativity flow? There the heart of Earth speaks within you. And this may be something that is not related to the usual sense of the word "work". It can be a hobby, or it can be something very simple: your bare feet on the beach, enjoying the Sun on your skin, playing with an animal, laughing heartily in a conversation with a good friend. Do not limit yourself when it comes to finding your joy and your passion. It is precisely where you find it in the little things of everyday life that it also comes to you in the bigger things that you want to manifest on Earth.

Take your passion seriously, take *yourself* seriously! Wherever you find joy and passion, your star-light touches Earth, and something beautiful ignites: a creation that holds the balance between heaven and Earth. Where there is joy and inspiration, where your body relaxes free from the external pressures that you impose upon yourself through thinking, there I flourish. I, the angel Gaia, can then flow and express myself through you. I can flourish in your beauty.

Embrace me in your everyday life, and have respect for your body and the signals that it sends to you when you really listen to it. Have respect for the spontaneous emotions in you that are often described as childish, or not acceptable, because they do not meet the requirements of the society around you. But it is specifically those natural movements in you that tell you where your true destiny lies.

I ask you, children of Earth, to trust me. A long tradition has weighed down on you in which this trust was discouraged, and in a sense was taken away from you. Now you, as the forerunners of a new tradition, can see my beauty and experience my natural urge for balance, and can make it a reality within you. *Be a child of Earth again*. Believe in the beauty of your body and the natural urge of the body to restore balance within yourself.

Have faith in your emotions, even when you feel "down" and dissatisfied and restless and depressed. These emotions are all very natural – *you are human!* You are a carrier of these emotions, so believe they have something to tell you. Embrace them as part of your creation so they may be heard. Allow the angry and sad children within you to have their say. It is precisely these aspects within you that can tell you more about how you can ground yourself, and in a much better way, than all the high-flying theories about spirituality and how you should "transcend Earth". Your concern lies not with ways to transcend Earth, but to anchor your light here, ever more deeply.

Believe in yourself, the nature in you, the Gaia in you, that is seeking balance. Have faith in my impulses, allow yourself to be taken up into the flow of my love, and you will feel secure and deeply rooted in Earth, till your last breath – at peace and safe. Know yourself to be secure and safe, and become the flower of the Earth that you are meant to be.

33. Live from your center

I am the voice of Earth. I greet you all from my living and beating heart. I am present in the ground beneath your feet, and in your body and heart. I knock at your door – I want to belong with you – I want to celebrate the adventure of being human with you. Will you let me do that?

Let me flow through your feet – make that connection. Feel how light and heat flows through your feet – they connect you with me. Feel how you are supported by Earth, by my living presence. Venture out from your head – be present in the *now* – and let go of your mind. Feel how all excess thoughts are blown away from you by a soft, gentle wind, until there is only silence in your heart – *that is where I am.*

It is difficult for many people to find a connection with their heart, a connection with their body. You have been taught to approach reality from your head: from thinking, organizing, planning, and then you often feel powerless. There *is* something you want, that you long for in life, but you can not get there through thinking.

You can push and pull at reality as hard as you want with your thinking, but the mental process is often impotent and powerless here. That happens when your thinking does not move along with the flow of life: the changing, swirling, and sometimes turbulent dynamics of life.

Why is it difficult for you to connect with the primal flow of life that exists outside your head? Because you were discouraged from doing so by your upbringing. From an early age, you learned to trust in your head more than in your feeling, your emotion, your passion. Often, people are taught that these types of energy are dangerous and should be controlled. Who decided that and who taught you that?

This ancient doctrine stems from fear: fear of the dynamics of life – the fervor of the emotions and the passions – and feeling unsafe with *nature*. But when you close yourself off from the energy of nature, you drain life of its "life", and that is what happens with many people.

From this lifeless, estranged state, there develops a desire for something different, a life that is more passionate and full, more open and expressive of who you are. You yearn for this, both in the area of work and in your relationships. What you desire most deeply is to live from your center, and that center is not to be found in your head; it resides lower, in your heart and in your abdomen.

There you find the "living water" that is your soul, which wants to flow with me here on Earth, and in connection with me, wants to radiate and shine. Try to make that connection with your soul, the living light that you are and that is incorruptible. Observe where your soul resides and flows most naturally in your body. Look to see if in the area of your heart this flow stirs up enthusiasm, or desire, or perhaps homesickness.

Allow the light that you are to flow through your abdomen. See if you can breathe into your depths and allow the light to flow through your abdomen and your legs until it connects with the ground beneath your feet. That is the purpose of your soul on Earth; to truly connect with all parts of your humanity: your body, your emotions, your passion.

Next, look at how the light of who you *really* are, your soul, flows into your everyday life. Travel in your imagination to a situation – work, for example – where you express your creativity, and observe how you are present in this situation. Where is most of your energy located, and does it flow out smoothly? Do you feel welcome from your heart and from your abdomen in these surroundings, or do you pull back a bit? Does your energy continue to remain in your head, and do you experience that you actually receive too little inspiration from this environment? Are you properly grounded in these surroundings and connected through your body with me, Earth?

Become aware of what you would like. How would you develop best? In these familiar surroundings or possibly in a very different one? Maybe you do not belong here any more – that can happen. Trust the signals that you are receiving. If something calls up resistance, if you do not feel at ease, then that is the language of your heart, of your soul – trust that.

Finally, I would like to ask you to simply feel how Earth receives you – *I am always here*. Through the trees, the plants, the animals, everything that surrounds you in nature, I talk with you – *I welcome you*. I want us to dance together! You are a soul made of star-light and I am the potter's hand that receives you and makes it possible for you to give shape to your Self on this planet. I am inspired by your light and I am glad when you recognize me; when you dare to enjoy the beauty of nature in and around you and all the possibilities that the body gives to you. Honor your body, create enjoyment in eating, drinking, touching, feeling.

Be truly human – that is the way you honor me. It is not the denial of your humanness that brings you Home, but precisely the opposite: the embrace of everything you are *as a human being* and everything that goes with it. It is the ups and downs, the peaks and the valleys, that make life worthwhile. Learn to rely on the flow of feeling within you. That flow is what brings you Home, and it is always there. You can for a while oppose it – but you can not destroy it. Do not hold back the flow any longer – *live!*

34. Receive yourself

I am the voice of Earth. I am beneath your feet and greet you all with warmth and a deeply felt welcome from my heart. I am with you, so very close by. Feel my presence in the air you breathe, the water you drink, in your own body, which accompanies you in this life from beginning to end.

I want to feel you, to absorb your presence, because your consciousness enriches me. I can learn from you and you can learn from me. We are here to create and work together. You have a consciousness that by its nature is both creative and resourceful, and because of that special type of consciousness you are distinct from other living creatures on Earth.

Everything that exists has a consciousness, a soul, but you have a creative power in you that distinguishes you from all other living beings. You are on your way to becoming gods – *you are gods in the making* – and you are learning how to become aware of and to accept your creative power. You are often not conscious of your creative power, or you do not know how to utilize it.

There is a part of you that feels lost, rejected in this life on Earth; a part of you that is *not* connected with the Source of everything, the Source that carries the whole of life. I want to encourage you today to engage in this connection with the greater whole, the Source – God if you will – that carries you throughout your life. It is the only connection in which you can truly feel unconditional security and absolute acceptance of who you are.

That connectedness is what you are looking for, and from that grounded connectedness your creative power will take on a positive expression. When you try to create without that basic security of feeling carried in a larger field of love, when you stand separately with your creative power, you feel lonely and lost. Then this creative energy will often turn against you.

Just look at your everyday life, how often you feel cut off from that source that carries you and you then begin to fret, your emotions confused and chaotic. All this has to do with that lack of connectedness and not being able to let go of trying to control life; not knowing that you are being carried by the Source.

How do you make the connection with that Source, the essence of who you are? Wherever that Source reveals itself, there you are also. You are not actually separated, there is a web of life that permeates all forms, all creatures. You are an inalienable part of this web, whether you know it or not. This is perhaps difficult to grasp with your mind, but you do not need to understand it with your intellect, *it is a feeling*. And my gift to you, what you can learn from me, is to surrender to this vast web of life.

Just look at the natural world, the non-human life. All beings in that web sense that they are carried and nurtured, supported by the environment while they develop their individual potential. A flower that blossoms in the field makes use of the forces of Earth: the sun, the wind, the rain. It asks not whether there will be sunshine at the right time, or water in the ground, or the shelter of a tree with sufficient shade. It expects the right circumstances will present themselves, and even when the right conditions do not come about, this natural life energy surrenders to what comes to it and, if necessary, it will die in order to flourish again in another form.

That power of surrender is present in the whole of nature: the animals, the plants, even the stones. Everything that lives instinctively knows how to function within this all encompassing web – except you, who so often seem to be confused and without roots, adrift. And why is that? You are confused and adrift precisely because of your great abilities and talents, your creative powers.

The path back to clarity, and to feeling rooted once again, is the path to a peaceful implementing of your creative power. And the joyful experience of that is by way of Earth; by returning to a oneness with all other life around you – that is the key, the solution. Try to feel that unity for a moment, starting with your body, which is my gift to you. Feel life flowing there, feel your body as a living field of energy. Do not look at what is wrong, or where there is a problem, but merely feel life itself for a moment, flowing and pulsing throughout your body.

This body is beautiful and innocent. Allow the Sun to shine on it, and imagine that all the cells in your body drink in the power of the Sun, which symbolizes so much more than just physical light. In the Sun, a heart is beating, the same as in me. In the Sun pulsates a memory, a knowing. The Sun is the fundamental creative force in this solar system; I absorb its light and energetic force which I then transform into life forms.

You are part of the Sun, and you could say that you come from the Sun, although I mean that metaphorically. You carry the creative force of the Sun in you, and you are here to instill that force into me so as to bring forth flourishing and abundant life on Earth. In return, my gift to you is that I receive you, I provide shelter for you in which to live, so you can enjoy this life.

Trust in me. Many of you mistrust me, not consciously perhaps, but there is so much that you were taught by the traditions of the many dominant cultures. Doctrines and theories that say that the body is in one way or another inferior, that nature is below humans and is less developed, less important. That this nature in you, your lust for life, your senses and emotions, and what the body wants, must all be transcended for the benefit of "spiritual truth" – although no one knows exactly what that entails.

You are so alienated from your human nature, your unity with me, Earth, and this makes you sad and lonely. I see your alienation daily. You are bombarded with stimuli from around you and especially from your own confused thoughts. You have lost your way because your fundamental connectedness with the field of power that I am has escaped you.

Now give yourself over to my strength and let me receive you. Let yourself be *who* you are and do not try so hard to be different than *what* you are. *You are good as you are*. Your "way" is to become who you are and never to be someone other than who you are – your way is to be always yourself.

Like a flower that blooms reveals its deepest purpose, so you come into flourishing when you allow your heart to radiate as it naturally wants to, without trying to restrict and stifle it by ideas that are not of your nature.

To return to your natural state of being, it is necessary that you rely on *yourself*, and not on a so-called "higher self" on which you should focus. Rely on your own humanness and put a listening ear to that.

What does the human being in you want? This whole idea that you should focus on a higher order of existence, a hierarchy that is elevated above Earth, is a misconception. You are *not* here to transcend your humanness. It is precisely in your humanness wherein lies the connection between heaven and Earth, between solar power and earth power. Precisely by being human can you become complete and whole. Herein lies your destiny. It is not by suppressing your humanness, but by embracing it that you come Home to yourself and you become that beautiful flower that you are destined to be.

What is this humanness that has become so suppressed, judged, and condemned from the head through thinking? *Your humanness has to do with your feelings.* You are here on Earth to learn by daring to feel, by allowing your emotions to be, and by riding the waves of those emotions. Learn to really listen to your emotions, and dare to trust that doing this will bring true understanding and sense of purpose. The flow of feelings inside you naturally strives for balance and growth. You do not believe that concept because your emotions often seem confused and difficult to understand, but your emotions want to bring you Home, your emotions are the messengers of your soul.

By listening *without reservation* to your emotions, or what you call the inner child, you will discover where things have become unbalanced within yourself. Your inner child, mirroring your emotions, is leading you to your roots. Imagine for a moment that you see a little child come to you, a child that arises from your body, from that deep place within yourself where you maintain a balance of energies. Take it on your lap. Let this image unfold by itself, or simply create a connection with your feelings; you do not have to see anything.

In you *is* a living child: a child born from Earth and heaven. It wants to tell you what it needs, it wants to point the way to feeling peaceful and secure on Earth. Let this child tell you how it feels, what emotions run high in it, and allow this child to express them. If you allow the child to do this, you will see that it becomes more peaceful and happy, and you can take it by the hand and, together with this child, move through life in close connection with your humanness.

What you all need most profoundly on your path is to receive yourself, to really say "yes" to all aspects that arise within you. Only when you actually say "yes" to everything within *you* – your thoughts, your emotions, your fears, your confusions – can your creative power extend to, and embrace, everything.

Your creative power, which I compare here with the Sun, is a radiant power that extends from within to without, that wants to give and unite and manifest. I, on the other hand, am a receiving power, the receptive Earth that absorbs. These two forces need each other to actually arrive at a balanced creation, a *co-creation*.

You have both forces within you, Sun and Earth, giver and receiver. You can more and more develop the receiving strength – Earth power – in you by truly saying "yes" to your own humanness, by truly having compassion with the deepest needs within you, as well as with the darkness and negativity that prevail there. Can the light from your Sun shine upon you? Can it warm you? That is why you are here, to form that bridge from heaven to Earth.

If you truly know how to receive, and *to not judge any aspect of yourself*, then your creative power, the rays of this Sun, really penetrate to the core of your humanness *and* to the core of Earth. Then you become illumined within by your own light, your own warmth. Allow that to happen.

Be Earth. Imagine that you *are* Earth and let this Sun shine upon, and penetrate, you. See how this Sun puts everything within you into the light, without judgment, so everything is allowed to be. Feel the relief of that – nothing is forbidden, nothing is bad. Allow this Sun to shine. Imagine that you are lying flat on your back on Earth and that you take in everything and feel: "I am allowed to be who I am."

By being who you are, you become who you are *meant* to be – the Sun and the Earth united within you. This union of forces manifests itself as a sense of peace, clarity, and well-being. These are the signs that you have made the connection, that you have put up the bridge. You do not have to do more than that, all else will fall into place.

I ask you to especially pay attention to this receiving from Earth, knowing that you are one with me and saying "yes" to yourself. If you know how to receive and embrace yourself, you truly bring down the light to Earth, and you become a giver, a creator, a radiant Sun. You will see that these two apparently different things are one and the same thing – the giving and receiving are one, not two.

A beautiful flower, a rose, gives by being itself, instinctively knowing that it is sustained by all the nurturing elements around it. *You* are like that. Be like a rose, trust that you are nurtured by the elements. The giving and sharing of your beauty happens by itself, by being who you are.

35. Dealing with the old energy

I am Earth who speaks to you. I greet you all in this new time that has arrived. This is a new time, and all of you present here are its guardians. Through you all, this new time will be born on Earth.

Feel how you are a channel for the new energy that wants to flourish in the hearts of people. You are engaged in connecting yourself anew with me, Earth, as a living planet and with yourself as a living body and soul, who in this world – my world – wants to manifest itself. You are engaged in a birthing process, where you free yourself from the conditioning and energy of the past – from your birth family, the generations before you, and your country and the traditions in which you grew up – and where you appear in a totally new way in the present. This is an intense and grand process.

Have respect for yourself and for what you intended to accomplish in this life. You are doing quite well. It is true that you occasionally drift off course. Each birth process is unique and strenuous and you have no certainties. On the way to the new, only the old is familiar and you want to cling to that from a need for certainty and control. But you have to let go of everything, just as a baby is called out of the womb by the light. It has nothing to hold on to, and has to surrender entirely to the new, trusting that everything will be well – so it is with you.

The old energies of fear, of power and authority, of duty, of coercion, do not suit you any more and are even painful for you. You experience that pain as dissatisfaction, gloom, not feeling at peace, and always wanting and seeking something else. That energy propels you forward and eventually leads you to break with those things to which you were accustomed – the old. You begin to feel the new attracting you. You feel the thrust of the new world, but you still have trouble completely letting go of the old. Cords of fear, of duty, and responsibility bind you to the world of the old.

Do you know the best way to liberate yourself from that? Simply put, it is to help the old to transform along with you. Too often, you see yourself embroiled in a fight with the old; you think: "I should be liberated from

211

this by wrestling myself free." At the same time, it feels like a massive presence that restrains you – almost imprisons you, but by looking at the situation in that way, you give the old too much power.

What or who is that old energy and where is it? It exists in people who have built up the old world, or who maintain it. However, those people are just like you. They, too, are on a search and all too often became lost and lonely within the old systems.

There is now a wave of new consciousness at work in the world; it is flowing throughout the whole world. It is a wave of enlivening light, which gently reminds people of who they are – a soul – and of the opportunities that exist to live differently, from the heart, and from gentleness and joy. This wave permeates the world and all systems are touched by it. You are the forerunners of this new consciousness and you sense this wave in your heart very clearly – *you want it!* And you *want* to move forward, but the pull of the old restrains you.

The truth is that all things move and vibrate together along with this new flow of consciousness and you can help the old – *you need not flee from old energies.* Rather, you can be a guide for those persons who also crave more inner freedom, more joy on their path, and a release of old burdens. They are not your enemies, but rather your students who reside in that old system; drawn in a little more tightly into the fears and the tyranny of the past than are you.

Change now your image of how you stand in this world – *you are the carrier of a new dawn.* Even though this transformation process, the birth in which you find yourself, feels heavy and you find it difficult to see the way to more freedom, you still are the first to pave a way for others. You set an example through your intention to give form to the new.

Perhaps it does not happen as you think it should, or it may be slower than you want it to be, and sometimes you lose sight of the totality of the process in which you find yourself. However, the transformation is underway in the area of your work and in the field of your self-development. You are establishing your originality and allowing yourself to be seen on me, Earth.

There is in each of you the soul's desire to give shape to the new consciousness in one way or another; to be a guide and an example; to offer a vision to others through which they begin to feel and think: "This way works; this road provides a new perspective and a new energy; it feels light and joyous". When you express your essential being, when you experience joy and inspiration in what you do, you radiate light to others, and that has been your soul's intention. Therefore, you do not have to do battle with the old. *You are the ones who encourage the old and who help it to transform.*

You are needed on Earth, *now*. With that, I do not want to put you "to work", in the sense of traditional work, because it is precisely by falling back into your natural being that you are doing the work that you intended for this life. It is *not* the intention that you carry the burdens of other people. The intention is simply that you let go of the burden of the old energies that are not really in harmony with who you are. It is then that your light radiates more brightly toward others.

Being yourself, without worry and concern for being different, daring to express your light and your own originality, that is lightwork, and that frees and releases energy for others. Then, you are literally doing "nothing" and no longer hiding yourself, you simply *are*. You let nature flow through you as it is meant to flow, just as your nature is meant to be expressed. To help and to assist another is thus not a doing, a task that takes energy, but an expressing of who you really are and daring to be different; *it is allowing the child within you to awaken!*

There is nothing more encouraging and inspiring for another person than to see you as your true being: free and spontaneous and effortless. That is what people see in what you call a great teacher: spontaneity, a natural light and joy; gentleness, but firmly grounded and connected to Earth. These qualities also live in you. Your only mission is to free this "beingness" within yourself; then you do the work for which you have come.

This freeing of yourself has to do especially with letting go of the old and feeling deeply within yourself: "What do I want?" Relax into your body and from that tranquility and peace allow the voice of your natural self to speak to you. Feel for a moment the energy of your body and how it flows. Escape from the prison of your mind and in that freedom experience the energy of your soul, which is always present within your body.

For your soul is not somewhere far away from you, it is present in all the cells of your body, and your soul wants to say something to you now: "What do you wish for most deeply? What feeling, what mood, what energy?" Allow yourself to receive that message. And when you listen deeply and trustingly to the voice of your soul – your heart – then you do the work for which you have come, and you anchor the New Earth.

36. Get out of your head!

I am the voice of Earth. Feel my energy and my strength. Make the connection with me through your body, which is the bridge between us. Let me into your life, so I can give to you what you need, which is only possible when you *allow* yourself to receive. You have become human here on Earth by your body receiving the elements of Earth, and only through a deeply felt connection with me can you manifest in flesh and blood who you are *truly* – a most profound and complete being.

I want to receive your soul, your inner warmth and light, and in return, to give to you everything you need as human beings to flourish and shine; to manifest and radiate what you are. However, when it comes to receiving, there is a barrier in humans that prevents me from giving to you all that you need. There is an inability in people to connect with Earth and to receive my energy, not only at the individual level, but also at the collective level. This is the reason why humanity as a whole is so lost in its head and stands on shaky and uncertain ground.

Many people disconnect from the *now* by losing themselves in constant, hectic thoughts, by being entangled in the past or driven by the future, and by being caught up in stress and pressure from the outside world. *I can not reach you when you are trapped in your head*, so I ask you to experience that gap between us for a moment. See a person before you who is completely in their head and enthralled by the thoughts that whirl and churn in there; they have become a prisoner of their own mind.

Meanwhile, their body becomes more lifeless, less vital and powerful. It receives too little nutrition from its own consciousness, and in this way can not be inspired by the powers of Earth and of nature. Such a person loses connection with their own feelings and with the energy flow within their body and, to some extent, each one of you is such a human. It can not be other than that, however, because you have been enormously influenced by the way human beings have been raised for centuries.

Why has all that energy become concentrated in the head? Orienting yourself mostly from your head happens only when there already exists a kind of rupture between yourself and Earth. An animal is naturally connected with its surrounding and with that surrounding forms an organic whole; first with its own kind, and then with its extended environment. It feels inextricably part of the whole and immerses itself in that. It feels it belongs and does not think about what it is like to be separate from the whole.

The natural experience of being connected is lacking in most people. If you are trapped in your head, there is a feeling of being lost: a loneliness, a consciousness of being separate, and a lack of meaning and the inability to make sense of your life. It is not strange then that people start behaving in a way that separates and drives them even farther from themselves, from others, and from me, Earth.

There is fear in people who live from their head, and as a result there arises in them a need to control and to eliminate that fear, or at least to conceal it. Unfortunately, their fear is never really relieved, if it is only driven by way of the head through mental activity. Actually, you then create only more barriers against life. So many judgments are located in the head about what should, or can, or might be.

Now imagine for a moment someone whose energy is *not* so concentrated around their head. See that person standing on Earth. You may see a human being who has a different kind of presence, and whose being inhabits its body in a unique and individual way. Maybe what arises in your imagination is the vision of a person who is barefoot or lightly clothed, a more natural person. Look at the heart and essence of that person. This human being is part of the whole; they listen to what nature has to tell them and to the flow of life within their body. That person *feels* what they need physically: food, clothing, shelter; and *feels* from the heart what they need emotionally: connection with other beings, passion, inspiration, creativity. This is the new human, the type of human that is to be born *through* you and is to inhabit the new Earth.

Call on that figure in your imagination; it is already within you, it is your future self. The activity in your head has become still; you have descended more deeply into your heart and abdomen. You no longer need to bring order and regulate life through your thinking mind; you easily allow things to be as they are. And it is from that more passive attitude –

seemingly passive, because in fact you are open and receptive, without wanting to grasp and control – that you can really receive your soul on Earth.

Your soul is like starlight from which a beam extends to Earth; a beam that can only penetrate and shine through the receptivity of a human being. Imagine for a moment that inside your soul is a star of light. Call on that star, which should be quite easy for you to do, because you *are* that star. Imagine that the light of this star falls on you, and look where in your body this light is the most readily received – *and that is not your head.*

Allow the light of the eternal star that you are to flow into your body; in through your heart, to your abdomen, tailbone, legs, and feet. As a human being you are a channel for your soul's light. *That* is why it is so essential to appreciate your own humanness and to understand and to love it. *Your humanness is not an obstacle for your soul, but a partner.* Your humanness, with all your emotions, thoughts, and body, is part of your life *here*. It is the channel through which your soul wants to flow. Embrace your dignity as a human being.

As a result of living from your head, you always try so very hard to prove that you are someone who is worth being loved. You overlook who you *really* are, because there is always something outside yourself that you want and reach for; but by doing this you can not be the receiving channel for your own soul's energy. Only when you really stand *with* yourself, and be who you are as a human being, with all the insecurities and uncertainties that are part of being human, can you be really at Home and one with your soul. You then do not need to prove yourself; you *know* you are good as you are.

Everything you are – all facets of being human – is part of this life on Earth and nothing needs to be removed. When you say "yes" to your humanness, you set yourself free. You no longer struggle within yourself, and you become part of the whole. Every human being is unique and walks their own path. That is precisely why you have so much to give to one another, because each has a unique perspective and is irreplaceable within the whole.

Finally, I would like to ask you to imagine that you are on the new Earth, a place where people live much less from their head and much more in harmony with themselves, with nature, and with other people. See yourself there and allow your imagination to roam free. Look, for a moment, at how you would live there. Is there a setting somewhere in nature, where you can be yourself completely, where you feel at peace and relaxed? You sense a connection with the entire environment and you sit there very calmly and tranquilly.

Maybe you have your own cottage there, one that completely reflects who you are. You feel safe and secure in that cottage. Allow the setting to influence you; it is important that you feel this. And then look around this setting to see if there are other people in the surrounding area. See if you feel a connection with these people and if this is a community of people with whom you belong on that new Earth.

And go a step further; imagine that you come together with these people in a central place or a square where you gather in a circle. How natural it feels to you to come together with these people, because you have nothing to prove to them, you can simply be yourself. That is your role in this community; to be yourself and to radiate your unique energy.

Feel for a moment how grateful people are that you are part of this community; how they appreciate you for who you are; how inspired they are by your presence and contribution. Experience these people together with you forming a circle by your all holding hands. Together, you generate something beautiful for Earth and for humanity. In this way, the flow of giving and receiving effortlessly come together. You know who you are and you receive what you naturally need in order to live well and in harmony with your surroundings. *Thank yourself for your value as a human being.*

My wish for you is that you take yourself really seriously and not denigrate yourself as you usually do. You are the channel for the new Earth that wants to arise from within the old, which was full of fear and judgment. The new Earth wants to manifest, so take yourself seriously as a forerunner of this new time. Totally embrace your humanness, for that is the channel for the manifestation to occur. Your unique humanness makes you part of the whole; indispensable and unique. This is my appeal to you: believe in yourself, appreciate yourself, and stand up and dare to shine. *Dare to give and to receive!*

37. Return to innocence

I am Earth. Feel me deeply; sense and experience me. I am present here in all things. I live and dance in the ground beneath your feet, in the chairs upon which you sit, in the flow of energy within your body. I want to be your constant companion by exploring and experiencing life together – *by dancing together.*

Often you resist me, because there is fear in most of you. There are many reasons why you might reject me, but the main reason is that you distrust my strength, just as you mistrust your own strength. As you distrust and are afraid of the forces of the wilderness, so are you afraid of the wildness of your own nature: the power of your emotions, the fluctuations of your moods, and the depth of your feelings. All too often, you retreat from these experiences in fear.

You have learned to lead life mostly from your head, by trying to organize life with your mind; to master life by trying to change and control it. That approach feels safe and manageable to you, but what you actually do when you do that is to smother the living flow that you are – you strangle it. You almost all do this, because you have been raised that way.

There is fear in you; fear to walk beyond well-trodden paths; fear to live according to your own wild nature, where "wild" means unspoiled, spontaneous, and natural, and not restricted by all sorts of external rules and social structures. How often do you repress your first spontaneous impulse and want to examine it with your mind? But something eventually dies in you as a result of this way of living and then you no longer are able to recover life's flow. You become cut off from who you are; you feel rigid and not alive and vibrant; you feel stuck. And eventually, by being devoid of the living light that you are, you become depressed

Living in this restricted way, you also can not connect with me, and with everything I want to give to you: the fun and light-heartedness, life according to your own nature. I want to ask of you at this time to have compassion with that part of you that is devoid of your own light, your own aliveness and spontaneity; the part of you that is hidden behind lock and key and was not allowed to flow into life. You need not examine the reasons why this happened by thinking about it, simply *feel* the part of you that has become imprisoned.

As a child, that part of you was uninhibited, and full of love and zest for life. Let that child in yourself come to you again, the child who could not express itself sufficiently; who was forbidden the free and boundless enjoyment of itself and of Earth; who was not allowed a life that flowed freely according to the rhythm of its soul. Who was that child and where has it gone? *It is still there*, and it is an inalienable part of you. You are unable to lose it even if it has been silenced for a long time. Have compassion for that part of you for it wants to return.

In earlier times, especially in societies heavily influenced by religion, people learned that this part of them – this sunny, enjoying, living, wild part – was their most sinful part. It was something about which you had to feel guilty and ashamed. It had to be governed and kept under control, and it had to be eventually transcended. But that is a reversal of the facts and a subversion of the truth, for it is just this radiant, spontaneous part in you, your life-light, that is the most spiritual part of you and comes here to Earth to dance with life and to experience and explore it. This is the part of you that is most alive.

See whether you can allow this energy to come to you by way of your feet. You may see this flow of energy in the form of a child, but it does not have to be that; it may also present itself as a bundle or flow of energy, or possibly an animal, if that is more fitting for you. Allow it to come through to you in the part of you that lies furthest from your head – your feet – because the head can not help you to make a connection with that energy.

Concentrate for a moment on the soles of your feet, and how they rest upon Earth. Feel the life in your feet; all those tiny cells full of flowing, vibrant life. Feel how the natural creature that you are – the human child who lives and enjoys and is not ashamed of who it is, who dares to be naked – feel how its energy flows back to you from the depths of my heart and up through your legs. Feel its presence.

Maybe you see it standing next to you in whatever form it presents itself, and make no judgment about how it presents itself. Maybe it has become a bit sad, because it has had to live too long in loneliness. Or maybe it is just happy and thrilled to see you again – *just imagine that*! This child, or this animal, or this flow of energy, belongs to you and wants to be with you; it wants to feel the embrace of your arms – *and it wants you to relax.* This is the part of you that connects you with me, Earth.

Your soul is a radiant light; it is not bound to Earth. At one time, it chose to connect to an earthly body, and even more than one time. And when you connect to an earthly body, you come to me; you live in my reality. Your soul's light is meant to flow through to me here, through the soil, the rocks, the plants, the animals, the flowers. The intention is that we make each other fertile and fruitful, and that we impregnate each other with our essences and enjoy the beautiful creation that arises as a result. You come here with your soul-energy, with your cosmic energy, and I receive you. I want to receive you and give to you what you need as a human being. I want to dance with you and to sing and have fun.

There is much that you give back to me, too, because I am inspired by your energy. How can that be? *Because I experience your consciousness.* When you pick up a flower and admire it, at that moment something lights up in me. I feel your attention and your loving admiration, and just as with a child, my eyes light up. It makes me happy and elated if you appreciate me for who I am. Just look at a field where you sow seeds; a field that you care for with love and attention. It begins to grow and flourish. It gives you something in return for your care, because it is so happy and pleased with your human attention.

You are gathered here on this visit (to southern France) because you are looking for a connection with your own deepest self, but also with my core and with who I am. I want to be known by you and be included in your conscious awareness. Your doing that makes me more alive and makes my consciousness grow and evolve. We are on a journey together and neither one of us is all-knowing. We are living, dynamic creatures, you and I, hand in hand.

I am your mother and I want to take care of you. When you listen to your body, I can give you guidance, nurture and inspire you, but you also give something to me in return. I am not only your mother, for in a way, I am also your child. You inspire me with your consciousness because of its cosmic quality. Just as the sun bathes me in its light, I also bathe in your light when it loves and is open to me. Feel the intimacy of our interaction for a moment. From this interaction, this union of energies, a gift comes to you, something you need at this moment in your life. Perhaps it has a form and you see an image, but that is not necessary. You can also just sense a vibrant and relaxing energy. Feel it come to you; allow it to flow through your feet and incorporate it – *you are so welcome to it.*

38. Healing the male and female energy in the body

I am your mother, Earth, who carries you. I flow through you constantly, and I want to nourish and inspire you with my energy. We belong together; we do this dance together.

Life in a body, male or female, is an interplay between your soul and that of Earth. Honor your beautiful body, the body I have given to you. It is an expression of female or male energy, so feel the beauty of that, and observe it from within. Experience the powerful energies in your body: the emotions, the feelings, the passions, the desires. They are powerful energies against which you sometime resist. However, try to feel the pure beauty of your body for a moment without wanting to control it. Feel the force field that you are as a physical being.

You continually receive information from your body and you often ignore that input because you think you know in your mind what is right for you or what is wrong for you. You often ignore your body, this gift from nature. I ask you to instead turn your attention downward toward the ground beneath your feet, the foundation upon which you stand in this life, and to return to your sacred body – the dwelling place of your soul. Make peace with your body and no longer resist those energies that manifest there – respect them. Your soul is invited to dance with the energies of Earth, with the energies of being a woman, of being a man, of being together.

Let us do this today. Try to let go of beliefs in terms of right or wrong, beliefs about what is to be allowed and what not. Try to let those ideas go, altogether. Let the energies speak for themselves. If you look around yourself in nature, you see a continual play of energies and powers: in the wind, in the water, in the temperature, in the seasons, in the weather.

Everything moves constantly, but tends naturally to a certain balance and equilibrium when things are allowed to take their own course. An overbearing need to control and organize eventually leads to imbalance, to a lack of equilibrium. And this happens also with your own human nature, because you are a part of earthly nature. Let go of trying to control and manipulate everything. Look at who you are, here and now, at this time. Allow your desires to be present and to "speak" to you.

Each of you present here longs for love. Love in relationships with others and love for yourself. Love to give and love to receive, and that is as it should be, because this desire is sincere. However, even though you have this strong desire, there is a part of you that is fearful and in the dark. This part makes you afraid of love. So although one part of you yearns for love, and reaches out for it, another part of you unintentionally closes you off from giving and receiving love.

You are forerunners of a new time, you are pioneers. You are taking steps on new ground, in unexplored territory. You want to live from your heart and your soul, and you want to get acquainted with what love really is. Not the images of love that are portrayed through the media, but a love that is more grand and more vast. A love that allows both partners to be completely who they are. A love as nature intended it to be.

This is a transitional time on Earth. More and more people desire depth in their relationships, a true meeting with the other person, and that is where your path leads you. But it is not a path that only leads to the heights; it is also a path that can lead to the depths, because on this path you encounter your own fears, the prejudices of your parents and ancestors, and the pain of generations before you. That is the choice you make once you choose for a relationship in the new era. You then choose for another way of being. You choose for an openness and sincerity that goes to the core of who you are, and therefore that choice challenges you to reveal, from the fullest extent of your soul, the part of you that still hides in the dark.

Let us today look in openness and without judgment at what still is to be revealed within you. What pain, what fear lives there? What hinders you from loving yourself and another? Let us first look at the past and to how the male and female energies have developed in centuries past. We then see that the male energy has played a dominant role for centuries and that both sexes, both women and men, have suffered because of that. The male energy that was dominant in your history was very much a mental energy of wanting to direct and determine earthly nature, as well as human nature. This form of energy wants to restrain and to control, often out of a desire for power.

In all layers of society, that energy has been at work. In governments, religions, and in daily life, the female energy, the emotional and the intuitive, was suppressed. The result has been that women felt inferior. The female qualities were less, or not at all, appreciated. That was the prevailing image. Women were regarded as second-class citizens, lesser human beings, and the female energy in general was regarded with suspicion.

If you are aggressive, and you focus on control, power, and manipulation through mental processes, the feminine soon becomes your enemy, because the feminine is by nature more flowing, more flexible, and more connected to qualities of feeling and emotion. The feminine is the source of *all* inspiration. She creates the bridge to your soul. Your soul flows through your feminine energy. The masculine energy is meant to support that inspiration, and to make it possible for this inspiration to become established in the material world.

That is the way it would be if the masculine and feminine worked well together, but throughout history the natural cooperation has become fractured, and men and women have become strangers who stand opposite one another. And this has not only happened outwardly between men and women, but also within the hearts of men and women. Men became alienated from their own emotional life, barred from it, and women increasingly began to feel insecure about who they are and what they can do. In both sexes, the male dominance has left wounds.

I would like you to join with me in an exercise of guided visualization. Imagine that you see a man and a woman standing side by side. I would like to sketch an image here of the male and the female soul on the collective level. A very sketchy picture, thus a general image, but something that you can recognize, or to which you might identify. When you see how a man looks historically, at the pain he has suffered, then you see a man whose emotions are not allowed to flow sufficiently. Men have identified with thinking, doing, and acting, but the connection with their heart is broken or difficult to find.

If you look at the figure of this man, you can see that he lives partly within a shell or an armor. This armor gives him a feeling of security, but at the same time restricts him, because his heart is stifled. You can see his tide of passion and love, but that current may not flow very freely through his armor; there is congestion and blockage within him. Men can not express their feelings very well, because they have to contend with an old armor that actually no longer fits them, and you can perceive there are already cracks in the armor of this representative male.

Men fight against this ancient armor, because they want to express their feelings more openly. But because of these restrictions, which are the result of the judgments of the past, it is still so that, as a man, you can not express certain emotions from your heart and you can not truly connect with another. From the point of view of these restrictions, you will give up your security when you release your inhibitions, and that is dangerous and scary.

Let us now look by way of this visualization at how the woman looks as a result of her long past of pain and suppression. If you look at this representative female, the first thing you see is that something is missing. The woman is not entirely present, because of the suppression and the sexual violence she has experienced in the past thousands of years. Something has been shut down, especially within her abdomen in the lower chakras.

The pain from the violence has been too heavy to process. And what people do, if traumas are too much to bear, is they flee from it in some way. They try to leave their body and are no longer sufficiently grounded and are no longer connected to their inner power, because it is too painful to be completely present in their bodies. That is what has been globally true for women.

Ask yourself to now connect in your imagination to both these figures, and let us begin with the man. Imagine that you go with your awareness inside that man. Feel the pain that lives there, and also the desire in him to be able to feel again, to live from his heart. See if you also recognize within yourself some of that same restrictive armor. To what extent do you also carry that with you, this armor that seemingly gives you the certainty of control, but that also stops you from allowing your soul to radiate on Earth? See if you can tell that man, and thereby also yourself, that you can put down this armor, piece by piece, releasing it more and more. You can let go of what is there in excess and no longer needed. Do that now, but do not do it by force. See what can fall away by itself.

Observe what feels freer in your energy field and in your emotions, and to where the released energy can flow. Maybe there is a place in your body to where it spontaneously flows. Yet, it may be that part of the armor remains or refuses to yield. If so, just let it be; it need not all go at once. In this way, you have now helped yourself, as well as the broader spectrum of the entire male energy here on Earth, which wants to transform in this time, wants to change. Now step outside the figure of that man that you envisioned.

Bring your awareness to a point of focus, leaving the figure of this man, and look at the woman. Notice how you see the figure of the woman, the uncertainty and insecurity, the fragility and delicacy in her, the not daring to be here fully. Go there for a moment with your awareness and allow it to descend into her consciousness and into her body. You can connect with her fear and the resistance to being here fully, to descending into that fragile area of her abdomen, into her womb.

I, Mother Earth, am with you when you do this, so you are safe. I will support you, so do not be afraid. Become present in the energy within that female figure. Let her know that you are there for her, that you will receive her. Tell her how beautiful she is, how welcome she is in this world on Earth. We *need* her intuitive gifts and the connection that she creates with the soul, with her inner knowing and the beauty that she brings to life. We need her again on Earth.

Imagine that some kind of ladder appears from heaven and the full and authentic female energy slowly descends downward, and do this for yourself as well as for the entire female energy at this time. She needs to feel welcome on Earth, as she has pulled away from Earth, because of the aggression and pain she has experienced.

This pain is present in you all, whether you are now a woman or a man. That is why it is so difficult to allow your emotions freedom of expression and to dare to be who you are in the depths of your soul. See if you succeed in bringing the rungs of the ladder closer, but allow it the freedom to do as it will; it does not have to come down all at once. Now leave this imaginary figure of a woman and come back to yourself, into your body, into the *here* and *now*.

You can visualize yourself in a triangle with these two figures, the male energy and the female energy. These are images that have to do with you, with your life as an individual and, at the same time, these images also transcend your individual life, because they are force fields that permeate society as a whole.

By recognizing the wounds of the past through these imaginary figures in this visualization, you also heal a part of yourself. You can once again become an inspired, feeling man, and a powerful, self-confident, intuitively gifted woman. In this way, you free yourself from the pain of the past, as well as add healing to the collective consciousness.

39. Communicating with animals

It fills me with joy to be present in your midst and to be welcomed by you. You who are present today see me, Mother Earth, as a full partner in Creation. You welcome me because you value my beauty and you are concerned about nature, and you feel connected with the animal kingdom. You are open to a connection with me and I thank you for being open, because a connection between us is something that can very much benefit us both.

Ultimately, we are one. We are born of one consciousness, the consciousness of God, who manifests in many ways and takes on many types of experience. Through us all flows one consciousness: through the human, animal, plant, and mineral kingdoms. Feel the unity that makes it possible that we, in our diversity, can communicate with each other, can learn from each other, and can enrich each other's lives. This is the purpose of our lives being woven together: that you feel enriched by all that lives on Earth.

We speak today, in particular, about the animals that surround you as loyal companions. Anyone who feels attracted to this topic has experienced a deep connection with animals, now or in the past. This connection extends beyond the taking care of an animal; something moved in your heart and was stirred emotionally. When this inner stirring happened, you gave something worthwhile to the animal kingdom. By your attention and openness to an animal in your life, you gave an important energy to the animal kingdom.

Animals desire to be acknowledged and appreciated by humans and valued for who they are: a part of Creation. When you treat animals with care and respect, it makes them happy. You sometimes worry whether you are doing enough to alleviate the suffering of animals. You observe how animals are treated disrespectfully and this knowledge affects you with a heavy and despondent feeling, and some of you even become depressed as a result.

I would like to tell you something about the spiritual significance of the animal kingdom and about the possibility of a joyful cooperation between humans and animals. I want you to understand clearly about your role relative to animals: what you can do for them and what you can receive from them.

The connection between humans and animals

All life forms on Earth have a particular purpose. Everything that lives is in a process of progression and development; is in a creative dance. Humans have free will and this distinguishes them from all other living beings on Earth. With this free will, humans can shape reality in a way that is unknown to animals. Animals live from a natural inborn instinct. Energetically, they are strongly linked with their own kind and live largely from the essence of their own species. Their individuality is not yet as strongly awakened as it is in humans.

Humans possess individuality and with that they give shape to their life. You use your head and willpower to manifest your ideas into material reality. The freedom to create is, on the one hand, a gift to humans and a source of their power, while on the other hand, this ability can also lead to imbalance, violence, and destruction. When you live too much from your thinking and willing, and you want too much to direct and organize – to manipulate – you lose connection with the totality to which you belong. You no longer experience the natural bond with other living beings and find yourself feeling separate and lonely.

As history shows, humans try to assert their might over nature and want to subject nature into servitude using that might. This impulse has a destructive impact on nature, animals, plants, and minerals – and you also suffer because of that impulse. You become estranged from your own nature, your spontaneity, and your feelings. No other living creature on Earth can feel as lonely and lost as do humans. Animals instinctively feel a connection with the whole and this is natural for them. They do not doubt this connection and therefore surrender easily to life. Animals live in the *now* and do not think about the future. Sadly, humans have lost this natural connection with life.

Self-awareness and the creative power of humans do not only constitute a source of power and a gift; these capabilities can also be a trap, into which humanity has obviously fallen. However, this does not take away from the fact that you also carry a sacred promise within you to enrich all living creatures on Earth. On a subconscious level, the animal kingdom knows of this promise, so in the animal kingdom there is still respect for humanity and the possibilities that humans carry.

What is this promise, this spiritual goal of the journey that humans are taking on Earth? When you are willing to use your creative consciousness in cooperation with nature, from a mutual giving and receiving, life on Earth can really develop into an innovative dance of creation. Nature can provide for your needs and can inspire you by her beauty, balance, and harmony, and you can give something to nature in return. I would like to explain this process in more detail.

The birth of individuality in animals

Consciousness is present in everything that is alive on Earth, even in plants and stones. Animals are the most identifiable to humans as conscious, sentient beings, because they are present in the world as the most individuated. You can see an animal move purposefully, deliberately, and in response to its environment. In plants and stones, this is less visible; their consciousness is naturally more passive and dreamy. From a certain perspective, it is easier for you to connect with animals than with other forms of life on Earth.

When you approach an animal with loving attention, you help the animal to realize that it is unique; that it is a particular individual with its own experience, its own inner world, and not just one of its kind. In this way, humans contribute to the birth of an individuated consciousness in animals. In connection with humans, the animal feels its consciousness grow. At the moment you connect with an animal with your attention and love, it awakens to itself. This happens very clearly in your relationship with pets, so you develop a unique bond with such an animal.

This kind of connection effects, on a wider scale, the entire animal kingdom. Your connection not only increases the self-awareness of the particular animal, it also increases the awareness of the entire species of which that animal is part. By receiving your human consciousness, the animal becomes acquainted with different experiences than those it knows through its animal nature, and the animal is open to this experience. It wants to explore more deeply the entire range of feeling and living. Pets often pick up on the emotions of their owners, even though they may be negative emotions. It is something that animals choose from their soul. They want to learn something from the kinds of awareness and emotions that people carry.

Sometimes it can tax an animal to feel the moods of its owner. This sensing can cause even physical complaints and behavioral problems in animals. Still, animals take this as part of their compact with humans. They want to be with you from a desire to come into greater consciousness themselves and also *because they love you.* As many of you know, pets show an incredible loyalty and willingness to serve humans. The attention and love that you give to them, they return doubly.

Spiritually, the connection with animals can also be very helpful for people. Through their presence, animals can stimulate you to open up emotionally and to come out of your head and to trust life. Animals can bring to you grounding, relaxation, and peace. The pure love of an animal can make you realize that *you are loved*, regardless of how you perform or how you look. Animals can bring you back to your essential core. From an energetic viewpoint, a beautiful interaction takes place between humans and animals. You stimulate the birth of individuality in animals and, in turn, animals stimulate in you a feeling of belonging.

What animals want, and where all life on Earth is moving toward, is growth in consciousness: to become more aware of oneself and to grow in the formation of free will and individual self-expression. With the birth of self-awareness arises individuality, and with individuality arises true creativity. When you are an individual – a conscious, creative being – you can act outside the laws of nature and create something new, and that can happen only if you are able to depart from learned habits and innate instincts. The birth of individuality in a living being is something truly majestic on its path of development – it is essentially the same as the birth of the soul.

Animals are living beings who are in the process of being born as an individual soul through a long process of inner development. Humans have an individual soul already and, in fact, are so advanced that you have also experienced the excesses and pitfalls of a too strongly developed free will. People can help animals to self-awareness, and animals can bring people Home on Earth and back to a connectedness with nature.

Easing the suffering of animals

Now, I would like to comment on the question of how you can alleviate the suffering of animals. Many of you are touched in your hearts by the disrespectful treatment of animals in the world. Some of you become disturbed and feel a heavy burden of pain and sadness and powerlessness when confronted with this suffering. I want to give a few suggestions to you by which the relating to animals, and the assisting of them, can become a joyful cooperation, where you both become inspired.

Realize that your consciousness is creative, and realize that in your deepest essence and core you are a healer, a guardian of Earth. From your soul, you are deeply connected to me. There is an ancient agreement between you and me – you wanted to incarnate as a soul to enrich me, Earth, with your loving consciousness. You also wanted to come here to enjoy your connectedness with the wealth of life that manifests on Earth. By being here, by appreciating the beauty and the harmony in nature, and by radiating your natural vibration wherever you go, you already help to bring healing to the animals on Earth.

You may doubt whether this is enough, but realize that consciousness is always creative. When you can hold to a consciousness on Earth that is imbued with the love of nature and with warmth and respect for animals, then this consciousness is felt and observed by animals and by me. It is natural for people to ask themselves whether they are doing enough, and then to look for concrete, visible results. However, it is through the radiance of your consciousness that something changes and *that something harmonizes without you doing or saying anything.*

Realize that animals have their own consciousness. They have chosen their life on Earth – to learn and to grow in consciousness here. Animals are inwardly prepared to give much and to be of service to humans, although it is certainly true that they suffer from disrespectful treatment. However, it does not help to see them as a victim, and to suffer along with them. *Honor their way!* It helps them most if you remain centered, not swept away by emotions of pity or indignation, and then ask yourself how you can contribute positively to their well-being. Animals are happy with little and need only the generosity of a small gesture.

Maintain a balance between giving and receiving

Attune yourself inwardly to the animal or animals that you want to help. Sense what is possible, what feels joyful for you, and by what you are inspired – this is your path for healing animals. Remember, you are here to express your own unique soul's light. Do what your feelings tell you to do and what brings you joy. Allow yourself to be inspired from within – follow the flow of your heart. As with everything, when it comes to changing the collective consciousness, so that animals will be honored more, there is a natural rhythm and timing that you can not force.

Helping animals needs to be something joyful, where you give and receive and are *mutually* inspired to growth in awareness. From your urge to eliminate suffering, you may give too much and lose sight of your boundaries, while animals have their own well developed sense of boundaries. To find out whether you are trying to give too much, you can inwardly consult an animal and ask what it wants from you. This is often something other than what you expected. You can also ask for an inner guide in the form of an animal. Allow an animal to enter your imagination and ask the animal for a message. Look at your dealings with animals as a two-way street. See yourself as receiver, as well as giver.

Trust your feelings

In the making of intuitive connections with animals, you come up against much self-doubt: "Do I sense this correctly? Is it all in my head? Is this not a projection on my part?" See this process of making connection with animals as a journey where you are asked to let go of your head and to set sail by the compass of your feelings. When you do find yourself being hampered by your head, your thinking, make no judgments about this – *all* of humankind lives too much in their head!

You feel attracted to communicating with animals because you want to let go of the overly mental and to sink more deeply into emotions and feelings, and in this way to come closer to your inner knowing. When you notice your hesitation, and become unsure of your ability to communicate with animals, see this as an opportunity to become aware of the fear in yourself and use this opportunity to encourage yourself. Animals are happy to help you here. In their eyes, you are forgiven quickly for your mistakes. They feel the sincerity of your intentions and that means a lot to them.

Feel for a moment the presence of the animals with whom you have connected in one way or another, both those living and those that have passed on. Animals that have died stay connected with you; their loyalty reaches so deeply and stretches across multiple incarnations and defies centuries. Feel their presence – they are gathered here around you. Let them tell you where they are, what they would be happy to receive from you. They speak not only for themselves, but also for the greater whole of the animal kingdom.

Feel and see for a moment how excited they are. Yes, some of them carry wounds, emotional wounds, and yet ... *look how much joy there is in them!* They feel honored by the connection that you made with them. They feel acknowledged and accepted by you. Open yourself to what they want to give to you. Feel how, in their own simple way, they invite you to be just yourself: to feel what you feel, to be who you are, to believe in yourself – just uncomplicated and in the *now*. See the power and full health of these animals. Feel their zest for life and their strength, their faith, their service, and their love – *enjoy their positive energy*! Answer their call for cooperation with them as equal partners in the adventure of earthly creation.

40. The love of Earth

I am the voice of Earth, and I bid you welcome. I carry you and, in love and surrender, I flow through you. I live within the cells of your body. You express yourself through me, but I also find expression through you. I enjoy being with you and to experience life through your human consciousness. I would like you to dare to surrender to me; to dare to give yourself over to your body, your feelings, and the flow of life that exists within you. *That is my wish.*

Feel the power of my love for you. You are my child, for I carry you as a mother. I want you to experience and accept me as a supporting energy in your life, but not to do that through your head and the thinking processes that you have been taught. My energy does not work in a determining and directive manner, but flows with a rhythm that is natural and spontaneous.

Whenever your soul connects with me from a letting go to life, we can dance and experience life together. You then unite your soul's energy, your cosmic heart, with my earthly energy in a connection that flows from above to below, in full surrender to the great forces of life and without the intervention of the head with its mental processes. This is the new human who will appear on Earth, the human being who recognizes and experiences both their earthly and cosmic roots, and feels as one with that experience. What is to now happen in the world is for people to connect with both their cosmic origin *and* their earthly life *by way of the body that carries them.*

Take a moment to regard the human body as a gateway for cosmic energy to flow into Earth. This week, you all have been in different caves (in southern France). These are physical gateways for cosmic energy to enter into Earth, as is your body such a gateway. Your body is composed of the powerful and fundamental energies of the Earth elements, which have as their basis solidity, stability, and peace; yet at the same time your body contains an energy gateway, an opening for the inspirational rays of light to flow from the Cosmic Sun into Earth.

Your body needs to be anchored on and in the Earth; to be entirely rooted here. And your body also needs nurturing, not only physical food, bread and water, but ethereal food as well: the feeling of being one with nature, of connecting with trees, plants, and animals; feeling the sun on your skin, floating on refreshing water, and feeling the heat of a fire. All these elements – my elements of water, fire, air, and earth – are just as much spiritual energies as are those of the teachers, masters, and angels whom you revere. My spiritual energies are here among you, and through the earthly elements I provide, you can unite with them.

These earthly-spiritual energies are everywhere on Earth. See around you the flowers that grow in the field, and the plants and herbs that provide you with what you need as human beings. Embrace these energies of Earth and feel my power – *this is your Home*! And whenever you are able to feel earthly and rooted, and dare to nourish yourself with everything you need, physically and energetically, then the gateway opens for the light of your soul. That gateway forms a connection with this earthly realm, and allows this realm to flourish by infusing it with cosmic light.

Feel for a moment what is needed in your own life in order to achieve this interplay in the best way possible. Start by feeling through your body that earthly foundation in yourself. Feel your body to be anchored into me. Here in this setting (southern France), where nature is wild and free, and has been cultivated and modified as little as possible, you can experience more easily the pure flow of the energy of Earth. Your body recognizes and responds to this energy and you do not have to do anything mental to make that happen. Simply lie on the grass and admire nature and the energy comes to you spontaneously.

Feel Earth energy flowing into your feet, and how your body regains a more full and solid feeling. Feel the peace and tranquility of the rocks beneath you, with their ages-old covering of soil. This earthly energy is there and it carries you because you are part of nature, just as are the animals and the plants, and the stones, the water, and the air. Just as are they, so also are you an important part and component of nature. Embrace and accept the reality and beauty of this fact.

This fact also means that when you return to your home from this visit and you are back in your everyday life, you will remember to feel what it is like to be connected with Earth, and with the calm that you need. Take seriously the rhythm that comes from your body and do not to let yourself be diverted by the many demands that come to you from human society. They do not bring you to where you have to be; they lead you away from your core. Take some rest, and relax by feeling the elements of Earth. Cherish these earthly elements and nurture yourself with them. Only then can the gateway open for your soul-light to truly manifest in your daily life.

Make a connection now with the light of your soul. You have felt what it is like to be rooted and connected with me, Earth, and you have felt what it is like to receive in your body the spiritual forces of the earthly elements. Now imagine what cosmic force, what soul-light wants to enter into you. Visualize it descending from heaven, from the sky above you. Feel your own sun-light, the strength of your soul, and receive that in your heart. *Feel it shine in your heart!* And see how the Earth energy receives and responds to that light within you. *How delicious it is to experience this radiance!*

The earthly and the cosmic are energies that respond to and need one another; they are not opposing energies. The Earth energy in your body becomes revitalized and filled with joy and is inspired by the cosmic light that you are, and this union of energies takes earthly form through you. The cosmic light wants nothing more than to be here, and to flow out through the cells of your body, so as to help Earth be fruitful and give birth to the new.

You are so welcome here – I need your light! Physically, as Earth, I can not live without the light from the Sun, and energetically, I also need *your* cosmic light. And that can only flow into me when you allow yourself to be received by me; when you trust me and feel at home here. Look how both energies are now joined in you: your cosmic star-light with your body, the earthly anchor. Let them embrace each other and let them together flow through your body.

Here then is the mating and union of both the male and female energies; the energies of both giving and receiving; the Sun and the Earth. Allow these mated and unified energies to flow over and through you in ever widening circles; not only in your body, but throughout your entire energetic field, your aura. Allow these energies to renew you and to remind you of who you truly are: a playful being of light; a living being temporarily present here to joyfully interact with my energy on Earth. Experience again the intimate union of both the Earth energy and the cosmic light that you are. Welcome and incorporate that feeling of intimacy, and take it with you as you return to your homes.

Now, for a moment, look at your everyday life from the perspective of that feeling of the intimate union of energies. Just feel intuitively, and without thinking about it, if you can find one part of your life that you would change so you are more in balance with your true nature. What can you do for yourself, physically or emotionally, through which you would feel more nurtured and experience more tranquility, relaxation, and inspiration? Promise yourself to give this to yourself. Make more space in your life to nurture yourself in both earthly and heavenly ways.

Finally, I would like to ask you to feel the great forces that welcome you in this life. From beneath your feet, receive the nurturing powers of the Mother, of Earth, and from above, the loving arms of the Father who protects and cherishes you. Feel this totality of forces from above and below you, and allow that union to happen. Just let go of the excessive thinking and doing; know that you are carried by greater forces that love you, that want the best for you. Relinquish control to them and allow yourself to be swept along by a great energy wave. A new world awaits you, and because you surrender to that energy flow, you become one of those who prepare and give shape to the new world. It is happening; *there is so much that is now evolving on Earth.* The biggest step for you is to dare to surrender to the forces of both Earth and Heaven. I love you and want you to feel my hand in yours – *you are never alone!*

Other books by Pamela Kribbe

Heart Centered Living

Heart Centered Living is living according to the calling of your soul. You can recognize the calling of your soul by the feelings of joy, peace and inspiration it brings to you. However, daring to trust your heart often involves a leap into the unknown. You may be confronted with deep-seated fears about your own worth and your ability to pursue your own path. This book is a loving guide on your way to heart centered living. It contains clear and informative channelings inspired by the Christ energy. They deal with different subjects, such as finding your true passion, how to create balanced relationships, parenting the new, sensitive children and emotional healing in the face of fear and depression. They also speak about the profound transformation humanity is going through, letting go of ego-based consciousness and evolving into heart-based consciousness.

This book is written for lightworkers, souls who feel compelled to go deep within and express their true soul's calling on Earth. The teachers who speak in this book (Jeshua, Mary and mother Earth) all encourage you to take the leap of faith and become who you really are. Their teachings gently inspire you to face and overcome whatever holds you back in listening to the voice of your heart.

ISBN-13: 978-1621412618
Paperback: 276 pages
Publisher: Booklocker.com, Inc.

The Jeshua Channelings

In clear and accessible language, Jeshua speaks about the origins and destiny of the lightworker family. He offers a detailed account of the transition from ego-based to heart-based consciousness. In the second part of the book, Jeshua deals with several aspects of everyday life, such as relationships, work and health. He addresses the most common questions and problems we struggle with in these areas.

Some books are filled with shining wisdom. Others radiate great love. A few – a very rare few – are overflowing with both. The Jeshua Channelings is one such book. If you want to know who you really are, why you're here, and what your life is truly about, look no further. This book gently and compassionately guides readers toward remembering their magnificence as divine souls. Brilliantly insightful and inspiring, it is true gem and a blessing to our world.

- Robert Schwartz, author, Your Soul's Plan: Discovering the Real Meaning of the Life You Planned Before You Were Born - yoursoulsplan.com

ISBN-13: 978-1601456823
Paperback: 264 pages
Publisher: Booklocker.com, Inc.